A Taste of
HERITAGE

the new
AFRICAN-AMERICAN
cuisine

CHEF JOE RANDALL
&
TONI TIPTON-MARTIN

MACMILLAN · USA

MACMILLAN
A Simon & Schuster Macmillan Company
1633 Broadway
New York, NY 10019-6785

Macmillan Publishing books may be purchased for business or sales promotional use. For information please write: Special Markets Department, Macmillan Publishing USA, 1633 Broadway, New York, NY 10019.

MACMILLAN is a registered trademark of Macmillan, Inc.

Library of Congress Cataloging-in-Publication Data

Randall, Joe.
    A taste of heritage : new African-American cuisine / Joe Randall,
Toni Tipton-Martin
      p.   cm.
    Includes index.
    ISBN 0-02-860382-6 (alk. paper)
    1. Afro-American cookery.   I. Tipton-Martin, Toni.   II. Title.
TX715.R2145   1998
641.59'296073—dc21   97-43736
                                   CIP

Some of the text in this book is reprinted with permission of *The Cleveland Plain Dealer.*

Manufactured in the United States of America

10 9 8 7 6 5 4 3 2 1

Book design by Nick Anderson

Dedication

To Barbara Zachary Randall, my devoted wife and the loving mother of my three wonderful children, J. Christopher Randall, Kenneth Alexander Randall, and my baby Cari Patrice Randall, and in memory of my natural father Washington Glascoe and my natural mother Margaret Randall Glascoe, for without them there would not have been a beginning. Also in loving memory of my Granny Ada B. Lewis and (Brother Bob) Elder Robert B. Holman Sr., my father in the Gospel who taught me to love old folks, and in loving memory of my Uncle and Aunt Dr. Joseph A. Randall and Laura Pan Randall, who adopted and raised me from the age of two weeks. Daddy Joe, who taught me to fight for the things I believed in. Mom Pan, who showed me how to have faith enough to believe in the things worth fighting for.

To my family, Aunt Lynnis Wise, my cousins Monroe Young, Sam Ross, Kenny Stotts, Arthur and Realure Glascoe, my sisters Mary Frances Carter, Lorraine Stone, Carolyn Lewis, and Catherine Buchanan.

To Chef Robert W. Lee, formerly of the Biltmore and Henry Grady Hotels in Atlanta, Georgia, who trained me, and headed the kitchens at the Harrisburger Hotel in Harrisburg, Pennsylvania, from 1940–1967, and all the culinary professionals who worked with him: Leroy Hill, John Hooks, Jimmy Broton, George Hawkins, George Connors Sr., Douglas Lee, Willie Joe Darin, Pansy Erving, George Connors Jr., Joe Martin, Lucius Coleman, R. D. Bruno, Theodore "Reverend Mitch" Mitchell, Charles Murray, Sammy Davenport, Donald Mitchell, Anthony "Mr. Lee" Liggon, Bill Fouwiley, and Lawrence Kelly, to name a few. All worthy heirs to a great tradition of southern cooking.

To Frank Castelli, formerly executive chef of the Penn Harris Hotel in Harrisburg, Pennsylvania, and The Union League in Philadelphia, who exposed me to haute cuisine.

Joseph G. Randall

This book is dedicated to: My loving husband Bruce, who happily sampled dish after dish and served as kitchen helper in every capacity—from scrubbing dishes to washing and picking collard greens; to my extraordinary children: Brandon, Jade, Christian, and Austin, who discovered what life must be like for motherless children; to my giving mother, Beverly Hamilton, and brother Derrick, for their constant support; and most of all to my selfless father, Charles Hamilton, who I am sure smiled a prideful smile as he read each page of this book from his seat in Heaven.

Toni Tipton-Martin

Contents

Contents

Foreword

IT WAS WITH A GREAT DEAL OF ENTHUSIASM THAT I ACCEPTED CHEF JOE RANDALL'S INVITATION TO WRITE the foreword to his book *A Taste of Heritage: New African-American Cuisine.*

Although I am of French-Canadian heritage and was born in Rhode Island, for the last twenty-seven years I have been fortunate to make my home in Williamsburg, Virginia. I honed my skills in New York City, but my introduction to the soul of cuisine came while I was working for the Colonial Williamsburg Foundation. From the African-American cooks with whom I worked, I discovered that pride is an essential element in food preparation, whether the ingredients are few and the recipes simple or the pantry is abundant and extravagant. From Mary Humelsine, wife of the chairman of the Foundation and hostess to countless heads of state who visited Williamsburg, I learned the importance of cooking with fresh seasonal ingredients. And by noted research historian Dr. Jane Carson, I was stimulated to read books on Southern cookery that have served as a muse ever since.

Reading *A Taste of Heritage: New African-American Cuisine* has given me a feeling of nostalgia for that time in the early seventies. It reminds me of the important things African-American cooks have brought to American culture and its table. And most of all, it made me hungry. My tongue anticipates the pleasure of licking the spoon that stirs the pot of Sweet Potato Smoked Louisiana Sausage Bisque. My nose tingles with the fantasy of the aroma of slowly baking Country Corn Pudding. It doesn't take much imagination to know the pleasure of savoring Steamed Littleneck Clams with Clam Nectar, Frizzled Leeks, and Hot Pepper Butter Sauce.

I could tease you with countless other selections from this noteworthy book; to stay friends, I suggest you indulge in it yourself. I feel certain that *A Taste of Heritage: New African-American Cuisine* will become a classic and that it will invigorate a tremendously deserved interest in what is arguably the original American cuisine.

Marcel Desaulniers
Executive Chef and Co-owner
The Trellis Restaurant
Williamsburg, Virginia

Acknowledgments

GIVING HONOR TO GOD THE ALMIGHTY FOR ALL CREATION AND HAVING HIS WAY IN MY LIFE. I WANT TO express my sincere, deepest gratitude:

To my coauthor Toni Tipton-Martin, for her historical presence, who believes like me that our heritage is the truth that lives within our souls. I spoke to her from my soul in a traditional language that she has translated deliciously.

To the chefs who are the best friends a man could have in cooking: Clifton Williams, Darryl Evans, Earlest Bell, Edna Lewis, John Harrison, Kym Gibson, Leah Chase, Patrick Clark, Patrick Yves Pierre-Jerome, Prince Akins, and Timothy Dean for their help in providing their recipes, insights, and creativity, and for preserving our culinary heritage by continuing the traditions and developing new ones.

To my friends for their continued support, encouragement, and love. A special expression of thanks must be given to Marcel Desaulniers, Dr. Rudy Lombard, Tom and Joan Costello, Billy and Jeannine Peterson, Gary and Pat Miller, Allen and Rose Smith, Dred and Katherine Scott, Tony and Jean Fennoy, Robert and Mary Holman, David and Rosie Brazelton, Jason and Dorothy Wallace, Martha Robinson, Willie Stinson, Roosevelt and Marilyn Jackson, Monica Turner, Shedric Wallace, Morton Tadder, Dr. James Bell, Dr. Sidney W. Mintz, Dr. Owen B. Ellington, Dr. Fred Parrott, and Thomas "T" Glass.

Joe Randall

WITH EACH WORD THAT I WRITE I THANK GOD FOR PLACING IN MY LIFE ALL THE INFLUENTIAL WRITERS AND editors who have in their own delicate way inspired and encouraged me along this journey. They are: Alice Marshall, my city editor at *Wave Newspapers*, a Los Angeles weekly, who gave my career as a food writer its start; Ruth Reichl, former food editor for the *Los Angeles Times* and now a restaurant critic for *The New York Times*, who took the rough edges off my copy and taught me to be faithful to my standards and ethics, however controversial. Thank you, Ruth for your candor and honesty. Also from the *Los Angeles Times*, Bill Farr, who saw potential in a young journalism student and encouraged me to pursue a food writing career. I am indebted to my staff and the editors at the *Plain Dealer* for their understanding and patience; and to my friends and family, who have eaten more mediocre meals than I want to admit making, just so I could become a better cook. Most of all, I wish to thank my coauthor, Chef Joe Randall, for giving me the opportunity to share a vision.

Toni Tipton-Martin

Introduction

THE ROOTS OF NEW AFRICAN-AMERICAN HERITAGE CUISINE

A Taste of Heritage began with our simple observation that African-American chefs and their unique cooking styles are getting more attention from the press and public than ever before. Virtually every time we talked, we delighted in the media coverage African-American chefs were suddenly receiving and in our observation that non–African-American chefs had begun embracing traditional African-American foods.

"Collards and other greens, barbecue sauce, grits and black-eyed peas, the stuff of soul food and the rural South in fancy duds," were showing up on some very upscale, high-profile menus, noted *New York Times* food writer Florence Fabricant. Recognizing that African-American chefs have a broad appeal, Julia Child began inviting African-American chefs to appear on her syndicated cooking show and the White House selected Patrick Clark as a finalist for the prestigious position of White House chef.

We couldn't have been happier. Other Americans had discovered what we knew all along: African-American cooking was food you could fall in love with.

Before 1993, Chef Randall had been alone in his quest to nurture talented African-American chefs like Patrick Clark. Through his annual Taste of Heritage dinners, he had spotlighted the country's best African-American chefs, and presented multicourse dinners to raise scholarship funds for aspiring young chefs. His efforts to honor the contributions to American food made by such contemporary African-American chefs as Clark, Edna Lewis, and Leah Chase led to a feeling of community among African-American chefs.

His lead was followed in 1993 by Matanzas Creek Winery in Sonoma County, California, which at the urging of the area's 100 Black Men organization, assembled some of the nation's most prestigious food writers and educators to select African-American chefs to honor at its annual Wine Country dinner.

It became crystal clear that African-American cuisine was quietly experiencing a renaissance. This book was born out of that revelation.

We wanted to create a cookbook that combined the sophisticated techniques of chefs without forgetting the humble origins of African-Americans. Though contemporary African-American cuisine has its roots in Africa, the slave experience in the South, and the "soul food" phase of the 1960s, we didn't want to publish just another book on soul food.

A Taste of Heritage conveys a culinary account of the evolution of African-American cooking through more than 300 recipes developed over the past thirty years by Chef Joe Randall and his colleagues around the country. Years of experimenting—trying new ingredients in old recipes and changing cooking techniques—have helped create these epicurean delights. The accompanying anecdotes tell the story of the recipes and offer historical perspectives on them.

Because a single chef does not a cuisine make, Chef Randall invited twelve of America's premier chefs to share some of their favorite recipes in these pages. Representing some of the finest hotels and restaurants in the nation, these professionals bring a traditional as well as a refreshing, innovative approach to the table. Representing many different areas of the country, the guest chefs who have contributed their recipes present the diversity found in today's sophisticated African-American kitchens. Their contributions have been invaluable.

This is a cookbook you don't have to be adventurous to enjoy. You don't need extravagant equipment or a larder stocked with unusual ingredients. You don't even need to be an experienced cook.

A Taste of Heritage is a colorful tapestry containing many threads. It is intended to help you experience the wonder of contemporary African-American cuisine with ease while you learn a little something about its history.

Our approach may appear unusual. While other books on African-American cooking highlight the peasant aspects of the food by offering recipes for soul food heaped on a plate, *A Taste of Heritage* presents recipes that are far more complex, reflecting the inspired skill of contemporary African-American chefs. Indeed, the African-American cuisine characterized on these pages reflects a broad, creative style that uses modern ingredients and has an emphasis on

freshness and simplicity yet doesn't bastardize our ancestry with unnecessarily lofty ingredients and expressions. At the same time as the book features the sophisticated recipes of chefs, it offers many accessible heirloom recipes that have been handed down through generations of many diverse families.

We share with you what has been learned over the years about basic, classic cooking through recipes that are unparalleled in their excellence, ingenuity, and scope—those originally crafted by ingenious slaves who learned to take advantage of the natural beauty of food, and whose visions have ultimately been revised by African-American chefs who weave professional techniques with rich ethnic traditions.

You'll be amazed at how years of experimenting in African-American kitchens has influenced what you've eaten in non–African-American restaurants every day. This is food you'll want to serve at parties, food you'll want to develop entire menus around. To some extent the food is rooted in classic French. But it always has been, ever since those early days when the Africans were influenced by their style, and we will reveal that. Then you too will feel as energized about African-American cuisine as we do and realize that it is about much more than cooking and survival; it is about dining and enjoying.

The African Influence

Though today's African-American chefs are utterly contemporary in their cooking, their success owes a debt to the past. The precolonial African diet in many ways resembled the much-lauded Mediterranean diet, in that it was basically healthy, country cooking utilizing fresh ingredients. African-American cuisine takes a cue from that style.

In Africa, our ancestors consumed mostly foods from the garden and the sea. They ate all sorts of vegetables and fruits, including yams, wild greens, okra, dates, watermelon, and more. Grains, such as millet, rice, and couscous, played a major role in the African diet. In coastal regions where seafood was plentiful, fish was the dominant protein; in other places, chicken was the meat of choice.

Foods ranged from bland to highly seasoned. Cornmeal porridges; West African fufu, made by boiling starchy cassava; yams; plantains or rice pounded into a mass; Kenyan dumplings; and injera, the flat bread of Ethiopia, were indispensable accompaniments to flavorful stews, wats, and tagines. Jollof rice and other rice dishes, lentils, and other legumes also contributed to the wholesomeness of the early African diet.

Vegetable dishes were as varied as the African countries themselves—curries, beans spiked with coconut milk, and spiced black-eyed peas are just a few. Spices such as cardamom, cumin, cloves, coriander, fennel, fenugreek, garlic, ginger, mint, saffron, and sesame lent allure to the fare.

African cooks prepared meats over a hot fire, simmering them into exotic, slow-cooked mixtures that allowed the flavors in the stockpot to mingle. This technique—suited to so many ingredients—kept them alive in the New World.

The Slave Experience in the South

Life after the Middle Passage was difficult for African women trying to feed their families on foreign soil. Their rough, tired hands worked arduously to bring dinner to the table, whether through the monotonous task of picking over wild greens or the messy job of cleaning the visceral organs of the master's hog. The slave woman reached deep into a tub of intestines, then picked, rinsed, soaked, and picked over again the pile of wrinkles. If she was lucky, she'd get three pounds of edible meat from more than ten pounds of pork waste. Suppertime was a lot of work, but ingenious cooks made food palatable under Stone Age conditions.

The fruits of this creative and resourceful nature remain at the core of the distinctive Southern cooking style that so many Americans, black and white, continue to enjoy today. It's possible that African-American cooking was universally popular in the South because of its blend of culinary attitudes, including Indian, French, and Spanish. Indeed, just about any group of people the slaves encountered embellished their style.

The Africans brought techniques from the Motherland that helped them use food their owners had thrown away—internal organs, hooves, ears, and tails of hogs, and bottom-feeding garbage fish (catfish). They overcame adversity by transforming unwanted foods—wild game and vegetables, which were plentiful—into savory dishes. Meat played only a supporting role in the theater of African-American cooking; vegetables and grains were the stars.

Simultaneously, Africans created delicacies: They pickled pigs' feet and ears; adopted the French way of serving brains and scrambled eggs for breakfast; and found use for chitterlings just as the French had crafted andouiettes from pork entrails in Europe.

Indeed, no part of the hog was wasted. They rendered the fat into lard, saved the blood for pudding, ground the scraps into sausage, and barbecued the bones to put a meager amount of meat into their family's diets. Neck bones, ham hocks, and fatback seasoned the vegetables. Even the pigskin was utilized. Cut into pieces, fried until crisp and golden brown, the cracklings were eaten as a snack or crushed into cornbread or spoon bread to give a dish a rich taste and pleasing texture.

The slave diet included chicken cooked in every way, from stewed to fried. Rabbit and game birds were also enjoyed. But fish, which was readily available in streams, rivers, and lakes in the rural South, was a major source of protein for slaves. It was usually deep- or pan-fried or used as the basis of the murky soup-stew called gumbo.

Gumbo, a hodgepodge dish fancied by Creole cooks, became a trademark of slave cooking. It mingles the peppery blends of African cuisine with the sultry savoir faire of the French. Its name comes from the African word for okra, which is used in many recipes as a thickener, in addition to the French-style roux. This technique, which combines fat and flour, is preferred for thickening gumbo. This pasty but rich mixture gives gumbo the dark, earthy flavor and smooth consistency for which it is famous.

Like many other hearty soups and stews in African-American cuisine, gumbo acted as a substantial supper. It is made with just a bit of meat and fish, which is simmered with hearty vegetables—sweet potatoes, tomatoes, greens, black-eyed peas, and a medley of dried beans, all of which slaves grew in their gardens—then served over rice.

Taking their cue from American Indians, slaves also grew corn in their gardens. The kernels were dried and ground into meal, which was used for everything from making bread to coating vegetables, chicken, and fish before frying. They were fond of white corn, which they made into hominy. Finely ground hominy grits are still a Southern tradition today.

Desserts comprised a major part of Southern African-American diets. Recipes for ambrosia and Waldorf salads still flood the pages of church and community cookbooks. The collection of simple sweets appears endless, with jelly cakes and bread pudding at the top of the list.

Because of their reputation for polished culinary skill, masters brought slave women into their kitchens and depended upon them to feed, pick up after, and help raise their children. The master and his family also survived on and enjoyed African-American cooking.

Effects of World War I and the Depression

Following World War I, African-Americans continued to serve in the homes of white Americans. Many carried their culinary expertise into restaurants, hotels, city and country clubs, cafeterias, trains, nightclubs, and army galleys. Many began as dishwashers because they lacked professional training, but eventually their experience helped them perfect the craft. In time, many built catering businesses and opened small restaurants of their own. During the 1930s and 1940s and into the 1950s, good Southern cooks adopted the gourmet style of epicures to make their cooking shine.

They arranged glorious affairs, with European-style dishes they had seen and helped prepare in restaurants, including truffle-stuffed filet mignon and chocolate soufflé. They also made the food they knew and loved and simply spruced it up. They still baked buttermilk biscuits, but they rolled them thin and cut them small. They tied herbs and spices into bouquet garni, peeled tomatoes, cooked with olive oil, and made salad dressing from scratch.

Some African-Americans overcame the myriad racial obstacles that marked the first half of the twentieth century, but most, because of segregation and low wages, still struggled with poverty. Although those who had worked in food service may have had the culinary tastes and skills of the upper class, their meals continued to mirror their poverty. The heavy foods associated with slavery were no longer necessary for survival in the fields, but their economical ingredients and techniques still suited the African-American way of life. The descendants of slaves survived the Depression and World War II with the cuisine of their ancestors, forever mindful of their expanding family's needs, yet confined by foods of necessity.

As America recovered from depression and war, it entered an era of less conscientious cooking. Processed foods and ready-to-eat foods infiltrated even the homes of well-to-do housewives. Americans began to eat more meat, dairy products, fats, oils, cheese, and ice cream and fewer fresh fruits and vegetables, finding their canned, frozen, dried, and other processed forms more convenient. Potato chips and French-fried potatoes became extremely popular.

The trend manifested itself somewhat differently in the South, which clung to its food habits more closely than the North. From the Gulf Coast to the

Midwest, poor African-Americans continued to rely on greens, cabbage, souse, chitterlings, beans, and pork for sustenance. The same inexpensive meats were roasted, smothered, and barbecued. When fresh meat didn't fit into the budget of urban blacks, smoked and pickled meat helped them get by. Blacks in metropolitan areas relied on the same cheap meat from the fifth quarter—skin, feet, organs, and ears. They ate fruits that were in season.

Families on farms in rural America foraged for wild berries during spring and summer and harvested dandelion and other wild greens for their deliciously bitter, assertive taste when possible. They ate more wild rabbit and fish than city dwellers because it was so readily available.

As was the case for most of middle America, canning, preserving, and stretching foods was important. Farm and city dwellers put up pickles from watermelon rinds and made chowchow from cabbage, a spicy condiment served with greens and other vegetables. Hot water corn bread, baked in heavy, black cast-iron skillets, made a small amount of vegetables go a long way. So did eggs, rice, and potatoes, which were relatively inexpensive.

New American Cuisine and the French Infusion

The test kitchen cook at the *Plain Dealer* used to say that soul food was something that tasted so good it made you wanna slap your momma. For many of us it was that and more. A radio disk jockey on early morning African-American radio explained to her listeners that if she had to choose her last meal, it would be collard greens, black-eyed peas, corn bread, fried chicken, apple pie, and sweet potato pie.

Although this was the same food African-Americans had been cooking for decades, during the soul movement, the moniker "soul food" made the style sound a whole lot sexier. Rhythm characterized everything black, including food. The translation of soul food was food cooked with the senses. Pastry had

to be felt, fried chicken was turned when it made that just-right crackling sound, greens were seasoned by touch, with a pinch of this and a shake of that, as were all foods that came straight from the soul.

Whether it was a rib joint in Harlem or a soul food restaurant near Watts, white Americans sought a taste of the food they so fondly recalled from childhood.

At about the same time—in 1971—a young woman named Alice Waters opened a tiny eatery, Chez Panisse, in Berkeley, California, after having traveled in France and fallen in love with its food. The style of cooking she introduced—based on fresh, seasonal ingredients—was virtually unknown to the descendants of processed foods. With Jeremiah Tower at her side, she helped create the New American Cuisine. New American Cuisine opened new avenues for chefs in America. It spawned the wildly popular California cuisine, in which recipes were prepared with fresh, low-fat ingredients, artfully arranged on a plate.

A better appreciation for chefs was born and those African-American chefs who came into the industry reaped some unique benefits. They also traveled abroad, to study in France. Some accepted the challenge to learn as much as they could about what was being projected as the "established technique."

When the door closed on nouvelle cuisine, with its tiny portions and artsy presentation in the 1980s, chefs looked to regional fare as a way to infuse excitement into restaurant menus. They inevitably turned to African-Americans, realizing we brought to the table the same things French, Italian, and other ethnic people brought: A sense of wholesome good cooking learned at Mother's knees.

Today, more than at any other time in history, food that is spicy, flavorful, and well-seasoned is on the front burner, in a mélange of cultural influences. Contemporary American chefs have confirmed that any food can assimilate into the realm of haute cuisine simply by shifting its emphasis.

We still have hogs-head cheese, but now it's julienned and served on a bed of fresh California baby greens and tossed with a light vinaigrette. We still adore the warm peach cobbler we ate at Mother's kitchen table, yet we can nestle that peach and sun-dried cherry filling in light dumplings and crown them with a brandy custard sauce.

Indeed, we haven't closed the door to Grandma's kitchen; we've opened it and let in a breath of fresh air.

TOOLS AND TECHNIQUES

Throughout this book you will notice cooking techniques, equipment, and terms that are used repeatedly to describe preparation of African-American cuisine. They are things that seem routine to chefs because they are always part of the mise en place, that is, prepared ahead of time in a restaurant kitchen.

BEURRE MANIÉ. A classic French technique used for thickening soups and finishing sauces. It is a mixture of equal parts softened butter and flour worked together to form a paste. Very small pieces of beurre manié are dropped into the simmering liquid and stirred with a whisk until it thickens and is smooth.

BRAZIER. A round, broad, shallow heavy-duty pot used for browning, braising, and stewing meats. During cooking, the braising liquid doesn't boil over because the sides are straight and it is sturdy enough to handle oven temperatures. A Dutch oven can be substituted.

BUTTER. Most butter sold in supermarkets is lightly salted to prolong its shelf life. Sweet or unsalted butter is more perishable but has a fresher, sweeter taste. For the recipes in this book, unsalted butter is recommended.

CAST-IRON SKILLET. The heavier the pot, the better it is at conducting heat. Cast iron diffuses heat evenly at low temperatures making it an excellent vessel for frying. It can take a long time to heat, however, so it is less efficient at short-term cooking and

preparation of delicate foods and sauces. African-American cooks have always preferred cast iron for making corn bread and for frying.

CHIFFONADE. This is a classic French technique, which means to cut leafy vegetables (lettuce, sorrel, greens) into thin or wide strips or shreds. Sometimes the vegetable is rolled first, then cut. This is not the same thing as julienne, which is to cut food into thin, matchstick strips. Usually it is a preparation used for vegetable side dishes and garnishes.

COULIS. A thick puree or sauce made from fruit or vegetables. When lightly sweetened it makes a nice accompaniment for plain cakes and desserts.

DEGLAZE. A liquid, usually wine or stock, is poured into a pan in which meat or fish has been cooked, then it is heated and stirred to loosen the browned bits of meat that remain in the pan. The two become the flavorful beginning for a sauce.

DEGREASE. To remove all visible fat from a hot liquid (stock, soup, sauce, or gravy). Use a spoon to skim the fat from the surface of the liquid. If you have time, you can chill the liquid in the refrigerator until the fat becomes solid and lift it off the surface.

HERBS. When many people think about herbs the dried variety is what comes to mind. But there is a whole world of flavor awaiting in fresh. To cook with fresh herbs, always strip the leaves away from the stem by pulling against the direction of leaf growth. Discard the stems and finely chop the leaves. You will need about three times as much fresh herb as dried, or about 1 tablespoon fresh for every $1/2$ to 1 teaspoon dried. Frozen herbs require about twice as much as fresh.

NAP WITH SAUCE. For a pleasing presentation, evenly spoon a thin layer of sauce over finished dishes so that the food is lightly but completely coated.

REDUCTION. Instead of using a roux to thicken a sauce, many chefs depend upon this method. An amount of stock or wine is boiled or simmered

rapidly until the volume is reduced by evaporation. Once reduced, it has a thicker consistency and concentrated flavor. Cream or butter may be added to the liquid to give body to the sauce.

RENDERING FAT. To melt a solid fat, such as streak-of-lean and streak-of-fat. Accomplished with a hot skillet.

ROUX. This is a cooked mixture consisting of equal parts flour and fat, used to thicken soups, sauces, and gravies. There are three classic roux—white, blond, and brown. The cooking time determines the color and flavor. White and blond roux are made when butter and flour are cooked and stirred rapidly and briefly, no more than about 5 minutes. Brown roux can be made with any number of fats, such as vegetable oil, beef fat, lard, chicken fat, duck fat, and bacon drippings. It is achieved with long, slow cooking and frequent stirring. Creole dishes such as gumbo and étouffée rely upon a brown roux.

SAUTÉ. To sear food quickly and prevent it from cooking in its own juices. It means to cook quickly in a small amount of fat in a preheated skillet or sauté pan on top of the stove over medium-high heat.

SIFT. The process of passing dry ingredients through a fine-mesh sifter so any large pieces can be removed, or to incorporate air to make the ingredients lighter. Sifting is important when weighing ingredients for baking, especially bread and cake flour. It is not necessary to sift all-purpose flour. To measure all-purpose by volume, lightly spoon the flour into a dry measure and level the top with a table knife. Do not pack the flour in the measuring cup.

SIMMER. To cook food in a liquid that is bubbling gently, just below boiling, about 185° to 205°F.

TOMATO PUREE, SAUCE, AND PASTE. All of these ingredients are called for in this book because each one has slightly different qualities that affect the finished dish. Tomato paste consists of tomatoes that have been cooked for several hours, strained, and reduced to a deep red, richly flavored concentrate. Tomato puree consists of tomatoes that have been cooked briefly and strained, resulting in a thick liquid. Tomato sauce is a slightly thinner tomato puree, often with seasonings and other flavoring added so that it is ready to use. It is not recommended that you interchange them in the recipes in this book.

TRUSSING. A way to keep poultry in compact and uniform shape. It means to tie the wings and legs against the body to make it into a solid unit.

VANILLA EXTRACT. It can be tempting to substitute vanilla flavoring or imitation flavorings for pure extract in recipes. Don't. Extracts are concentrated and have pure flavor; flavorings contain only a small amount of pure flavor and it takes more to get the right taste.

Chapter 1

Appetizers
and
Starters

T HERE IS PERHAPS NO BETTER EXAMPLE OF THE ARTISTRY EVIDENT IN CONTEMPORARY African-American cuisine than what lies ahead on the following pages. These appetizers are delicious. Each one is perfect for entertaining, whether your party includes a gathering of well-traveled professionals, adventurous friends with an exotic palate, or just plain folks who are eager to see Grandma's cooking in a whole new light.

It's true that appetizers are not native to the African-American cooking scene, with the exception of crudités, chips and dips, and relish trays. To the contrary, dinner tables sagged under the weight of a veritable feast of delicious foods served all at once, overwhelming guests. All that has changed. People have begun to wonder how all the wonderful heirloom recipes in our history can be presented as part of an exquisite, multicourse menu.

1

The idea isn't a new one for chefs who, early in their careers, learn the French principle of mise-en-place, which means "everything in its place." Chefs are used to spending their time planning, organizing, chopping, and blending ahead of time so that dishes that appear complex can be served quickly at the last minute. Meanwhile, home cooks struggle with timetables and overcrowded ovens, juggling dishes and serving glorious menus that no one can possibly eat all at once. Home cooks will benefit from learning the techniques of planning ahead.

Although I created some of these original appetizers for Elegant Taste of Heritage dinners featuring a hundred guests or more, they translate well to the home kitchen. Some have dressings and other components that can be made entirely in advance; others actually benefit from standing overnight so the flavors have a chance to mingle.

Don't be intimidated by the rest. Crab cakes and crispy fried chitterlings do require more last-minute preparation. The key is to make sure you have planned and paced the evening carefully, utilizing shortcuts wherever possible, and allowing yourself plenty of time so you stay calm, organized, and ready before serving each course.

If you plan to serve a sit-down dinner, which is usually more formal than a family meal or buffet, you will want to fill your most attractive serveware with those recipes that can be made into tiny, nibble-size portions and pass them around before dinner. Or if you have some help in the kitchen, you can arrange individual servings on salad plates and allow your guests to enjoy their starter at the dinner table with glass of wine before the rest of the meal is served.

At less formal occasions, such as family gatherings, when the atmosphere is more relaxed, you can still set out nibble-size portions on serving trays, but invite your guests to join you in the kitchen as you serve the plates, to keep the theme casual.

Whichever style party you decide to host, plan your guest list ahead and think about the menu. With these appetizers, the evening will be first class.

Baked Oysters Wrapped
in Country Bacon

MAKES 8 SERVINGS

The rustic flavor of country smoked bacon tastes delicious with oysters.
Be sure to serve them hot with plenty of cocktail sauce.

$^1/_2$ cup olive oil

1 teaspoon salt

$^1/_2$ teaspoon freshly ground
    black pepper

2 tablespoons fresh lemon juice

3 dashes Tabasco sauce

48 large Eastern oysters,
    shucked and well drained

16 slices country bacon, each
    slice cut into thirds

Cocktail Sauce (recipe follows)

Combine the olive oil, salt, pepper, lemon juice, and Tabasco in a large bowl and mix thoroughly. Add the oysters and refrigerate for 2 hours. If you wish to marinate the oysters longer, add the lemon juice just before wrapping them. Drain the oysters, discarding the marinade.

Preheat the oven to 350°F.

Wrap each oyster with a piece of bacon and secure with a wood pick. Place the wrapped oysters on a baking sheets and bake until the bacon is brown and crisp, about 6 to 8 minutes.

Serve the baked oysters hot, napped with Cocktail Sauce.

Cocktail Sauce

MAKES 2 CUPS

2 cups chili sauce

1 tablespoon prepared
    horseradish

1 tablespoon fresh lemon juice

2 teaspoons Worcestershire
    sauce

1 teaspoon Tabasco sauce

1 tablespoon chopped
    fresh parsley

Salt, to taste

In a bowl, combine all ingredients; mix well. Cover and refrigerate.

Catfish Fingers with Remoulade Sauce

Fried catfish is so popular on African-American dinner menus, it is a logical candidate for starting the meal. What is unusual here is the sauce. The Creole remoulade is magnificent on the crispy fish.

2 pounds boned catfish fillets, trimmed of fat and patted dry

1 teaspoon salt

1 tablespoon freshly ground black pepper

$1/2$ teaspoon cayenne pepper

$3^1/2$ cups yellow cornmeal

$1/4$ cup all-purpose flour

1 cup peanut oil

2 cups Remoulade Sauce (see page 289)

Cut the fillets into $1/2$-inch strips. Lightly season them with salt, black pepper, and cayenne. In a large bowl, combine the cornmeal, flour, and any remaining salt and pepper; dredge each strip of fish in the mixture.

Heat the oil over medium-high heat in a large frying pan or cast-iron skillet until hot. Fry each strip of fish until golden brown, about 2 to 3 minutes, then turn and cook it on the other side. Do not crowd the pan. Drain the fish strips on paper towels.

Serve immediately with Remoulade Sauce or your favorite Louisiana hot red pepper sauce.

CHIT'LIN PIZZA ON A CORNMEAL CRUST

MAKES 4 TO 6 SERVINGS

*I began experimenting with this recipe for Chit'lin Pizza after hearing about Bob McCall,
a young black chef and restaurateur who had tried a similar dish in Pittsburgh, Pennsylvania,
in the early 1980s. The recipe came together years later and appeared at the fashionable
Southern-style restaurant, Georgia, on Melrose Avenue in Los Angeles.*

$1/4$ cup all-purpose flour

1 teaspoon salt

$1/2$ teaspoon freshly ground
black pepper

$1/2$ pound Simmered Chitterlings
Country Style with Hog Maws
(see page 214), hog maws
removed and reserved for
another use

2 eggs, beaten

1 cup yellow cornmeal, spooned
into a medium-size bowl

$1/4$ cup peanut oil

Cornmeal Pizza Dough
(see page 6)

1 cup Pizza Sauce (see page 288)

6 ounces shredded mozzarella
cheese

$1/8$ teaspoon red pepper flakes

In a large bowl, thoroughly mix the flour with the salt and pepper. Cut the chitterlings into pieces, dust in the seasoned flour, dip in the beaten eggs, and roll in the cornmeal.

In a cast-iron skillet, heat the oil over medium-high heat until hot and fry the chitterlings on both sides until they are light brown and crisp, about 2 to 3 minutes. Being careful not to crowd the pan. Drain the chitterlings on paper towels and set aside.

Preheat the oven to 400°F.

Lightly oil two baking sheets and dust them with cornmeal. Cut the Cornmeal Pizza Dough in half. Roll each piece into a 9- to 10-inch circle, about $1/4$-inch thick, then crimp the edges and place on a baking sheet. Top each with Pizza Sauce, spreading it evenly, and cover with cheese, chitterlings, and red pepper flakes. Bake until the cheese melts, about 4 to 6 minutes.

CORNMEAL PIZZA DOUGH

1 package active dry yeast

2 cups warm water

2 cups all-purpose flour

1 cup yellow cornmeal

$^{1}/_{2}$ teaspoon salt

1 tablespoon honey

2 tablespoons peanut oil

In a large mixing bowl, dissolve the yeast in the warm water and allow to rest until it is frothy, about 10 to 15 minutes. Add the flour, cornmeal, salt, honey, and oil to the yeast mixture. Beat the dough until it forms a round ball that is dry to the touch. Cover the dough with plastic wrap or a damp towel and store it in a warm place to rise for 1 hour.

CORNMEAL PIZZA CRUST WITH SMOKED CATFISH

MAKES 4 SERVINGS

Cornmeal Pizza Dough
   (see recipe above)

1 cup sour cream

4 ounces cream cheese

2 tablespoons prepared
   horseradish

1 teaspoon fresh lemon juice

$^{1}/_{2}$ teaspoon chili oil

1 pound Smoked Catfish fillets
   (see page 273), sliced on a bias

1 tablespoon chopped fresh chives

Preheat the oven to 400°F.

Lightly oil two baking sheets and dust them with cornmeal. Cut the pizza dough in half. Roll each half into 9- or 10-inch circle $^{1}/_{4}$ inch thick, then crimp the edges and place on a baking sheet. Bake the pizzas for 4 to 5 minutes, then remove from oven and set aside to cool.

In a bowl, combine the sour cream, cream cheese, horseradish, lemon juice, and chili oil. Mix the ingredients well. Spread some of the mixture evenly on top of each baked pizza crust. Arrange slices of smoked catfish on top of the sour cream mixture and return the pizzas to the oven until hot, about 3 to 4 minutes. Put the remaining sour cream mixture in a squeeze bottle and drizzle a zigzag design on top of each pizza. Sprinkle each with chopped chives, cut, and serve. Serve hot or at room temperature.

DEEP-FRIED CHIT'LINS AND MAWS

Chitterlings are one of those things: You are either a fan or you are not. If you already love chitterlings, you'll appreciate this new approach to the dish, which takes a cue from the Chinese, who also enjoy them fried.

2 eggs

2 cups milk

$1/4$ cup cornstarch

3 cups all-purpose flour

2 teaspoons salt

1 teaspoon freshly ground black
  pepper

5 pounds Simmered Chitterlings
  Country Style with Hog
  Maws (see page 214)

4 cups peanut oil

In a medium-size bowl, combine the eggs and milk and beat well. In another bowl, mix the cornstarch, flour, salt, and pepper. Separate the chitterlings and hog maws and drain them well. Separately dip the chitterlings and hog maws into the egg-milk mixture, coating evenly, then dredge them in the flour mixture.

Heat the oil in a large cast-iron skillet over medium-high heat. Fry the chitterlings and hog maws in batches until golden brown on both sides, about 2 to 3 minutes. Drain well on paper towels.

Serve hot with your favorite hot pepper sauce on the side.

Duo of Lump Crabmeat Cake and Gulf Shrimp Cake with Herb Mustard Sauce

MAKES 6 SERVINGS

It can be frustrating to order crab cakes in restaurants. There is usually too much cake and not enough crab. This combination of crab cakes and shrimp cakes served side by side is a real winner. The fresh herbs make a difference you can taste.

CRAB CAKES

1 pound lump crabmeat, picked over for cartilage and bits of shell

$1/4$ cup mayonnaise

2 teaspoons prepared mustard

1 egg, beaten

2 dashes Tabasco sauce

1 teaspoon Worcestershire sauce

14 club crackers, crumbled into fine crumbs (you should end up with $1/2$ cup crumbs)

1 teaspoon chopped fresh parsley

Salt and freshly ground black pepper to taste

SHRIMP CAKES

1 pound (10 to 15) jumbo shrimp

2 egg whites

$1/4$ cup mayonnaise

1 tablespoon chopped fresh dill weed

$1/2$ teaspoon dry mustard

1 teaspoon fresh lemon juice

Salt and freshly ground black pepper to taste

3 cups fresh bread crumbs

1 cup peanut oil

Remove and discard all shell and cartilage from the crabmeat and place the meat in a bowl. In a separate bowl, combine the mayonnaise, mustard, egg, Tabasco sauce, Worcestershire sauce, crumbs, parsley, salt, and pepper. Toss gently with the crabmeat, mixing thoroughly. Form six cakes about 1 inch thick (each will be about $3^1/2$ ounces). Coat each cake with bread crumbs and set aside.

Peel and devein the shrimp and remove the tails. Place half of the shrimp meat in a food processor fitted with the metal blade and puree until smooth, 1 to 2 minutes. Add the egg whites and puree 1 minute longer. Pour the mixture into a large bowl and stir in the mayonnaise, dill, mustard, lemon juice, salt, and pepper to taste. Mix well. Chop the remaining shrimp coarsely and add to the mixture. Form into six cakes about 1 inch thick (each about $3^1/2$ ounces). Coat each cake with fresh bread crumbs and set aside.

Heat the oil in a cast-iron skillet over medium-high heat and fry each of the crab and shrimp cakes until golden brown, about 3 to 4 minutes on each side. Drain on paper towels. Keep the cakes warm in a preheated 200°F oven.

Mustard Sauce

2 cups mayonnaise
$^1/_2$ cup Dijon mustard
2 teaspoons dry mustard
1 tablespoon finely chopped
   dill weed

Combine the mayonnaise, Dijon mustard, dry mustard, and chopped dill, and pour the mixture into a squeeze bottle. Drizzle the sauce onto warm plates in a crisscross design and place one crab cake and one shrimp cake in the center of each plate. Serve hot.

Timothy Dean's Jumbo Lump Crab Cakes with Ratatouille

MAKES 8 SERVINGS

This appetizer was inspired by Jean Louis, says Timothy. Their melt-in-your-mouth lightness is derived from the rich, smooth scallop mousse. To complete the presentation, the crab cakes are perched on a bed of ratatouille. Timothy says he adds ham to the vegetable dish so the flavor jumps off.

RATATOUILLE

3 ounces extra-virgin olive oil

$1/4$ cup diced Virginia ham

2 cloves garlic, minced

1 Italian eggplant, trimmed and cut into $1/4$-inch dice

1 yellow onion, peeled and cut into $1/4$-inch dice

1 zucchini, ends trimmed and cut into $1/4$-inch dice

1 yellow crookneck squash, ends trimmed and cut into $1/4$-inch dice

2 cups clam juice

2 tablespoons tomato paste

$1/8$ teaspoon salt

$1/8$ freshly ground black pepper

CRAB CAKES

3 ounces scallops

1 cup heavy cream

1 pound jumbo lump crabmeat, picked over for cartilage and bits of shell

1 teaspoon salt

1 teaspoon white pepper

2 tablespoons butter

$1/2$ tablespoon chopped fresh parsley

Preheat the oven to 350°F.

In a large sauté pan, heat the olive oil and sauté the ham, garlic, eggplant, onion, zucchini, and squash until tender, about 3 to 5 minutes. Add the clam juice and tomato paste. Reduce the heat and simmer 3 to 4 minutes. Season with salt and pepper. Keep warm, but do not allow to overcook.

Place the scallops in a food processor and puree until smooth. Blend in the cream until smooth. Place in a bowl and mix in the crabmeat. Season with salt and pepper, being careful not to break up the lumps. Form mixture into 3-ounce cakes and place on a buttered baking pan. Bake until golden. Remove and garnish with chopped parsley.

To serve, place about $1/3$ cup ratatouille on a serving plate. Top with a crab cake and garnish with chopped parsley. Serve immediately.

Fettuccine with Chitterling Sausage and Roasted Red Pepper Vinaigrette

MAKES 6 SERVINGS

Grilled chitterling sausage has a unique flavor that is even more appealing when napped with a tangy roasted red pepper vinaigrette and perched regally atop spicy, fresh homemade noodles.

4 cups unbleached all-purpose flour

1 teaspoon cayenne pepper

4 eggs

2 tablespoons olive oil

$^1/_8$ teaspoon salt

1 tablespoon peanut oil

$2^1/_4$ pounds Chitterling Sausage, poached (see page 203)

$1^1/_2$ cups Roasted Red Pepper Vinaigrette (see page 81)

6 sprigs fresh basil

Sift the flour and cayenne into a mound on a work surface and make a well in the center. Break the eggs into the well and add the olive oil and salt. Using a fork, beat the eggs and then gradually incorporate them into the flour. When the dough has begun to form, knead it with your hands until it becomes dry and elastic, about 10 to 15 minutes. Add a little more flour, if needed. Form the dough into a ball, dust with flour, and wrap it in plastic. Refrigerate for $1^1/_2$ hours until ready to roll and cut. (The dough can be refrigerated overnight.)

Divide the dough into four pieces and shape each into a ball. Flatten the pieces with a rolling pin until they are thin enough to pass through the largest setting on a manual pasta machine, then begin rolling the pasta through the machine, dusting with flour between rollings. The dough gets wide as it passes through the machine, so it needs to be folded in thirds lengthwise before each run through the machine. Keep lowering the setting on the rollers until the pasta has been rolled through the thinnest setting. Then cut the pasta into long strips for fettuccine, toss the strips with flour, and allow them to dry for at least 15 to 30 minutes before cooking. Drape them over a broomstick to dry. Repeat with the remaining dough.

Pan-fry the sausage in 1 tablespoon of the peanut oil over medium-high heat for 3 to 4 minutes on all sides. Cut it into 1-inch thick medallions and set aside in a covered dish in a warm oven to keep warm.

Bring a large pot of salted water to boil on high heat. Add the pasta. When the water returns to a full boil after the pasta has been added, cook for 30 seconds, then drain. In each of six serving dishes, arrange the sausage alongside the pasta, nap with Roasted Red Pepper Vinaigrette, and garnish with basil. Serve immediately.

Clifton Williams's Sautéed Shrimp with Linguine

African-Americans from Carolina to Louisiana love shrimp and some of us grew up with a seafood day every Friday. The marriage between pasta and shrimp in this dish is a delicious one.

24 large shrimp

$1/2$ cup Shrimp (Shellfish) Stock (see page 280)

$3/4$ cup ($1^1/2$ sticks) butter

1 cup finely chopped green onions, green part only

$1/2$ teaspoon minced garlic

$1/8$ teaspoon minced fresh basil

$1/8$ teaspoon minced fresh thyme

$1/8$ teaspoon minced fresh oregano

1 cup thinly sliced button mushrooms

$1/2$ teaspoon salt

$1/4$ teaspoon freshly ground black pepper

$1/8$ teaspoon cayenne pepper

1 pound linguine, cooked according to package directions

$1/8$ teaspoon minced fresh parsley

Peel and devein the shrimp. Reserve the shells for the stock and refrigerate the shrimp until needed. Melt $1/2$ cup of the butter in a sauté pan over medium heat. Add the green onions and garlic. Add the shrimp and sauté just until they turn pink, about 1 to 2 minutes, shaking the pan. Add the basil, thyme, oregano, and mushrooms and continue to shake the pan. Add the salt, black pepper, and cayenne. Add the Shellfish Stock and simmer 1 minute. Add the linguine and stir. Stir in the remaining $1/4$ cup butter and sprinkle with fresh chopped parsley. Arrange the pasta on hot serving plates with four shrimp per plate. Serve immediately.

Grilled Shrimp Wrapped in Smoked Bacon with White Bean Cakes and Roasted Red Pepper Vinaigrette

MAKES 8 SERVINGS

White toast made from French and Italian breads is a common canvas for chefs creating new and unusual appetizers. White bean cakes are a nice change of pace for hosts who are eager for a change. In this dish, Asian seasonings create an alluring backdrop for the shrimp.

24 large shrimp (16 to 20 per pound), peeled and deveined

$^1/_2$ cup peanut oil

$^1/_8$ teaspoon dark sesame oil

2 tablespoons seasoned rice vinegar

1 clove garlic, minced

$^1/_2$ tablespoon chopped fresh cilantro

12 strips thinly sliced smoked bacon, each strip cut in half crosswise

8 White Bean Cakes, cooked (see page 113)

Roasted Red Pepper Vinaigrette (see page 81)

Put the shrimp into a large bowl. In a separate small bowl, combine the peanut oil, sesame oil, rice vinegar, garlic, and cilantro and mix well. Pour the oil mixture over the shrimp, cover, and refrigerate for at least 8 hours or overnight.

Preheat the grill until white ash forms on top of the coals or preheat the broiler to high. Place the broiler pan under the broiler to heat.

Remove the shrimp from the marinade and discard the marinade. Wrap each shrimp with half a strip of bacon and secure the bacon. Arrange the bacon-wrapped shrimp on long wooden skewers, about six shrimp per skewer. Grill the shrimp on each side over hot coals or under the heated broiler until the bacon browns and the shrimp turn pink, about 3 to 4 minutes. Remove the long skewers.

Drizzle a pool of Roasted Red Pepper Vinaigrette onto a serving plate. Place a hot bean cake on top of the pool and arrange the shrimp around the bean cake. Serve immediately.

Grilled Quail Stuffed with Collard Greens with Creamy Grits

Leftover greens are common in African-American refrigerators. For something elegant, serve them to guests stuffed in quail on creamy grits.

6 whole quail, breastbones
   removed
2 tablespoons olive oil
Salt to taste
Freshly ground black pepper
   to taste
1$^1/_2$ cups Southern Collard
   Greens (see page 109)
$^1/_2$ cup Chicken Stock
   (see page 279)
2 tablespoons red currant jelly
$^1/_4$ teaspoon red pepper flakes
2 cups Creamy Grits, cooked
   (see page 95)

Preheat the oven to 375°F.

Rub the quail with the olive oil and season them inside and out with salt and pepper. Place the quail on the rack of a large roasting pan, and roast for 15 to 20 minutes or until juices are clear. Remove the quail from the oven and set aside to cool. Stuff each bird with 4 tablespoons of cooked Southern Collard Greens.

Preheat the grill until white ash forms on top of the coals or preheat the broiler to high. Place the broiler pan under the broiler to heat.

Start reducing the sauce after the bird is in the oven. In a small saucepan, bring the chicken stock, jelly, and red pepper flakes to a boil, then reduce until syrupy or it coats the back of a spoon, about 1 hour. Meanwhile, grill the quail evenly over medium-hot coals, basting with the syrup until thoroughly cooked, 4 to 5 minutes on each side.

Perch each quail on a bed of Creamy Grits and serve immediately.

Sautéed Sea Scallops with Black Bean Cakes and Citrus Vinaigrette

MAKES 8 SERVINGS

These feisty bean cakes can be made in advance and reheated while the scallops are cooking. The vinaigrette can be made a few days ahead. The bean cakes can be served with any number of steamed or sautéed vegetables.

24 large sea scallops, connective
   muscle removed
$^1/_2$ tablespoon salt
1 teaspoon freshly ground
   black pepper
$^1/_4$ cup all-purpose flour
   (optional)
2 tablespoons olive oil
2 tablespoons butter
1 tablespoon minced garlic
8 Black Bean Cakes, cooked
   (see page 112)
2 cups Citrus Vinaigrette
   (see page 80)
1 tablespoon chopped chives

Season the scallops with the salt and pepper. If you care to use flour, lightly dust the seasoned scallops with it and shake off any excess. Heat the olive oil and butter in a cast-iron skillet or sauté pan over medium-high heat. Add the scallops and garlic and sauté for 3 minutes on each side.

Place a bean cake in the center of each serving plate. Arrange the warm scallops around the cakes and nap with Citrus Vinaigrette. Garnish with chopped chives and serve hot.

SAUTÉED FOIE GRAS, CRISP MUSTARD GREENS, WATERCRESS, AND CARAMELIZED RED ONION WITH COUNTRY SMOKED BACON DRESSING

MAKES 8 SERVINGS

Chefs are always looking for new ways to add flair to menus. Adding foie gras, the epitome of aristocracy, takes humble mustard greens to new heights. Be careful not to overcook this dish.

1 tablespoon butter

1 pound fresh foie gras, cut into eight 2-ounce slices

2 bunches mustard greens, washed thoroughly, stems removed, and cut into a broad chiffonade

1 bunch watercress, washed and trimmed

2 strips smoked bacon

8 slices red onion, cut ¼ inch thick

½ tablespoon sugar

1 cup Country Smoked Bacon Dressing (see page 78)

Heat a cast-iron skillet over high heat. Add the butter and sauté four slices of foie gras for 30 seconds on each side and keep warm on a plate. Repeat with the remaining foie gras. Mix the mustard greens and watercress in a large serving bowl. In the same skillet, fry the bacon until it is brown and crispy. Remove the bacon and drain it on paper towels. Crumble the bacon into small pieces.

Sauté the red onion in the bacon drippings over medium-high heat. Sprinkle them with the sugar to help caramelize them. Sauté until they begin to caramelize and are almost brown, about 3 to 5 minutes.

Toss the greens with the Country Smoked Bacon Dressing. Arrange the coated greens on individual serving plates and place a piece of foie gras on each plate. Top the pieces of foie gras with onion and crumbled bacon and serve at once.

Sautéed Salt Mackerel, Wild Mushrooms, Smithfield Ham, and Oyster Broth

MAKES 4 SERVINGS

My father loved fresh oyster stew; my grandmother adored fried salt mackerel. Fond memories of both inspired me to create this dish. It was a huge hit, served at the first Elegant Taste of Heritage benefit dinner in the spring of 1993 at the Hay-Adams Hotel in Washington, D.C., which was hosted by Chef Patrick Clark.

Four 4-ounce Cured Salted
    Mackerel fillets (see page 269)
$^1/_2$ cup all-purpose flour
$^1/_4$ teaspoon freshly ground
    black pepper
$^1/_2$ teaspoon paprika
$^1/_2$ cup peanut oil
1 cup Sautéed Wild Mushrooms
    (see page 107)
$^1/_4$ pound Smithfield ham, thinly
    sliced and cut into julienne
2 cups Oyster Broth
    (see page 282)
1 tablespoon chopped fresh chives

Remove the mackerel from the brine and rinse under cold running water. Place the mackerel in a bowl and cover it with cold water. Allow the fish to soak for at least 12 hours or overnight. Just before use, drain the mackerel and pat dry with paper towels.

In a bowl, mix the flour, pepper, and paprika. Heat the oil in a sauté pan over medium-high heat, dust the mackerel fillets with seasoned flour, and sauté them for 2 to 3 minutes on each side. Remove the fillets from the pan and drain them on paper towels; keep hot in a preheated 200°F.

Place each mackerel fillet in the center of a large soup plate. Place 3 tablespoons of mushrooms and 3 of the oysters reserved from the Oyster Broth around each fillet; top with slivers of Smithfield ham and pour Oyster Broth into each bowl. Garnish with chopped chives and serve immediately.

SAUTÉED SHRIMP AND CREAMY GRITS WITH TASSO TOMATO BROTH

MAKES 8 SERVINGS

When Norm Nixon and Brad Johnson asked me to create the menu for the opening of Georgia, the popular Melrose Avenue restaurant in Los Angeles, I knew it would have to be something really special. This recipe was just for them.

$^1/_2$ cup clarified butter

48 large shrimp, peeled and deveined

6 cloves garlic, minced

1 tablespoon chopped fresh thyme

$^1/_4$ teaspoon freshly ground black pepper

2 cups Tasso Tomato Broth (see page 282)

1 cup Creamy Grits (see page 95)

8 sprigs thyme

In a large sauté pan, heat $^1/_4$ cup of the butter over medium-high heat and sauté 12 shrimp and 2 cloves of the minced garlic on each side until the shrimp turn pink and are firm, about 3 to 4 minutes. Repeat with the remaining shrimp and 2 more cloves of minced garlic. Add half the thyme and pepper, stir in 1 cup of Tasso Tomato Broth, reduce the heat, and simmer for 2 minutes. Remove from the heat and keep warm in a double boiler or hot water bath. Repeat with the remaining butter, shrimp, garlic, thyme, pepper, and broth.

To serve, spoon 2 tablespoons of hot Creamy Grits in the center of each heated soup plate; arrange 6 shrimp and some broth around the grits. Spoon extra broth over the shrimp, garnish with a sprig of fresh thyme in the center of the grits, and serve immediately.

Sautéed Shrimp with Tomato Broth and Pan-fried Grits

MAKES 8 SERVINGS

This is an original creation I prepared for an Elegant Taste of Heritage benefit dinner held in the spring of 1995 at the Grand Hyatt Hotel in Washington, D.C. It was a hit with the attendees.

24 large shrimp, peeled and
    deveined
$^1/_4$ teaspoon salt
$^1/_4$ teaspoon freshly ground
    black pepper
2 teaspoons chopped fresh thyme
$^1/_2$ cup (1 stick) butter
4 cloves garlic, minced
16 cooked Pan-fried Grits
    Triangles (see page 105)
2 cups Tomato Broth
    (see page 283)
8 sprigs fresh thyme

Place the shrimp in a bowl and season with the salt, pepper, and thyme.

Heat the butter in a sauté pan over medium-high heat. Sauté half the garlic and 12 shrimp until the shrimp are firm, about 2 to 3 minutes on each side; do not overcook. Set aside and repeat with the second batch of shrimp.

To serve, place a Pan-fried Grits Triangle in the center of each of eight soup plates. Place a second triangle at an angle across the top. Arrange 3 shrimp around the triangles. Spoon the Tomato Broth around the shrimp. Garnish with a sprig of fresh thyme in the center and serve immediately.

Shrimp Custard with Roasted Red Peppers and Remoulade Sauce

MAKES 6 TO 8 SERVINGS

Shrimp remoulade is a standard in New Orleans and there are many versions,
of which this is a lighter, more delicate version.

$^1/_4$ cup ($^1/_2$ stick) butter

8 large shrimp, peeled, deveined, tails removed, and cut into small pieces

$^1/_2$ tablespoon minced shallots

1 teaspoon fresh lemon juice

$2^3/_4$ cups milk

4 eggs, beaten

1 teaspoon finely sliced fresh chives

$^1/_2$ teaspoon salt

$^1/_8$ teaspoon cayenne pepper

2 marinated Roasted Red Peppers (see page 272)

2 tablespoons extra-virgin olive oil

$^1/_2$ tablespoon red wine vinegar

Salt to taste

Freshly ground black pepper to taste

$^1/_2$ head green leaf lettuce, shredded

1 cup Remoulade Sauce (see page 289)

1 tablespoon sliced chives, for garnish

Heat the butter in a sauté pan over medium-high heat. Sauté the shrimp for 2 to 3 minutes, then add the shallots and lemon juice and sauté 1 minute more. Remove from the pan and set aside to cool.

In a medium-size saucepan, bring the milk just to a boil. When the milk is scalded, turn off the heat and cover the pan so the milk will remain hot.

In a large mixing bowl, whisk the eggs until they are light and just frothy; whisk in the chives, salt, and cayenne. Gradually whisk the hot milk into the mixture, beating well.

Preheat the oven to 350°F. Grease six 4-ounce soufflé molds, or any nonstick 3- to 4-ounce cup or dish.

Divide the shrimp evenly among the six soufflé molds, then pour in the custard. Set the molds in a 13 × 9-inch baking pan; pour very hot water 1-inch deep into the pan. Put the baking pan in the oven and bake the custards until a thin-bladed knife inserted in center comes out clean, about 35 to 45 minutes. Remove the soufflé molds from the water, cool, and refrigerate until ready to serve. They will keep 1 to 2 days in the refrigerator.

Cut the roasted peppers into strips. In a large bowl, combine the olive oil, vinegar, salt, and pepper. Pour the mixture over the roasted pepper strips and refrigerate until needed. They will keep 1 to 2 days in the refrigerator.

To serve, place shredded lettuce in the center of six serving plates. Unmold the chilled custards onto the center of each plate. Spoon 2 tablespoons of Remoulade Sauce over each custard, arrange the marinated peppers around each plate, and garnish with fresh chives.

SMOKED CATFISH WITH CORN CAKES, CREOLE SOUR CREAM, AND HOT CHILI OIL

MAKES 8 SERVINGS

I have always enjoyed smoked fish of all kinds—salmon, trout, sturgeon, and catfish. This was my contribution to the Black Culinarian Alumni Chapter of the Culinary Institute of America benefit dinner, held at the Loew's Hotel in New York City in February 1995. The smoked catfish along with the corn cakes stole the show. This version of smoked catfish is juicy and moist and has a real smoky flavor.

CORN CAKES

3 cups fresh or frozen sweet
   corn kernels

1/2 medium onion, finely chopped

1 cup milk

3 eggs

1 1/2 cups all-purpose flour

3/4 cup yellow cornmeal

1 teaspoon salt

1/2 teaspoon freshly ground
   black pepper

3 tablespoons melted butter

3 green onions, finely sliced

1 cup corn oil

TO FINISH THE DISH

2 pounds Smoked Catfish, thinly
   sliced (see page 273)

2 cups Creole Sour Cream
   (see page 287), poured into
   a squeeze bottle

1/2 tablespoon hot chili oil

1 tablespoon chopped fresh chives

In a blender, puree the corn, onion, milk, and eggs until smooth. Pour the mixture into a mixing bowl and whisk in the flour, cornmeal, salt, and pepper. Stir in the butter and green onions.

Lightly oil a griddle preheated to a medium-high heat. Ladle about 2 tablespoons of the batter for each cake onto the hot griddle. Cook until lightly brown, turn, and repeat on the other side. Keep warm, covered, on a plate in a preheated 200°F oven.

To serve place 3 corn cakes on each serving plate near the center. Arrange 4 ounces of sliced catfish on top. Drizzle Creole Sour Cream in an attractive zigzag pattern over the entire plate, and place 3 drops of hot chili oil around the plate. Sprinkle with chopped chives.

CHEF'S TIP

Look for hot chili oil in Asian markets or in the Oriental section of your supermarket.

John Harrison's Clams Casino

Clams are among John's favorite shellfish and he says this dish is a good example of how a little bit of the country can spice up any meal.

$^1/_4$ cup ($^1/_2$ stick) butter

$^1/_2$ cup diced onion

$^1/_2$ cup diced green pepper

$^1/_4$ teaspoon paprika

$^1/_2$ cup diced pimiento

2 dozen cherrystone clams, washed

6 slices slab bacon, cut into quarters

Preheat the oven to 375°F.

Heat the butter in a sauté pan and sauté the onion, pepper, and paprika about 2 minutes. Stir in the pimiento and set aside. Open clams, discarding top shells and removing the muscle. Arrange clams on a baking pan and top with about 1 tablespoon of the sautéed vegetables. Place a piece of bacon on top of the vegetables. Bake until bacon is browned, about 20 minutes.

CHEF'S TIP
This dish is wonderful with a squeeze of fresh lemon juice.

Steamed Littleneck Clams with Clam Nectar, Frizzled Leeks, and Hot Pepper Butter Sauce

MAKES 8 SERVINGS

Steamed shellfish always make a nice first course and these spicy clams are no exception to the rule. Be sure you discard any clams that arrive unopened. Hot Pepper Butter Sauce is also great with steamed cracked crabs.

3 cups julienned leeks, white
  part only
1 quart clam juice
1 cup sauternes
8 dozen littleneck clams,
  scrubbed

HOT PEPPER BUTTER SAUCE
1 cup clarified butter
$1/2$ cup Frank's Red Hot Sauce
  or other Louisiana hot pepper
  sauce
$1/4$ teaspoon fresh lemon juice
1 teaspoon finely chopped fresh
  parsley
2 cups peanut oil

Chill the leeks in ice water until ready to use.

Heat a stainless-steel pot over medium-high heat until hot, then add 2 cups of the clam juice, $1/4$ cup of the sauternes, and 4 dozen clams. Cover and cook for 6 to 8 minutes, shaking the pot so the clams cook evenly. As the clams open, remove them immediately to a heated bowl to keep them warm. (Be sure to remove the clams as soon as they open; they become chewy and tough if overcooked.) Repeat with the remaining juice, wine, and clams. Strain the cooking broth and pour a little in each heated serving bowl. Place the bowl in a preheated 200°F oven for 10 minutes before serving.

For sauce, in a blender, puree the butter, hot sauce, lemon juice, and parsley until the mixture reaches an even consistency. Place in a saucepan and boil over medium-high heat, then reduce the heat and keep warm.

Drain the leeks and dry them on paper towels. Heat the oil in a skillet over high heat and deep-fry the leeks until frizzled, crispy, and crunchy. Drain the frizzled leeks on paper towels. Place a mound of leeks in the center of the clams. Pass the Hot Pepper Butter Sauce at the table.

Chapter 2

·········

Gumbos, Stews, and Soups

THROUGHOUT OUR CULINARY HISTORY, AFRICAN-AMERICANS HAVE DEPENDED UPON
soups, stews, and gumbos to make a little go a long way. With bits of meat and lots of
vegetables and starches including potatoes, rice, and pasta, we have created hearty soups that are
suitable as savory beginnings to more substantial suppers or, when accompanied by corn bread
or biscuits and salad, as complete meals.

Consider gumbo, the murky soup-stew that started as a hodgepodge of a cook's favorite
ingredients. In New Orleans, where the dish originated in Creole kitchens, the pot is rich with
crab, shrimp, and other sea animals because they are so plentiful in the gulf region. Another cook
might have stirred smoked sausage and chicken into the mix; still others would have flavored the
brew with okra and tomatoes. Whichever you prefer, authentic Creole-style gumbo is a dish with

a kick. So is my Jamaican Pepper Pot, which is something for fanciers of the exotic. Better taste it as you go along; some palates might find this version incendiary.

Gumbo is truly a dish with numerous influences. The peppery blends of Africa, mingled with the sophistication of France, make for a palate-haunting experience. Gumbo takes its name from the African word for okra, the vegetable that provides thickening in some recipes. Okra, in concert with the French technique of combining flour and fat, called a roux, gives the soup body. Long, slow cooking of this pasty, rich mixture, is what gives gumbo its characteristic dark, earthy flavor. You may think roux making is a tedious, time-consuming process, but it's one that is well worth mastering. Trust me.

Filé, a seasoning made from dried, tender sassafras leaves, also contributes flavor and texture to gumbo. Sprinkle the powder over the pot near the end of cooking time or it will make your soup thready and gummy. Here's a trick from a friend in New Orleans: Keep a bottle of filé powder next to the salt and pepper shakers and the hot sauce on the dinner table. Then sprinkle it over the rice before spooning on the gumbo.

Understated but creamy bisques and vegetable soups make up the remainder of our soup repertoire. Catfish Stew with Cornmeal Dumplings is so hearty you'll want to serve it on chilly winter nights. If you're hosting a meal for a few of your adventurous friends, Caribbean Fish Tea is ideal.

CATFISH STEW WITH CORNMEAL DUMPLINGS

Catfish stew is a dish found all over the South. The addition of cornmeal dumplings in this version adds extra body to the broth.

2 pounds catfish bones

6 cups water

1 tablespoon salt

1 cup minced onion

3 cloves garlic, minced

4 potatoes, peeled and diced

$1/2$ cup diced celery

2 cups canned whole peeled
tomatoes, chopped with their
liquid

1 teaspoon freshly ground
black pepper

1 teaspoon cayenne pepper

CORNMEAL DUMPLINGS

$3/4$ cup all-purpose flour

$1/4$ cup yellow cornmeal

$1^1/2$ teaspoons baking powder

$1/2$ teaspoon salt

1 egg, beaten

$1/3$ cup milk

2 tablespoons bacon drippings

$2^1/2$ pounds catfish fillets

2 teaspoons chopped fresh
thyme

2 tablespoons chopped fresh
parsley

In a large soup pot, combine the fish bones, water, and salt. Bring to a boil, then reduce the heat and simmer for 30 minutes. Strain the stock into a clean pot and discard the bones. Bring the clear stock to a boil and add the onions, garlic, potatoes, celery, tomatoes, black pepper, and cayenne, stirring occasionally.

To make the cornmeal dumpling batter, in a bowl, combine the flour, cornmeal, baking powder, and salt. Mix in the egg, milk, and bacon drippings.

When the stock returns to a boil, reduce the heat and simmer until the potatoes are half done (cooked but still firm), about 10 to 15 minutes. Stir in the catfish and cook for 5 to 6 minutes. Stir in the thyme and parsley. Drop teaspoons of the cornmeal dumpling batter into the boiling catfish stew, one at a time, cover, and allow to simmer until the fish is cooked, potatoes are soft, and dumplings are cooked through, about 10 to 15 minutes. Serve three dumplings in each bowl with the stew, making sure there is plenty of broth. Add water if there isn't enough broth.

CHEF'S TIP

Store leftover dumplings and stew in separate containers in the refrigerator so that the dumplings don't absorb all the liquid from the stew.

CHICKEN AND SHRIMP STEW

In the middle of the week when you are in need of a recipe that goes together fast with just a few ingredients, but with hearty flavor, this is just what you're looking for.

¹/₄ pound finely diced salt pork

Four 6-ounce boneless, skinless chicken breasts

¹/₂ cup diced onion

2 tablespoons all-purpose flour

6 cups water

1¹/₂ cups peeled and diced potatoes

1 teaspoon salt

¹/₂ teaspoon freshly ground black pepper

¹/₄ teaspoon cayenne pepper

2 pounds large shrimp, peeled and deveined

2 teaspoons chopped fresh thyme

In a large skillet or small stockpot over medium-high heat sauté the salt pork until lightly brown, about 3 to 4 minutes. Add the chicken and sauté for 2 to 3 minutes. Add the onion and cook 1 minute more. Stir in the flour and cook until it browns. Add the water, potatoes, salt, black pepper, and cayenne. Cover and simmer over low heat until the potatoes are almost tender, 15 to 20 minutes. Stir in the shrimp and thyme and cook until the shrimp turn pink, about 3 to 5 minutes longer.

CHICKEN BREAST STEW COUSCOUS

MAKES 8 SERVINGS

One of my students at Cal-Poly (California State Polytechnic University) in Pomona, California, named "Mama Do," considered couscous the national dish of Senegal, his home, though it is most often thought of as a North African dish. He pleased visitors to an international food fair sponsored by the International Club of the School of Hotel and Restaurant Management with this couscous soup. Guests at a Real Men Cook benefit enjoyed it, as well.

Eight 8-ounce boneless, skinless
  chicken breasts
2 teaspoons salt
2 teaspoons freshly ground
  black pepper
$1/4$ cup ($1/2$ stick) butter
$1/4$ cup extra-virgin olive oil
$1^1/2$ cups onions, cut into
  $1/4$-inch dice
3 cloves garlic, minced
2 teaspoons minced gingerroot
$1/4$ cup all-purpose flour
1 quart Chicken Stock
  (see page 279)
2 dozen large pimento-stuffed
  Spanish olives
$1/2$ cup dried dates
$1/2$ cup dried black currants
2 cinnamon sticks
$1/2$ teaspoon saffron threads
1 teaspoon cayenne pepper
$2^1/2$ cups quick-cooking couscous

Season the chicken with the salt and black pepper.

In a large saucepan or braising pan, heat the butter and olive oil over medium-high heat. Sauté the chicken breasts in two batches until golden brown, about 3 to 4 minutes on each side. Remove from the pan and set aside.

In same pan over medium-high heat, sauté the onions, garlic, and ginger 2 to 3 minutes. Stir in the flour and cook for 2 to 3 minutes. Add the chicken stock, olives, dates, currants, cinnamon, saffron, and cayenne. Bring the mixture to a boil, then reduce the heat to a simmer. Return the chicken to the pan and cook for 20 to 25 minutes, stirring occasionally. Add more chicken stock or water if the stew seems too thick.

Prepare the couscous according to the directions on the package. Place the hot cooked couscous on a large platter. Pour the liquid over it, arranging the chicken on top. Garnish the dish with dates, currants, olives, and more stewing liquid.

CREOLE SEAFOOD GUMBO

MAKES 8 TO 10 SERVINGS

Some foods have the ability to do strange things to some people. Gumbo is one such dish. In the early 1980s, while living in Sacramento, I was shopping for the ingredients to make a pot of gumbo for entertaining at home. I saw a friend and told her what I was cooking. After purchasing the groceries, I returned home to get started. About two hours before our guests arrived, a complete stranger stood at the door inquiring whether the gumbo was ready. The woman said someone had told her I was preparing a pot of gumbo and she had to have some.

She introduced herself and offered to help vacuum or do anything to earn a taste of gumbo. My wife and I declined her offer to help, but seeing her passion for gumbo, we invited her to join us for dinner. She was elated, thanked us, and promised to return, but wondered if she could bring her daughter also. From that day on I knew that gumbo was a very special dish, much more than just a seafood soup.

1 chicken, cut into 10 pieces

2 cups all-purpose flour

$2^1/_2$ cups peanut oil

$^3/_4$ pound Chaurice Sausage, cut into $^1/_2$-inch pieces (see page 201)

$1^1/_2$ pounds large shrimp, peeled and deveined

4 large blue crabs, cleaned and cut into pieces

2 medium onions, diced

1 large green pepper, diced

3 ribs celery, diced

3 cloves garlic, minced

1 cup smoked hot sausage, cut into $^1/_2$-inch pieces

1 cup smoked ham, cut into $^1/_4$-inch dice

3 quarts Shrimp (Shellfish) Stock, strained (see page 280)

Dust the chicken pieces with 1 cup of the flour. Heat $1^1/_4$ cups of the peanut oil in a skillet over medium-high heat and fry the pieces of chicken in batches for 6 to 8 minutes on each side. Drain and set aside.

Cook the Chaurice Sausage in the same skillet over medium-high heat until most of the fat has rendered or the sausage has become firm and most of the fat has melted, about 4 to 5 minutes. Drain and set aside.

Refrigerate the shrimp and crab in separate containers.

In a heavy bottomed, 8-quart stockpot, heat 1 cup of the peanut oil over medium heat. Whisk in 1 cup flour, whisking constantly until the roux is reddish-brown, about 8 to 10 minutes. Reduce the heat to low. Add the onions, green peppers, celery, and garlic to the roux and cook over low heat until the vegetables are wilted. Add the smoked sausage and ham. Continue to cook and stir for 2 minutes. Add the Shrimp (Shellfish) Stock, 2 cups at a time, stirring constantly, until it is evenly incorporated. Bring the mixture to a boil, then add the fried chicken, crab, parsley, paprika, thyme, salt, and cayenne. Return to a

1/4 cup chopped fresh parsley

1 tablespoon paprika

1 tablespoon chopped fresh thyme

1 teaspoon salt

1 teaspoon cayenne pepper

1 pound fresh okra, sliced

30 Eastern oysters, including
their liquor

1 tablespoon filé powder

3 cups Steamed Buttered Rice
(see page 114)

boil, then reduce the heat and simmer for 30 to 45 minutes, stirring occasionally.

Heat the remaining 1/4 cup peanut oil in a sauté pan over medium-high heat and cook the okra until almost dry, about 4 to 5 minutes. Drain and set aside. Add the sautéed okra, shrimp, and oysters with their liquor to the gumbo pot and continue to cook 15 minutes more. Remove from the heat. Add filé powder, stirring well. Serve warm over Steamed Buttered Rice.

Store well in the refrigerator for 2 to 3 days in shallow containers. This gumbo can be frozen and kept for up to 30 days.

J.R.'s Oyster Stew

Dr. Joseph A. Randall, my father, loved fresh oysters and while he studied at Howard University in Washington, D.C., this was one of his favorite dishes. While working at the Harrisburger Hotel in the Jack Room I perfected this simple but wonderful oyster stew.

$^1/_2$ cup (1 stick) butter

1 pint Eastern oysters, shucked, with their liquor

$^1/_2$ teaspoon Worcestershire sauce

1 quart half-and-half

1 teaspoon salt

$^1/_4$ teaspoon white pepper

$^1/_8$ teaspoon cayenne pepper

$^1/_2$ tablespoon finely chopped parsley

Heat the butter in a large sauté pan over medium heat. Add the oysters with their liquor and the Worcestershire sauce. Reduce the heat to low and cook until the edges of the oysters curl, about 2 or 3 minutes. Add the half-and-half and heat until bubbles form around the edge. Do not boil. Season with the salt, white pepper, and cayenne.

Pour the soup into heated bowls, sprinkle with parsley, and serve with your favorite oyster crackers.

EARLEST BELL'S OLD-FASHIONED BEEF AND OXTAIL STEW

This dish will knock your socks off and it tastes even better the next day. Earlest's oxtail stew deviates from traditional versions a bit, but it still resonates African-American heritage.

2 pounds oxtails, cut into pieces

2 pounds stew beef, cut into cubes

1 teaspoon salt

$1/2$ teaspoon freshly ground
    black pepper

1 cup all-purpose flour

$1/2$ cup vegetable oil

2 medium carrots, diced

1 medium green pepper, seeded
    and diced

1 medium onion, diced

1 rib celery, diced

2 cloves garlic, minced

One 8-ounce can whole tomatoes

1 quart Veal (Brown) Stock
    (see page 281) or water

3 cups potatoes, peeled and
    cut into 1-inch dice
    (about 5 medium potatoes)

$1/4$ teaspoon dried oregano

2 bay leaves

Season oxtail and stew meat with salt and pepper and sprinkle with flour.

In a large Dutch oven, heat half the oil and brown the meat evenly on all sides. Remove the meat from the pan set aside. Add the remaining oil and cook the carrots, green pepper, onion, celery, garlic, and tomatoes. Stir in the meat and stock and cook over medium heat until meat is tender, approximately 1 hour. Add potatoes and continue to cook until potatoes are tender. Mash half the potatoes to thicken the liquid. Add the oregano and bay leaves and adjust seasoning with salt and pepper. Let simmer over low heat 15 minutes longer. Serve with white rice, mashed potatoes, or millet.

PATRICK CLARK'S BAY SCALLOP CHOWDER

MAKES 12 SERVINGS

Patrick's father, a New York chef, loved seafood and often brought scallops home for dinner. "It was one of his favorite things." This thick, creamy soup is a tribute to Dad.

3 tablespoons butter

2 slices bacon, finely chopped

2 medium onions, diced

1 clove garlic, minced

$1/2$ teaspoon crushed red pepper flakes

1 bouquet garni (bay leaf, parsley stems, fresh thyme, and black peppercorns)

3 quarts clam juice or chicken stock

3 cups diced Yukon Gold potatoes (about 8 to 10 potatoes)

2 tablespoons cornstarch

$2^1/4$ cups heavy cream

2 large leeks, split lengthwise, washed, and thinly sliced, white part only

$1^1/2$ pounds Nantucket Bay scallops, cleaned, with the tiny muscle removed

Salt and freshly ground black pepper to taste

$1/2$ cup minced chives

In a large Dutch oven or enameled cast-iron pot, melt the butter. Add the bacon and cook until bacon is no longer pink, about 1 to 2 minutes. Add the onions and cook until tender and transparent, about 5 to 7 minutes. Add the garlic and crushed red pepper and cook an additional 2 to 3 minutes. Drop in the bouquet garni and add the clam juice. Bring to a simmer and cook about 20 minutes. Add diced potatoes and cook until just tender. Dissolve the cornstarch in $1/4$ cup of the cream, then mix with the remaining cream. Remove the bouquet garni, then increase heat and bring the soup to a boil. Whisk the cream into the boiling soup, then add the leeks and cook for 3 to 4 minutes. Reduce the heat to medium, add the scallops, and cook 3 to 4 minutes, being careful not to allow mixture to boil. Season with salt and freshly ground pepper. Serve immediately, dividing evenly among warm soup bowls. Sprinkle with chives.

Prince Akins's Black-eyed Pea Soup

Now that black-eyed peas and collards have become more mainstream and are so readily available in supermarkets, more cooks are experimenting with new ways of preparing them, like this delicious soup.

1 pound dried black-eyed peas

$^1/_4$ cup bacon drippings

$1^1/_2$ medium onions, finely diced

2 cloves garlic, minced

2 ribs celery, finely diced

$1^1/_2$ pounds smoked pork neck bones, cut into pieces

3 quarts water

1 teaspoon chopped fresh thyme

2 bay leaves

1 teaspoon salt

1 teaspoon cayenne pepper

1 teaspoon freshly ground black pepper

2 cups Steamed Buttered Rice (see page 114)

Place the peas in a large bowl with 1 quart of water and soak 8 hours or overnight.

Heat the bacon drippings in a soup pot and add the onions, garlic, and celery. Sauté 2 minutes. Add the neck bones and water, stir, and bring to a boil. Cover and reduce the heat to medium. Allow to cook until the meat easily comes away from the bone, about $1^1/_2$ hours. Drain the peas and add to the pot along with the thyme, bay leaves, salt, and cayenne and black peppers. Return to a boil, then reduce the heat and cook until the peas are tender, $1^1/_4$ to $1^1/_2$ hours. Do not overcook. Remove the neck bones from the pot, remove the meat from the bones and chop. Return the meat to the pot, stir in the cooked rice, and correct seasoning and consistency. Serve hot.

BEEF TENDERLOIN SOUP

MAKES 10 TO 12 SERVINGS

A trip to San Francisco's theater district used to be a special treat, as long as it included a visit to Geary Street for a bowl of Pam East's superb steak soup. This is my version, which can be made with round steak, but tenderloin gives the soup an air of sophistication.

2 pounds trimmed and finely
   diced beef tenderloin

$^1/_2$ cup (1 stick) butter

1 clove garlic, minced

1 medium onion, finely chopped

1 large carrot, finely chopped

4 ribs celery, finely chopped

1 cup all-purpose flour

Two 16-ounce cans whole
   tomatoes, finely chopped

2 quarts Veal (Brown) Stock
   (see page 281)

1 tablespoon Worcestershire sauce

1 teaspoon salt

1 teaspoon freshly ground
   black pepper

2 cups half-and-half

1 teaspoon chopped fresh
   parsley leaves

In a 8-quart stockpot over medium heat, brown the meat 4 to 5 minutes. Add the butter, garlic, onion, carrot, and celery and sauté for 2 to 3 minutes. Stir in the flour and cook for 10 minutes. Add the tomatoes, veal stock, Worcestershire sauce, salt, and pepper. Bring the mixture to a boil, then reduce the heat and simmer for 45 minutes. Add the half-and-half and simmer 15 minutes more.

Sprinkle with parsley and serve at once with hot crusty bread.

CARIBBEAN FISH TEA

While visiting lifelong friends Gary and Patricia Miller in Montego Bay, Jamaica, I discovered this magnificent dish, which is highly regarded by the islanders. The flavorful broth is another example of black folk making the best of what's available. The original recipe probably called for fish heads or the leftover carcass of filleted fish. This rich broth is eaten like a soup.

2 quarts water

2 pounds parrot fish, cleaned and cut into pieces, or use any firm white fish

4 medium Yukon Gold potatoes, peeled and diced

1 medium carrot, diced

$1/4$ cup peeled and diced mirliton (also called chayote, a pale green squash readily found in the produce section of your supermarket)

2 green onions, sliced

1 teaspoon ground allspice

1 sprig fresh thyme

1 whole Scotch bonnet pepper

1 teaspoon salt

$1/2$ teaspoon freshly ground black pepper

In a large soup pot, bring the water and fish to a boil. Reduce the heat and simmer, covered, for 30 to 40 minutes. Strain the stock and set the fish aside to cool.

In a large soup pot, bring the stock to a boil. Add the potatoes, carrot, mirliton, onions, allspice, thyme, Scotch bonnet pepper, salt, and black pepper. Reduce the heat and simmer. Remove fish flesh from the bones and add the fish to the soup. Discard the bones. Simmer the soup, stirring occasionally, until the potatoes and squash are tender, about 15 to 20 minutes. Remove the whole Scotch bonnet pepper, being careful not to break it, and discard it.

Serve the soup hot in cups.

EARLEST BELL'S CHICKEN AND DUMPLING SOUP

When Earlest was growing up, his mother prepared chicken and dumplings on Sundays before church. Not only did the dish taste great, but it kept him full for hours. That memory was the catalyst for this soup, which Earlest has served at hotels and restaurants all over the United States.

1 stewing chicken, cut into
    8 pieces
2 ribs celery, chopped
1 green bell pepper, seeded and
    chopped
1 medium carrot, peeled and
    chopped
1 medium onion, chopped
$1/2$ bay leaf
$1/2$ teaspoon fresh thyme
Salt and freshly ground black
    pepper to taste

DUMPLINGS
1 egg, beaten
3 tablespoons milk
1 tablespoon cold water
1 cup all-purpose flour
$1/4$ teaspoon salt
1 teaspoon baking powder

Place the chicken in a large Dutch oven and add cold water to cover. Bring to a boil, then reduce the heat to simmer, skim the broth, and continue to cook until chicken is tender and easily comes off the bone, about 1 hour. Remove the chicken from the stock, then remove and discard the skin and bones. Dice the meat and reserve. Add the vegetables, seasonings, and diced chicken to the stock, adding more water, if needed. Bring to a boil, then reduce the heat to simmer and cook 15 minutes.

Meanwhile, for the dumplings, beat the egg, milk, and water together until light. Beat in the dry ingredients to form a soft dough. Drop the dumplings into the soup, cover the pot, and cook until dumplings are done, about 15 minutes longer.

LEAH CHASE'S CORN AND CRAB SOUP

*When Leah prepares crab soup, she usually browns whole blue crabs in the oil for
her roux, then mixes it with the flour that forms the basis of the soup. This version, with
butter and corn, looks at crab soup from another view.*

3 cups fresh corn kernels

$^1/_4$ cup ($^1/_2$ stick) butter

3 tablespoons all-purpose flour

1 medium onion, chopped

1 rib celery, chopped

1 small green pepper, chopped

2 cups water

3 cups milk

1 teaspoon salt

1 teaspoon Lawry's Seasoned Salt

$^1/_2$ teaspoon cayenne pepper

1 pound lump crabmeat, picked
over for cartilage and bits of
shell

Place $1^1/_2$ cups of the corn in a food processor, chop fine, and set aside. In a 2-quart saucepan, heat the butter. Add flour to make a roux, stirring well, but do not brown the flour. Add the onion, celery, and green pepper, stir, and cook until the onion is transparent. Add the water, stirring with a wire whisk, making sure there are no lumps. Bring to a boil. Add the chopped corn, stir well, and reduce the heat. Slowly add the milk and stir in the whole kernels of corn. Add the salt, seasoned salt, and pepper. Let simmer for 10 minutes, then add the crabmeat and cook for 5 minutes longer on low heat. Serve with garlic rounds or crackers.

PATRICK YVES PIERRE-JEROME'S CHILLED DUO OF MELON SOUP

MAKES 4 SERVINGS

As a kid, Pierre ate a lot of melons like honeydew, watermelon, and cranshaw. This soup is very cool and refreshing and very, very simple, with only four ingredients in each recipe. It is divine when melons are at their seasonal best, in the heart of summer.

CANTALOUPE SOUP

1 large cantaloupe

4 pinches saffron threads

1 tablespoon grated gingerroot

2 tablespoons honey, or to taste

HONEYDEW SOUP

1 medium honeydew melon

$1/4$ cup Midori liqueur

1 tablespoon honey

1 teaspoon chopped fresh mint

Cut the cantaloupe in half and scrape out the seeds. Scoop out the flesh and place in a blender with the saffron and ginger. Puree until smooth, about 30 seconds, then add honey to desired sweetness. Strain through a fine sieve. Chill about 2 hours.

Cut the honeydew melon in half and scrape out the seeds. Scoop out the flesh and place in a blender with the liqueur. Puree until smooth, about 30 seconds, then add honey to desired sweetness. Strain through a fine sieve. Stir in the mint. Chill about 2 hours.

Chill four bowls. Pour $1/3$ cup cantaloupe puree into a small cup. Pour $1/3$ cup honeydew puree into another cup. Simultaneously pour the purees into a chilled bowl.

Chilled Georgia Peach and Sun-dried Cherry Soup

MAKES 8 SERVINGS

Fruit soups have always been a refreshing way to savor the flavor of the season's harvest. The addition of sun-dried cherries makes this one a perfect addition to contemporary menus.

2 cups Chicken Stock
(see page 279)
1 cup sun-dried cherries
4 cups peeled and sliced fresh peaches
1 cup fresh peach juice
2 tablespoons fresh lemon juice
$^1/_2$ cup sugar
1 teaspoon ground cinnamon
$^1/_8$ teaspoon ground cloves
$^1/_4$ cup peach brandy
2 cups light cream
1 cup heavy cream
1 tablespoon powdered sugar
$^1/_8$ cup chopped pecans

In a saucepan, bring the chicken stock to a boil. Put the dried cherries in a bowl and pour 1 cup of the boiling stock over them; set aside.

To the remaining stock, add the peaches, peach juice, lemon juice, sugar, cinnamon, and cloves and return to a boil. Reduce the heat and simmer, stirring occasionally, until the peaches are tender, about 20 to 25 minutes. Drain the cherry juice into the peach mixture. To the drained cherries add all but 1 tablespoon of the peach brandy and stir to coat well. Pour the peach mixture into a food processor or blender in batches and blend until smooth.

Pour the pureed peach mixture into a shallow container. Add the cherries and peach brandy mixture and refrigerate until chilled well, 1 to 2 hours. Just before serving, stir in the chilled light cream.

Whip heavy cream to medium peaks, add the powdered sugar and continue to whip, adding the remaining 1 tablespoon peach brandy a little at a time while continuing to whip stiff peaks. Pour the soup into soup plates, dollop with whipped cream, and sprinkle with chopped pecans.

DARRYL EVANS'S CORN AND ROASTED PEPPER CHOWDER

MAKES 6 TO 8 SERVINGS

Roasting vegetables is a way to draw out their flavor and substituting roasted peppers for the meat and some of the salt usually called for in this dish gives it a robust flavor.

2 large shallots, minced

1 rib celery, minced

3 cloves garlic, minced

1 cup white wine

1 cup dry sherry

$1/4$ cup seasoned rice vinegar

Salt and white pepper to taste

2 pinches cayenne pepper

3 cups fresh corn kernels

3 cups heavy cream

1 cup half-and-half

$1^1/2$ tablespoons cornstarch

$1^1/2$ tablespoons water

$1/4$ teaspoon ground cumin

2 pinches ground nutmeg

1 tablespoon chopped fresh chives

1 whole Roasted Red Pepper,
   finely diced (see page 272)

Sweat the shallots and celery in a soup pot until tender. Add the garlic, white wine, and sherry. Reduce by half, then add the vinegar, salt, and white and cayenne peppers. Cook over medium-high heat to reduce by one third. Add the corn and sweat until tender. Add the heavy cream and half-and-half and bring to a boil. Reduce the heat and simmer 10 minutes. Puree in a blender or food processor.

If a thicker consistency is desired, thicken with a mixture of cornstarch and water. Season with the cumin, nutmeg, and chopped chives. Add the diced roasted red pepper.

CHEF'S TIP
To sweat vegetables is to cook them without added fat or liquid, which brings out their very best, natural flavor.

Cream of Boiled Peanut Soup

MAKES 10 TO 12 SERVINGS

In Africa, peanuts are the basis of a silky brew called groundnut stew. The tradition continued with the slaves when they arrived in the South. This is a refinement of that dish.

3 pounds raw, unshelled peanuts

1 cup salt

1 large sprig fresh thyme

2 quarts water

$^1/_4$ cup ($^1/_2$ stick) butter

1 small onion, finely diced

1 rib celery, finely diced

3 tablespoons all-purpose flour

4 cups Chicken Stock
   (see page 279)

2 cups light cream

Salt to taste

$^1/_2$ teaspoon ground white pepper

Place the peanuts, salt, and thyme in a saucepan. Add enough water to cover, bring to a boil, then reduce the heat and simmer until the peanuts are tender, about 30 minutes. Allow to cool in the cooking water. Drain the peanuts and remove the shells and skin. Set aside $^1/_2$ cup of peanuts. Place enough of the remaining peanuts in a blender and puree to yield 1 cup. Chop the reserved $^1/_2$ cup for garnish.

In a soup pot, heat the butter over medium-high heat and sauté the onions and celery until tender, but not brown, about 3 to 4 minutes. Stir in the flour and cook for 1 minute. Stir in the chicken stock. When evenly blended, stir in the cream. Simmer until the soup thickens, about 10 to 15 minutes. Strain the soup through a fine strainer into another pot and discard the solids. Bring the strained soup to a boil, then reduce the heat to a simmer. Whisk in the pureed peanuts until smooth. Season with salt and pepper.

Ladle into warm soup plates and sprinkle with chopped boiled peanuts.

CUBAN BLACK BEAN SOUP
WITH SAFFRON RICE

While teaching at Cal-Poly in Pomona, California, in the School of Hotel and Restaurant Management, I developed this recipe for the restaurant at Kellogg Ranch, a student-operated eatery. It was very popular.

2 thick slices streak-of-lean and streak-of-fat, about 2 ounces total

1 pound dried black beans, soaked at least 8 hours or overnight

2 cloves garlic, minced

2 quarts water

2 teaspoons chopped fresh thyme

1 teaspoon chopped fresh oregano

2 whole bay leaves

$^1/_2$ teaspoon celery salt

1 teaspoon freshly ground black pepper

$^1/_4$ cup white wine vinegar

1 cup Saffron Rice (see page 115)

$^1/_2$ small red onion, diced and marinated in 1 tablespoon white wine vinegar

Heat a large soup pot over medium heat. Brown the streak-of lean, being careful not to burn, 4 to 5 minutes. Drain the soaked beans, and add them, along with the garlic, to the pot. Stir to mix. Add the water and bring the beans to a boil over high heat. Add the thyme, oregano, bay leaves, celery salt, and pepper. Reduce the heat and simmer until the beans are tender, $1^1/_4$ to $1^1/_2$ hours. (If using canned beans, follow the heating instructions on the can.) Add more water, if needed. Remove the streak-of-lean and streak-of-fat with tongs and chop into very fine pieces and return to the soup. Remove 2 cups of cooked beans and place them in a food processor and puree. Return the pureed beans to soup to thicken it. Stir in the vinegar. Check the consistency and add more water if the soup is very thick. Correct the seasoning, if needed.

Ladle the soup into soup plates or bowls, place a spoonful of Saffron Rice in the center of each serving, and garnish with a little marinated chopped red onion.

FRESH CORN AND OYSTER SOUP

MAKES 8 SERVINGS

Oysters are popular on African-American tables all along the East Coast and in the Gulf states.
But they are especially elegant stirred into a creamy corn bisque.

$^1/_3$ cup unsalted butter

3 cups fresh corn kernels (about 9 ears or $1^1/_2$ pounds frozen corn)

1 cup water

2 cups Shrimp (Shellfish) Stock (see page 280)

$2^1/_2$ cups heavy cream

24 Eastern Oysters, shucked, with their liquor

$2^1/_2$ teaspoons salt

1 teaspoon ground white pepper

$^1/_2$ teaspoon cayenne pepper

1 tablespoon chopped chives

In a small soup pot, melt the butter over medium heat. Stir in the corn and sauté it for 12 to 15 minutes. Add the water and cook, covered, until the water has evaporated, about 5 minutes. Add the stock and cream, and bring to just under a boil. Simmer for 25 to 30 minutes. Remove the soup from the heat and allow to cool.

Puree the soup in a food processor or blender, then strain it through a fine strainer into a saucepan. Strain the oysters, reserving their liquor, and set aside. Add the liquor to the corn mixture, and bring it to a simmer, then cook 4 to 5 minutes. Season with the salt, white pepper, and cayenne. Add the oysters and continue to simmer until the oysters begin to curl at the edges, 3 to 4 minutes.

Pour the soup into hot soup plates, with about 3 oysters to each bowl, and sprinkle with chives.

Jamaican Pepper Pot (Callaloo)

There's a little bit of something for everyone stirred into this pot. Your guests will be pleasantly surprised by the soup's subtle hint of the exotic. Only you will know the secret ingredient: coconut milk.

1/2 pound finely ground salt pork

1/2 medium red pepper, diced

3 green onions, sliced

3 cloves garlic, minced

1 cup plus 2 tablespoons all-purpose flour

1 1/2 quarts water

3 cups coconut milk

1 1/2 cups peeled and diced fresh yellow yams (found in produce section of your supermarket)

1/2 Scotch bonnet pepper, seeded and thinly sliced

1 sprig fresh thyme

2 bunches callaloo greens or spinach leaves, washed, stemmed, and cut into chiffonade

16 fresh okra pods, sliced 1/4 inch thick

2 pounds soft-shell crabs, cleaned

1/4 cup peanut oil

1 teaspoon salt

1/2 teaspoon freshly ground black pepper

In a large soup pot over medium-high heat, cook the salt pork just until the fat is rendered, but do not brown. This will take 4 to 5 minutes. Remove the salt pork, pour off all but 2 tablespoons of fat, and sauté the red pepper, green onions, and garlic over medium-high heat for 2 to 3 minutes. Return the salt pork to the pot, add the 2 tablespoons flour, and cook for 1 minute. Stir in the water and coconut milk. Bring the mixture to a boil, then reduce the heat and simmer for 30 minutes. Add the yellow yams, Scotch bonnet pepper, and thyme. Simmer for 20 minutes. Add the callaloo and okra, and simmer for 15 minutes.

Dust the soft-shell crabs in the remaining 1 cup flour. Heat the oil in large skillet over medium-high heat. Sauté the crabs until golden brown, about 4 to 5 minutes on each side. Drain the crabs on paper towels and cut them into 1-inch pieces. Stir the crab pieces into the pot. Simmer 5 minutes, then correct the seasoning with salt and pepper. Serve hot.

CHEF'S TIP

If fresh soft-shell crabs are unavailable, you may substitute frozen, or use 1 pound lump crabmeat.

MARYLAND CREAM OF CRAB SOUP

MAKES 10 TO 12 SERVINGS

You don't have to live in the East to appreciate the deliciousness of a good crab bisque. Just be sure to purchase the very best crab you can find to preserve the flavor of this rich and creamy soup.

$^1/_2$ cup (1 stick) butter

1 small onion, finely chopped

2 cloves garlic, minced

1 rib celery, finely chopped

1 teaspoon salt

$^3/_4$ teaspoon ground white pepper

$^1/_4$ cup dry sherry

1 quart half-and-half

5 tablespoons butter, softened

4 tablespoons all-purpose flour

1 teaspoon celery salt

$^1/_8$ teaspoon cayenne pepper

$^1/_2$ cup shredded plain Havarti cheese

$^1/_4$ cup fresh lemon juice

$1^1/_2$ pounds fresh jumbo lump crabmeat, picked over for cartilage and bits of shell

Salt to taste

White pepper to taste

1 tablespoon chopped fresh parsley

In a soup pot, melt the butter over medium-high heat. Sauté the onion, garlic, and celery until the onion is translucent, about 2 to 3 minutes. Season with the salt and pepper. Add 2 tablespoons of the sherry and simmer for another 1 to 2 minutes. Stir in the half-and-half and bring the mixture to a boil. Reduce the heat to a simmer.

To make a beurre manié, in a small mixing bowl, combine the softened butter and flour well to make a paste. Whisk the beurre manié into the soup in small pieces and continue to simmer until the soup thickens. Stir in the celery salt, cayenne, cheese, lemon juice, and remaining 2 tablespoons sherry. Add the crabmeat and simmer until the soup is thoroughly hot, about 3 to 5 minutes. Correct the seasoning with salt and white pepper to taste, if needed.

Serve the soup hot. Garnish with chopped parsley.

Pennsylvania Dutch Chicken Corn Soup

MAKES 6 TO 8 SERVINGS

I was raised in central Pennsylvania, so nothing says summer better than a big pot of chicken soup made with freshly picked corn. Today, you don't need an outdoor fire or Granny's heaping kettle. Just be sure the corn is at its freshest and see what memories it conjures up.

1 whole stewing chicken, about 3 pounds

1 bay leaf

1 large sprig parsley

1 cup diced onion

3 quarts water

$1/4$ cup ($1/2$ stick) butter, optional

4 cups fresh corn kernels plus their milk (about 12 ears)

1 rib celery, diced

1 medium carrot, diced

$1/4$ cup all-purpose flour

1 teaspoon salt

$1/2$ teaspoon ground white pepper

1 tablespoon chopped fresh parsley

Place the chicken, bay leaf, parsley sprig, and $1/2$ cup of the onion in a large stockpot. Cover with water and bring to a boil, skimming off and reserving the fat. Reduce the heat and simmer until the chicken is tender, 1 to $1^1/2$ hours. Remove the chicken from the stock and allow to cool. Remove the meat from the bones, dice it, and set aside. Discard the bones. Strain the stock and set aside.

In a large soup pot, heat 3 tablespoons of the reserved chicken fat (or use the butter) over medium-high heat and cook the corn, celery, carrot, and remaining $1/2$ cup onion for 3 to 4 minutes. Stir in the flour to make a roux and cook for 2 to 3 minutes. Stir in the stock and bring to a boil. Add the chicken meat and reduce the heat. Simmer until the soup thickens, about 15 to 20 minutes. Season with salt and pepper and garnish with chopped parsley.

ROASTED TOMATO AND OKRA SOUP

A delicate hint of smoke is the foundation of this traditional soup. Stock made from ham hocks and roasted tomatoes provides a robust flavor. Toss in the meat from the hock to make the soup more filling.

2 tablespoons butter

1 medium onion, diced

1 clove garlic, minced

6 whole tomatoes, roasted, peeled, and diced (about 5 cups)

3 pints Smoked Ham Stock (see page 281)

1 cup half-and-half

1 1/4 pounds fresh okra, stems removed and sliced 1/2-inch thick (about 5 cups)

1 bay leaf

2 teaspoons chopped fresh thyme

1/2 cup diced ham hock meat

Salt to taste

Freshly ground black pepper to taste

In a soup pot, heat the butter over medium-high heat and sauté the onion and garlic until the onions are translucent, about 3 to 4 minutes. Stir in the tomatoes and cook for 2 to 3 minutes. Pour in the stock, bring to a boil, then reduce the heat and simmer for 30 minutes. Stir in the half-and-half and cook 5 minutes more. Remove from the heat and puree in batches in a blender or food processor until smooth.

Return the soup to the pot, bring it to a boil, then reduce the heat to a simmer. Add the okra, bay leaf, thyme, and ham. Simmer until the okra is tender, about 5 to 10 minutes. Remove the bay leaf and season the soup with salt and pepper to taste.

Serve hot in soup plates.

CHEF'S TIP

To roast tomatoes, cook them under a hot broiler until they are charred evenly on all sides, about 4 to 5 minutes. Set them aside to cool, then peel and dice into 1-inch pieces.

EDNA LEWIS'S SHE-CRAB SOUP
CHARLESTON STYLE

MAKES 8 SERVINGS

In Charleston, female crabs are prized for this famous soup because they contribute a potent but delicate flavor. Following tradition, she-crab soup should be prepared using female crabs exclusively, with their roe added for even more flavor. If crab roe is not available, you may hard-boil four eggs and crumble half a hard-boiled egg yolk into the bottom of each bowl before ladling in the soup. Serve this soup with Edna's Benne Seed Biscuits (recipe follows).

$^1/_2$ cup (1 stick) unsalted butter

3 cups milk

$^1/_2$ cup all-purpose flour

4 cups heavy cream

1 pound lump crabmeat, picked over for cartilage and bits of shell

$^1/_4$ cup dry sherry

2 teaspoons salt

2 cups crab roe or the yolks of 4 hard-boiled eggs

$^1/_4$ cup finely chopped fresh parsley

$^1/_2$ tablespoon cayenne pepper

Melt the butter in a heavy 4-quart soup pot over medium heat. In a saucepan, heat the milk, but do not allow it to boil. When the butter is hot, whisk in the flour to make a roux. Cook the roux 2 to 3 minutes, but do not brown. Slowly stir in the hot milk, whisking well. Cook over medium-low heat until hot, stirring occasionally to prevent scorching. Pour the cream into a large skillet. Bring to a boil, whisking occasionally, then reduce the heat and cook until the cream has thickened and is reduced by one quarter, about 10 to 15 minutes. Pour the cream into hot milk mixture. Mix well, then stir in the crabmeat. Cook 30 minutes to allow the flavor to develop, stirring occasionally. Season with sherry and salt. Add the crab roe. Ladle into serving bowls. Garnish with parsley and a generous sprinkle of cayenne.

EDNA LEWIS'S BENNE SEED BISCUITS

MAKES 2 DOZEN

The slaves brought benne (sesame) seeds to the New World with them from Africa and they have been a staple in Southern cookery ever since.

1 cup benne seeds
3 cups all-purpose flour
1 1/2 teaspoons Single-acting
   Baking Powder (see page 272)
1 teaspoon salt
2/3 cup lard
2/3 cup milk
Salt to taste

Place the benne seeds in a shallow pan in a preheated 425°F oven. After 5 minutes, check on the benne seeds. They should be the color of butterscotch and should have a delicious toasted smell. If not, shake the pan and return to the oven for 1 to 2 minutes longer, but watch carefully. They burn easily.

Sift the flour, baking powder, and salt into a large bowl. Add the lard and work the mixture with a pastry blender or your fingertips until it has the texture of cornmeal. Add the milk and mix well. Mix in the toasted benne seeds.

Place the dough on a floured surface, knead for a few seconds, and shape into a ball. Roll the dough out until it is about the thickness of a nickel. Using a 2-inch biscuit cutter, stamp out rounds and lay them on an ungreased baking sheet or a baking sheet lined with parchment paper. Bake until lightly browned, about 12 minutes. Remove from the oven, sprinkle with a little bit of salt, and serve hot.

CHEF'S TIP
You may store the cooked biscuits in an airtight tin or jar and reheat them before serving.

KYM GIBSON'S RED SNAPPER CHOWDER

MAKES 8 SERVINGS

From her grandmother, Kym inherited marvelous old Southern-style traditions, including gumbos and pies. Her grandparents also had two hobbies: They were herb fanatics and they enjoyed fishing. This dish is her testament to all the wonderful aromas that filled the house when red snapper was in the pot.

2 tablespoons butter

1 medium onion, finely chopped

1 rib celery, chopped

3 cloves garlic, minced

2 tablespoons chopped fresh thyme

1 teaspoon ground cumin

Pinch saffron

1 lime

1¼ pounds red snapper fillets, cut into cubes

1 cup Chicken Stock (see page 279)

2 potatoes, peeled and diced

2 cups Fish Stock (see page 279)

One 17-ounce can Italian plum tomatoes, crushed

2 cups white wine

1 teaspoon crushed red pepper flakes

¼ cup chopped fresh chives

Heat the butter in a 2-quart saucepan. Sauté the onion, celery, garlic, thyme, and cumin. Add the saffron. Cut the lime in half, squeeze the juice onto the red snapper and let stand 10 minutes. Place the lime halves in the pot and add the chicken stock. Add the diced potatoes, cover, and simmer for 7 to 8 minutes. Remove the lime halves. Add the fish stock, tomatoes, and wine and simmer for 15 minutes. Add the red snapper cubes and crushed red pepper, cover the pot, and let simmer for 5 to 7 minutes.

Pour in heated soup bowls and garnish with chopped chives.

Sweet Potato Smoked Louisiana Sausage Bisque

MAKES 6 TO 8 SERVINGS

Charlie's Restaurant in Lafayette, Louisiana, serves a very tasty sweet potato soup that inspired me to create this version using smoked Louisiana hot sausage. The sausage lends a very smoky flavor but if you can't get any, try substituting a spicy smoked link sausage. The sweet potato takes on a squashlike flavor when mixed, as it is here, with fresh thyme and garlic.

1 cup (2 sticks) butter

1 medium onion, diced

1 medium green pepper, diced

2 ribs celery, diced

4 cloves garlic, minced

1 pound smoked Louisiana
  hot sausage, diced

$1/2$ cup all-purpose flour

$1^1/2$ quarts Chicken Stock
  (see page 279)

$1^1/2$ pounds sweet potatoes,
  baked, cooled, and peeled

1 tablespoon chopped fresh thyme

1 teaspoon salt

1 teaspoon ground white pepper

4 dashes Tabasco sauce

Melt the butter in a soup pot over medium-high heat and sauté the onion, green pepper, celery, and garlic for 3 to 4 minutes. Add the sausage and continue to sauté for 2 minutes more. Stir in the flour to make a roux. Cook for 3 to 4 minutes, but do not brown.

In a separate saucepan, bring the chicken stock to a boil. Stir the hot stock into the soup pot, mixing until smooth. Reduce the heat to medium and simmer for 15 minutes.

In a blender or food processor, puree half the sweet potatoes and add them to the soup. Simmer and stir the soup for 15 minutes. Dice the remaining sweet potatoes and add them to the soup pot. Season with the thyme, salt, pepper, and Tabasco sauce. Simmer for 10 minutes more.

Serve hot in soup plates.

Virginia Country Ham Soup with Collard Greens and Black-eyed Peas

If you love the taste of collard greens you'll appreciate just one more way of preparing and serving them.

2 quarts water

One ¼-inch-thick slice Smithfield ham

2 bunches collard greens, stems removed and cut into chiffonade

⅛ teaspoon crushed red pepper flakes

2 cups cooked Black-eyed Peas with Ham Hocks (see page 89)

1 teaspoon salt

½ teaspoon freshly ground black pepper

In a soup pot, bring the water to a boil.

In a large skillet over medium-high heat, cook the ham until lightly brown, about 2 to 3 minutes on each side. Cut the ham in half and place it in the boiling water. Reduce the heat and simmer for 1 hour.

Add the collard greens and red pepper flakes to the soup pot and continue to simmer until the greens are tender, about 25 to 30 minutes, adding more water, if needed.

Remove the ham from the pot. Trim and discard the fat. Dice the meat and return it to the pot along with the black-eyed peas. Simmer for 10 minutes. Season with salt and pepper.

Serve hot.

White Bean Soup with Mustard Greens and Streak-of-lean and Streak-of-fat

This hearty soup isn't just good tasting, it's good for you too, thanks to the beans and mustard greens, which are a storehouse of fiber and vitamins.

2 slices streak-of-lean and streak-of-fat, cut $^1/_8$ inch thick

2 quarts water

2 cups cooked white beans (see recipe for White Bean Cakes, page 113)

2 bunches mustard greens, stems removed, washed, drained, and cut into strips

2 green onions, sliced

1 teaspoon salt

$^1/_8$ teaspoon freshly ground black pepper

$^1/_8$ teaspoon cayenne pepper

In a skillet over medium-high heat, cook the streak-of-lean on each side until golden brown, about 4 to 5 minutes Drain on a paper towel, dice, and set aside, reserving the fat in the skillet.

Bring the water to a boil in a soup pot. Add the diced streak-of-lean, reduce the heat, and simmer for 1 hour. Add the white beans and continue to simmer for 10 to 15 minutes. Heat the reserved fat in the skillet over medium high heat, add the greens and green onions and sauté for 5 minutes. Toss the contents of the skillet into the soup pot. Season the soup with salt, pepper, and cayenne. Simmer for 3 to 4 minutes longer.

Serve hot.

Chapter 3

Salads
and
Dressings

I T'S AMAZING THAT IN THIS DAY AND AGE WHEN MANY FOLKS THINK ABOUT SALAD, THEY conjure up recollections of Sunday dinners at Granny's and church socials where tuna-stuffed tomatoes, Jell-O molds, and concoctions with names like Tropical Delight, Exotic Waldorf Salad, and Slushy Fruit were par for the course. In my family, we depended upon Aunt Lynnis to bring deviled eggs, coleslaw, and potato salad to family reunions. At the dinner table, a cafeteria-style mixture of iceberg lettuce wedges with Thousand Island dressing completed the menu. Occasionally, a family gathering would turn up some homey surprises, but nothing that compared to the mellow blends you'd expect in first-rate restaurants.

While all of these salads remain classics, today African-American salads offer much more appealing and varied options. Okra marinated in oil and vinegar, for instance, is a heritage combination. But to make a contemporary salad from this legendary dish, we deep-fry the slippery okra pods so the slime virtually vanishes, and perch them atop fresh, pungent greens.

Indeed, this chapter takes you beyond the typical salad bar offerings of leaf lettuce, sliced carrots, beets, green beans, sprouts, shredded cheese, and croutons, with innovative salads you can depend upon for everyday, as well as for entertaining.

Don't expect a litany of rules; most of these salads are for easygoing cooks. We learned from our ancestors to rely upon whatever vegetables are in season plus a mix of vinegar, oil, and seasonings when tossing a salad that is cool and satisfying.

First consider the dressing. You can vary the taste and fat content of the mix once you become familiar with the formula. Usually, cooks begin with a ratio of half vinegar and half oil, then adjust the amount of each—adding more of one and less of the other to suit their taste buds. Then they add other ingredients. Flavored mustards, like Dijon, Creole, and coarse country-style mustards can double as substitutes for some of the oil, reducing the amount of fat in your salad while giving the dressing body and flavor. Mayonnaise and buttermilk are rich and creamy, and make dressings full-bodied. Although homemade mayonnaise is delicious, with increased concerns about salmonella and raw eggs, we recommend you stick to store-bought.

Another way chefs enhance the salads on their menus is by experimenting with fragrant oils infused with fresh herbs from the garden. You can do it too,

just tinker with the flavors you already enjoy—olive, walnut, hazelnut, even avocado oils.

Next, choose a vinegar. Not many chefs still use raspberry vinegar but balsamic vinegar is really hot on menus everywhere. For true African-American style, however, these recipes crave cider or wine vinegars and peanut oil, which capture the authentic flavor of the South.

Aromatic vegetables are another integral part of salad dressings. Alliums of every sort, including shallots, green onions, and Vidalias, which grow abundantly in the South, are part of these formulas. The shallots are good when a more subtle flavor is desired. Use garlic in your dressings only when your salad ingredients are substantial enough to stand up to its potent character. Roasting the vegetables before topping the mixed greens will give the salad a smoky accent.

When it comes to the actual salad foundation, the possibilities are endless. Over the years, African-Americans have enjoyed a respectable assortment of classic, meat, vegetable, fish and shellfish, and poultry salads, all perched on the old standbys iceberg and romaine.

Times have changed. To build a new salad repertoire, start slowly. Don't be afraid to visit the local farmers' market and learn more about all the baby field greens—watercress, arugula, mâche—and the qualities that make each one unique. Then, begin interchanging lettuces, toppings, and dressings you like in all sorts of recipes.

A good salad signals the beginning of a delicious meal to come. The next thing you know, you'll be tossing your favorite greens with the very best African-American ingredients, whether it's fried chicken livers, seared catfish fillet, or smoked chicken.

CREAMY COLESLAW

MAKES 8 TO 10 SERVINGS

This homey coleslaw is an ideal highlight of a summertime picnic.

1 large head green cabbage, shredded

1 carrot, peeled and shredded

3 green onions, trimmed and thinly sliced

1 medium green pepper, diced

$1/2$ cup mayonnaise

$1/2$ cup sour cream

$1/2$ teaspoon salt

2 teaspoons sugar

1 tablespoon cider vinegar

2 teaspoons prepared mustard

In a large bowl, combine the cabbage, carrot, green onions, and green pepper.

In a medium bowl, combine the mayonnaise, sour cream, salt, sugar, vinegar, and mustard. Stir until blended well. Pour the dressing over the vegetables and toss to coat well. Cover and refrigerate 2 to 3 hours to allow flavors to blend. Will keep 2 to 3 days in the refrigerator.

DOWN-HOME POTATO SALAD

MAKES 6 TO 8 SERVINGS

Serve this salad alone for lunch, as an accompaniment to fried chicken, or toss your favorite grilled sausage into the mix for a more substantial meal.

6 russet potatoes, scrubbed
   (about 2 pounds)
2 ribs celery, finely diced
$^1/_2$ small onion, minced
2 tablespoons sweet pickle relish
4 hard-boiled eggs, peeled and
   diced
$^1/_2$ cup mayonnaise
1 tablespoon prepared mustard
1 teaspoon salt
$^1/_2$ teaspoon ground white pepper
$^1/_2$ teaspoon celery salt
$^1/_2$ teaspoon paprika
$^1/_2$ tablespoon chopped fresh
   chives

In a large saucepan, cover the potatoes with water and boil until tender, about 30 to 40 minutes, testing them with a fork. Drain and set them aside until they are cool enough to be handled. Peel and dice them, then place them in a large mixing bowl. Add the celery, onion, relish, and eggs. Stir to combine.

In a small bowl, blend the mayonnaise, mustard, salt, pepper, and celery salt, mixing well. Mix the dressing thoroughly with the potato mixture. Sprinkle with paprika and chives to garnish.

Timothy Dean's Caesar Salad with Curried Scallops

MAKES 4 SERVINGS

Timothy's mother often cooked with curry. As he grew older, he became fond of Jamaican cooking. This dish is illustrative of both experiences.

8 sea scallops

2 tablespoons curry powder

2 tablespoons extra-virgin
   olive oil

1 French bread baguette

5 heads baby red romaine,
   washed, with ends removed

5 heads baby green romaine,
   washed, with ends removed

1 cup Caesar Dressing
   (see page 77)

1 yellow vine-ripened tomato,
   diced

1 red vine-ripened tomato, diced

4 tablespoons shaved Parmesan
   cheese

Dip the scallops in the curry powder, then cut them in half. Heat the olive oil in a small sauté pan and sear the scallops on the curried side until caramelized. Remove from the pan and set aside.

Cut the baguette into 3-inch sections. Remove the middle of the bread reserving it for another use and toast the crust until golden brown. Place baguette crusts in the center of individual serving plates, arrange the lettuce in the baguettes and pour Caesar dressing over the lettuce. Top with the tomatoes and Parmesan. Arrange scallop halves around the salad on each plate.

Baby Romaine and Spicy Fried Oysters with Caesar Dressing

Caesar salad has enjoyed renewed interest these days, as chefs crown crispy romaine lettuce with everything from grilled chicken and salmon to sausage and warm duck. This snappy version is appealing to the eye and the palate.

2 cups yellow cornmeal

1 teaspoon salt

1 teaspoon freshly ground black pepper

$^1/_2$ teaspoon cayenne pepper

48 medium Eastern oysters, shucked and drained

3 cups vegetable oil

8 heads baby red romaine, rinsed and trimmed

8 heads baby green romaine, rinsed and trimmed

2 cups Caesar Dressing (see page 77)

1 cup freshly shaved Parmesan cheese

In a bowl, combine the cornmeal, salt, and peppers. Dredge the oysters in the seasoned cornmeal. Set them aside on a plate until ready to cook.

Heat the oil in a deep skillet on medium heat. Cook the oysters in batches of sixteen for 2 to 3 minutes per side, turning to ensure that they cook evenly and brown all over. Remove the oysters with a slotted spoon and drain them on paper towels. Repeat with the remaining oysters.

Arrange the romaine lettuce on plates, alternating red and green leaves. Lightly pour Caesar dressing over the lettuce and sprinkle the shaved cheese on top. Place 6 fried oysters on each plate and serve immediately.

LEAH CHASE'S CREOLE TOMATOES AND GREEN BEAN SALAD

This salad is at its best at the height of the summer harvest.

2 pounds whole fresh green beans

$1/4$ pound country bacon, finely diced

$1/2$ cup extra-virgin olive oil

6 tablespoons red wine vinegar

1 teaspoon Creole mustard or other whole grain mustard

2 teaspoons chopped fresh parsley

$1/2$ teaspoon salt

$1/2$ teaspoon freshly ground black pepper

1 red onion, thinly sliced and separated

2 green onions, thinly sliced

1 pound fresh Creole tomatoes or fresh plum tomatoes,

Remove the ends and any strings from the green beans and wash. In a large pot, bring enough water to cover the green beans to a boil, add salt, and cook the beans until just tender, about 6 to 8 minutes. Drain the beans well and shock in ice water to stop the cooking. Remove from the ice water. Place beans in paper towels and refrigerate until serving time.

In a sauté pan, cook the bacon until crisp. Drain and set aside. In a large salad bowl, combine the olive oil, vinegar, mustard, parsley, salt, and pepper. Add the red and green onions and tomatoes, mix well, and refrigerate until ready to serve. Toss the chilled beans with dressing and serve.

Dandelion Greens, Bibb Lettuce, New Potatoes, and Green Beans with Country Smoked Bacon Dressing

MAKES 8 SERVINGS

When Northerners are cursing the dandelions that invade their gardens in the spring, Southern cooks are praising them and gathering the greens for zesty salads like this one. A tangy-sweet dressing takes the edge off of the bitterness of the greens, giving them a place on anyone's menu and a cottage industry all their own.

1 pound smoked slab bacon

1 pound green beans, washed and snapped 3 inches long

2 quarts boiling salted water

1 pound red new potatoes, quartered

2 medium heads Bibb lettuce, washed, drained, and trimmed

3 bunches dandelion greens, washed and stems removed (about 3 cups)

Country Smoked Bacon Dressing (see page 78)

Preheat the oven to 325°F.

Slice the bacon into $1/8$-inch strips, remove the rind, and cut the strips into $1/8$-inch cubes. Place the bacon cubes in a baking pan and bake them until the bacon is crisp and brown, about 20 to 30 minutes. Drain and set aside, reserving the bacon drippings.

Blanch the green beans in the boiling water until the beans are just tender, about 3 to 4 minutes. Remove with a slotted spoon and transfer them to an ice water bath to stop them cooking. Drain the beans and set aside. In the same water in which you cooked the beans, boil the potatoes until tender. Drain and cool the potatoes.

Form the Bibb lettuce leaves into cups and place in the center of eight serving plates. Divide the dandelion greens evenly among the Bibb lettuce cups, arrange the green beans and potatoes on top of the greens, and place a tablespoon of bacon cubes in the center of each salad. Stir the Country Smoked Bacon Dressing well, then spoon 2 tablespoons of it over each salad. Serve immediately.

Green Leaf Lettuce, Sliced Beets, Smithfield Ham, Bermuda Onion, and Georgia Peanuts with Peanut Oil Dressing

MAKES 6 TO 8 SERVINGS

Ever since George Washington Carver discovered a hundred uses for the peanut, peanut oil has been a favorite in African-American kitchens for frying. Together with Georgia peanuts (that you roast yourself for freshness), this recipe is an aromatic way to celebrate African-American heritage.

$1^1/_2$ quarts water

1 teaspoon salt

$1^1/_2$ pounds small beets, trimmed (about 6 beets)

1 cup unsalted peanuts, shelled, with the skin removed

2 heads green leaf lettuce, washed, drained, and cut into pieces

1 Bermuda onion, thinly sliced

4 ounces Smithfield ham, cut into strips $^1/_8$ inch × $1^1/_4$ inches

2 cups Peanut Oil Dressing (see page 78)

Place eight salad plates in the refrigerator to chill.

In a large saucepan, bring the water to a boil. Add the salt and beets. Boil the beets until just tender, about 20 to 25 minutes. Remove the beets from the water and shock them in an ice water bath to stop cooking. When they are cool enough to touch, peel the beets and slice them about $^1/_8$ inch thick. Wrap them in plastic wrap and refrigerate until needed.

Preheat the oven to 350°F. Lightly roast the peanuts on a baking pan for 20 minutes. Remove the peanuts from the oven and let them cool to room temperature.

Place portions of green leaf lettuce in the center of the chilled salad plates. Arrange the sliced beets and onion rings around the greens. Sprinkle the ham over the greens and spoon about 2 tablespoons Peanut Oil Dressing over each salad. Scatter the roasted peanuts on top of each salad. Serve immediately.

Leaf Spinach, Savannah Pickled Shrimp, and Marinated Peppers with Citrus Vinaigrette

MAKES 8 SERVINGS

*Marinated assorted peppers and jumbo shrimp create a colorful mosaic
that gives crisp spinach an unforgettable Southern flavor.*

2 quarts boiling water

1 tablespoon plus $^1/_2$ teaspoon
coarse sea salt

1 lemon, halved

3 ribs celery, cut into large pieces

2 pounds large shrimp, peeled
and deveined

1 medium onion, sliced

1 medium green pepper,
cut into strips

1 medium yellow pepper,
cut into strips

1 medium red pepper, cut into
strips

1 teaspoon pickling spice

2 teaspoons chopped fresh dill
weed

1 teaspoon red pepper flakes

$^1/_4$ teaspoon freshly ground
black pepper

2 cups peanut oil

$1^1/_2$ cups white wine vinegar

$^3/_4$ cup water

3 large bunches fresh spinach,
stems removed, rinsed, and
drained well

2 cups Citrus Vinaigrette
(see page 80)

In a heavy stockpot or kettle, bring the water to a rapid boil. Add 1 tablespoon of the salt, the lemon, celery, and shrimp and boil for 3 to 4 minutes. Remove the shrimp from the pot with a slotted spoon and shock them in a bowl of ice water to stop cooking. When the shrimp have cooled, drain them and place in a large bowl with the onion and peppers. Toss the mixture lightly.

In a separate bowl, combine the pickling spice, dill, remaining $^1/_2$ teaspoon salt, red pepper, and black pepper. Blend in the peanut oil, vinegar, and water. Mix well. Pour the marinade over the shrimp mixture, cover it tightly, and refrigerate overnight.

Place eight salad plates in the refrigerator to chill overnight.

When ready to serve the salad, toss the spinach with three quarters of the Citrus Vinaigrette. Place about $^1/_2$ cup spinach on each of the cold salad plates. Arrange the red, yellow, and green marinated peppers on top of the spinach. Place 4 shrimp on each plate around the peppers. Sprinkle the remaining vinaigrette over each salad. Serve immediately.

CHEF'S TIP

In the old days, cooks marinated shrimp and other perishables to give them a longer shelf life. These shrimp may be stored up to 10 days in their marinade, tightly covered in the refrigerator.

Patrick Yves Pierre-Jerome's Salmon Salad with Hot Onion Dressing

MAKES 6 SERVINGS

Onions are the one ingredient that showed up with "alarming frequency" in his childhood says Pierre, whose grandmother couldn't seem to get enough of them. That, coupled with his love of salmon, is the inspiration for this light dish. Grill the fish to heighten the flavor.

2 tablespoons extra-virgin olive oil
Six 3-ounce salmon fillets
2$^{1}/_{2}$ cups salad greens
1$^{1}/_{2}$ cups Hot Onion Dressing (recipe follows)

Heat the olive oil in a large sauté pan over high heat and sauté the salmon 1$^{1}/_{2}$ minutes on each side. Remove the salmon from the pan and cut each salmon fillet into 3 pieces; keep warm. Place a mound of salad in the center of a salad plate. Arrange 3 pieces of salmon around the salad. Spoon Hot Onion Dressing over the salmon and salad. Repeat with the remaining plates.

Patrick Yves Pierre-Jerome's Hot Onion Dressing

MAKES 2 CUPS

2 tablespoons butter
1 medium onion, finely diced
$^{1}/_{4}$ cup sherry vinegar
2 cups Chicken Stock (see page 279)
$^{1}/_{8}$ teaspoon salt
$^{1}/_{8}$ teaspoon freshly ground black pepper

Heat the butter in a sauté pan. Add the onions and sauté until they begin to brown. Add vinegar and reduce by half. Add the chicken stock and reduce by half. Season with salt and pepper.

Limestone Lettuce, Mâche, Warm Fried Okra, Diced Tomato, and Roasted Corn with Fresh Basil Vinaigrette

MAKES 8 SERVINGS

Limestone lettuce is a buttery leaf lettuce that makes a soft pillow for warm vegetables in this salad. If you can't find it, Boston lettuce is a fine substitute.

2 pounds fresh okra

$^1/_4$ teaspoon salt

$^1/_4$ teaspoon freshly ground pepper

$^1/_2$ cup Tomato Concasse (recipe follows)

1 cup Fresh Basil Vinaigrette (see page 81)

2 heads limestone lettuce, torn into pieces

3 bunches mâche

$^1/_2$ cup roasted fresh corn kernels

1 cup yellow cornmeal

Peanut oil for frying

8 sprigs fresh basil

Place eight salad plates in the refrigerator to chill.

Trim the stems from the okra and slice the okra crosswise into $^1/_2$-inch-thick slices. Season the slices with salt and pepper.

Place the Tomato Concasse in a small bowl and pour $^1/_4$ cup of the Fresh Basil Vinaigrette over it. Toss to mix.

In a large bowl, toss the limestone lettuce and mâche with $^1/_2$ cup of the Fresh Basil Vinaigrette. Arrange the greens in the center of the chilled salad plates and arrange the Tomato Concasse around the greens.

In a small bowl, mix the corn with the remaining Fresh Basil Vinaigrette. Arrange the corn mixture around the greens.

Toss the okra with the cornmeal and shake off any excess. Heat the peanut oil in a deep skillet over high heat and deep-fry the okra in three batches for 3 to 4 minutes. Drain the fried pieces of okra on paper towels, then place them on top of the salads.

Garnish each serving with a fresh basil sprig.

CHEF'S TIP

Roast the corn in its husk under a hot broiler about 4 to 5 minutes on each side. Soak the corn in its husk in cool water for 10 minutes before roasting.

TOMATO CONCASSE

MAKES ABOUT $1/2$ CUP

1 medium ripe tomato

Remove the stem end from the bottom of the tomato, then use a sharp knife to make an *X* on the bottom. Blanch the tomato in boiling water for a few seconds, just until the skin begins to loosen. Immediately remove it from the boiling water and plunge it into an ice water bath to stop cooking. Remove the peel and cut the tomato in half crosswise. Squeeze the tomato gently over a bowl to loosen the seeds, then use your fingers to remove the seeds and liquid, leaving the tomato as intact as possible. Discard the seeds and liquid. Dice the tomato flesh into $1/4$-inch cubes and reserve until ready to use.

Edna Lewis's Watercress, Romaine, and Green Leaf Lettuce with Cider Vinegar Dressing

MAKES 4 TO 6 SERVINGS

This salad is wonderful for entertaining because it can be held for up to an hour without wilting. It contains no oil.

$^1/_2$ cup cider vinegar

4 teaspoons sugar

$^1/_2$ teaspoon salt

$^1/_4$ teaspoon freshly ground black pepper

1 head romaine lettuce, washed, dried, and torn into pieces

1 head green leaf lettuce, washed, dried, and torn into pieces

1 bunch watercress, trimmed, washed, and dried

1 large Kirby cucumber, peeled and thinly sliced

5 green onions, thinly sliced, green part only

Place the vinegar, sugar, salt, and pepper in a bowl or bottle. Shake or stir with a wooden spoon until all the salt has dissolved. Arrange the lettuce, watercress, cucumbers, and onions on a plate. Pour dressing over all. Set aside until ready to serve.

Clifton Williams's Orange Slices and Watercress Drizzled with Spicy Oil

The inspiration for this dish comes from Clifton's grandmother.

1 small clove garlic, minced

$^1/_2$ teaspoon salt

3 tablespoons extra-virgin
   olive oil

$^1/_2$ teaspoon cayenne pepper

$^1/_2$ teaspoon ground cumin

$^1/_2$ teaspoon ground coriander

2 bunches watercress, cleaned
   and trimmed

4 navel oranges, peeled and
   sliced into 6 slices each

3 teaspoons minced fresh cilantro

1 tablespoon grated orange zest

In a small bowl, mix the garlic and salt into a paste. Combine with the olive oil, cayenne, cumin, and coriander. Refrigerate until serving time. Arrange the watercress and orange slices on chilled plates and drizzle with dressing. Sprinkle the salad with fresh cilantro and sprinkle the orange zest around the plate.

Mixed Baby Lettuces, Fried Chicken, and Tiny Corn Fritters with Buttermilk Dressing

This is another one of my popular inventions for Georgia, the Melrose Avenue restaurant in Los Angeles owned by Norm Nixon, Debbie Allen, and Brad Johnson. The tang of a buttermilk-based dressing is the perfect foil for the mild baby lettuces.

1 cup all-purpose flour

1 teaspoon salt

$^1/_2$ teaspoon freshly ground black pepper

$^1/_2$ teaspoon cayenne pepper

1 teaspoon paprika

$^1/_2$ cup buttermilk

$^1/_4$ cup water

1 cup peanut oil

2 cloves garlic, minced

4 whole boneless, skinless chicken breasts, cut into $^1/_4$-inch strips

4 cups mesclun

Buttermilk Dressing (see page 77)

24 Corn Fritters (see page 92)

Place eight salad plates in the refrigerator to chill.

In a bowl, combine the flour, salt, black pepper, cayenne, and paprika. In a separate bowl, thoroughly mix the buttermilk and water. Heat the peanut oil in a large skillet over medium heat and add the garlic. Dip the chicken strips in the buttermilk mixture and dust them with the seasoned flour. Fry the strips in two batches in the hot oil until golden brown, about 3 to 4 minutes on each side. Remove the strips from the skillet and drain them on paper towels. Keep warm in a preheated 200°F oven until ready to serve.

In a large bowl, toss the baby greens with 2 tablespoons of Buttermilk Dressing. Divide the dressed greens evenly among the chilled salad plates and top them with chicken strips. Arrange 3 to 4 corn fritters around each salad. Serve immediately.

Red Leaf Lettuce, Butter Leaf Lettuce, Grilled Spring Onions, Tomatoes, and Souse Meat with Champagne Vinaigrette

MAKES 8 SERVINGS

My Southern heritage provides the inspiration for this contemporary treatment of a familiar dish. Wherever hogs are killed souse meat becomes an end product. This dish was created in the summer of 1994 for An Elegant Taste of Heritage benefit dinner, at the Grand Hyatt Hotel in Washington, D.C.

2 heads red leaf lettuce, rinsed and torn into bite-size pieces

2 heads butter leaf lettuce, rinsed and torn into bite-size pieces

8 slices Souse Meat, cut $1/4$ inch thick and julienned (see page 215)

2 cups Champagne Vinaigrette (see page 79)

16 green onions, peeled and with the ends cut off

Extra-virgin olive oil

2 cups Tomato Concasse (see page 69)

8 sprigs fresh sage

Place eight salad plates in the refrigerator to chill. Preheat charcoal grill or the broiler.

Place the greens in a large salad bowl. In a separate bowl, combine the Souse Meat and $1/2$ cup of the Champagne Vinaigrette, tossing lightly to coat.

Brush the onions with olive oil and grill them over hot coals or broil them until lightly browned. Remove them from the heat and cool. Toss the remaining $1^1/2$ cups of Champagne Vinaigrette over the greens and divide the greens evenly among the chilled salad plates. Arrange the marinated souse meat on top of the greens, place the green onions on each side, and sprinkle each salad with Tomato Concasse.

Garnish with sage and serve immediately.

SOFT GREENS AND MARINATED BLACK-EYED PEAS WITH ROASTED RED PEPPER VINAIGRETTE

MAKES 8 SERVINGS

After just one bite of this salad, the president of Golden Bird Restaurants, the first African-American family-owned fried chicken chain in California, asked to add it to his menu. I created the dish for the Black Faculty and Staff Fund-raiser dinner at California State Polytechnic University.

4 cups mesclun

1 cup Roasted Red Pepper Vinaigrette (see page 81)

2$^1/_4$ cups Marinated Black-eyed Peas (recipe follows)

1 cup Tomato Concasse (see page 69)

$^1/_2$ cup diced red onion

Place eight salad plates in the refrigerator to chill.

In a medium bowl, toss the greens with the Roasted Red Pepper Vinaigrette. Arrange the salad in the center of the chilled plates. Top the salads with Marinated Black-eyed Peas, Tomato Concasse, and diced onions. Serve immediately.

MARINATED BLACK-EYED PEAS

Black-eyed peas in this dish is a true taste of heritage. It may remind some people of a popular black-eyed pea salad called Texas caviar.

1 cup diced Roasted Red Peppers
  (see page 272)
$^1/_2$ cup diced red onion
2 cloves garlic, minced
1 tablespoon chopped fresh basil
$^1/_2$ tablespoon chopped fresh
  parsley
3 cups Black-eyed Peas with
  Ham Hocks, cooled
  (see page 89)
$^3/_4$ cup peanut oil
$^1/_4$ cup red wine vinegar
$^1/_2$ tablespoon dark brown sugar
1 teaspoon Worcestershire sauce
1 teaspoon salt
$^1/_4$ teaspoon freshly ground
  black pepper
$^1/_8$ teaspoon crushed red pepper
  flakes

In a large bowl, combine the roasted red pepper, onion, garlic, basil, parsley, and black-eyed peas. In a small bowl, blend the oil, vinegar, sugar, Worcestershire sauce, salt, pepper, and red pepper flakes. Pour the dressing over the black-eyed pea mixture and refrigerate. Serve chilled.

WILTED SPINACH, MUSTARD GREENS, GRILLED RED ONIONS, SLICED ARTICHOKES, SMITHFIELD HAM, AND RED-EYE GRAVY

MAKES 8 SERVINGS

This unusual combination is an example of what happens when beloved Old World flavors are updated for the 1990s. It makes a fine impression on brunch or luncheon tables.

1 large red onion, sliced into $^1/_4$-inch slices or rings

4 medium canned artichoke bottoms, cut into strips

$^1/_4$ cup olive oil

2 slices Smithfield ham, cut $^1/_4$ inch thick

$^1/_4$ cup brewed black coffee

$^1/_2$ cup water

$^1/_4$ teaspoon freshly ground black pepper

$^1/_4$ teaspoon sugar

$1^1/_2$ bunches fresh spinach, stems removed, washed, and drained

$1^1/_2$ bunches fresh mustard greens, stems removed, washed, and drained

Preheat a charcoal grill until white forms on top of the coals or preheat the broiler in your oven. Place the broiler pan under the hot coils to get the pan hot.

In a large bowl, toss the onion and artichokes with the olive oil and grill for 1 to 2 minutes on a hot grill or broiler. Set aside.

In a heated nonstick skillet on medium-high heat, cook the ham slices until browned on both sides, about 3 to 4 minutes. Remove the ham from the skillet and cut into thin strips. Set aside. Place the plates in a preheated 350°F oven for 2 minutes to warm them.

Pour off the excess fat in the skillet. Deglaze the pan with the coffee, stirring to loosen all the browned bits and pieces of "red" ham. Add the water, pepper, and sugar and bring the mixture to a boil. Cook for 2 to 3 minutes to reduce by half. Add the spinach and mustard greens to the skillet and toss them until they are thoroughly coated with sauce. Place the warm greens on the heated plates and garnish with the grilled onion, artichokes, and ham strips. Serve immediately.

BUTTERMILK DRESSING

MAKES ABOUT 1 ³/₄ CUPS

1 cup mayonnaise

¹/₂ cup buttermilk

1 clove garlic, minced

1¹/₂ tablespoons minced Vidalia or other sweet onion

1 tablespoon cider vinegar

¹/₂ tablespoon chopped fresh parsley

¹/₄ teaspoon salt

¹/₄ teaspoon ground white pepper

In a bowl, combine the mayonnaise, buttermilk, garlic, onion, vinegar, and parsley. Season with salt and pepper. Refrigerate until ready to serve. This dressing will keep 2 to 3 days.

CAESAR DRESSING

MAKES 1¹/₂ TO 2 CUPS

1 egg yolk

1 tablespoon Dijon mustard

2 cloves garlic, mashed to a paste

1 tablespoon fresh lemon juice

1 cup extra-virgin olive oil

2 anchovy fillets, minced

¹/₂ tablespoon Worcestershire sauce

¹/₄ cup red wine vinegar

¹/₂ teaspoon freshly ground black pepper

2 tablespoons freshly grated Parmesan cheese

2 dashes Tabasco sauce

In a mixing bowl, beat the egg yolk, Dijon mustard, garlic, and ¹/₂ tablespoon of the lemon juice with a wire whisk until foamy. Add the olive oil in a slow, steady stream, beating briskly until it is incorporated and the dressing thickens. Stir in the anchovies, Worcestershire sauce, vinegar, pepper, remaining ¹/₂ tablespoon lemon juice, Parmesan cheese, and Tabasco sauce. Refrigerate until ready to serve. This dressing will keep 2 to 3 days under refrigeration.

COUNTRY SMOKED BACON DRESSING

MAKES ABOUT 1 CUP

$^3/_4$ cup peanut oil

$^1/_4$ cup cider vinegar

1 teaspoon brown sugar

2 teaspoons minced shallots

$^1/_4$ teaspoon salt

$^1/_8$ teaspoon freshly ground
   black pepper

In a bowl, whisk together the oil, vinegar, brown sugar, shallots, salt, and pepper. This dressing will keep overnight.

PEANUT OIL DRESSING

MAKES ABOUT 2 CUPS

$^1/_2$ cup cider vinegar

1 tablespoon peanut butter

2 tablespoons packed dark
   brown sugar

$1^1/_2$ cups peanut oil

1 teaspoon minced onion

1 teaspoon minced garlic

1 tablespoon chopped fresh thyme

1 tablespoon chopped fresh
   parsley

$^1/_8$ teaspoon salt

$^1/_8$ teaspoon freshly ground
   black pepper

In a mixing bowl, whisk together the vinegar, peanut butter, and sugar. Stir in the oil, onion, garlic, thyme, and parsley. Mix well. Season with the salt and pepper. Refrigerate until ready to serve. This dressing holds up to three days under refrigeration.

Balsamic Vinaigrette

2 cups olive oil

1 cup extra-virgin olive oil

2 tablespoons pickled ginger

1 teaspoon garlic

1 large shallot, finely minced

1/2 cup balsamic vinegar

1/4 cup seasoned rice vinegar

Salt and ground white pepper
to taste

In a mixing bowl, combine the olive oils, pickled ginger, garlic, and shallot. Slowly whisk in the balsamic vinegar, then whisk in the seasoned rice vinegar. Season with salt and white pepper to taste.

Champagne Vinaigrette

MAKES 2 1/4 CUPS

1 cup peanut oil

1/2 cup extra-virgin olive oil

1/4 cup champagne vinegar

1/4 cup champagne

1/4 cup minced shallots

1 tablespoon chopped fresh basil

1 teaspoon sugar

1/2 teaspoon salt

1/2 teaspoon freshly ground
black pepper

In a blender, combine the peanut oil, olive oil, champagne vinegar, champagne, shallots, basil, sugar, salt, and pepper and blend until thick. Refrigerate until ready to serve. This dressing will keep 2 to 3 days.

CHEF'S TIP

This dressing should be made several hours in advance for the best flavor.

Cilantro Vinaigrette

$^1/_2$ cup peanut oil

$^1/_4$ cup sesame oil

$^1/_8$ cup soy sauce

$^1/_4$ cup unseasoned rice vinegar

$^1/_8$ cup sake

1 teaspoon sugar

2 tablespoons chopped fresh cilantro

2 tablespoons minced green onions

1 teaspoon minced fresh gingerroot

1 clove garlic, minced

In a mixing bowl, whisk together the peanut oil, sesame oil, soy sauce, rice vinegar, sake, sugar, cilantro, green onions, ginger, and garlic. This dressing will keep 1 to 2 days in the refrigerator.

Citrus Vinaigrette

$^1/_4$ cup white wine vinegar

$^1/_4$ cup fresh lemon juice

$^1/_2$ teaspoon lemon zest

1 teaspoon sugar

$^1/_2$ teaspoon salt

$^1/_4$ teaspoon freshly ground black pepper

$1^1/_2$ cups peanut oil

Whisk together the white wine vinegar, lemon juice, lemon zest, sugar, salt, and pepper. Continue to whisk while pouring in the oil in a steady stream. Taste and adjust the seasoning, if needed. This dressing will keep 1 to 2 days in the refrigerator.

FRESH BASIL VINAIGRETTE

MAKES 2 CUPS

$1^1/_2$ cups extra-virgin olive oil

$^1/_2$ cup red wine vinegar

1 tablespoon chopped fresh basil

$^1/_2$ teaspoon crushed red pepper flakes

$^1/_2$ teaspoon salt

$^1/_2$ teaspoon freshly ground black pepper

In a bowl, combine the olive oil, vinegar, basil, red pepper flakes, salt, and pepper. Blend well. This dressing will keep 2 to 3 days in the refrigerator.

ROASTED RED PEPPER VINAIGRETTE

MAKES $3^1/_2$ CUPS

$2^1/_2$ cups peanut oil

$^3/_4$ cup red wine vinegar

2 tablespoons cold water

1 tablespoon chopped fresh basil

$^1/_2$ cup Roasted Red Peppers (see page 272)

1 tablespoon brown sugar

1 clove garlic

1 teaspoon salt

1 teaspoon freshly ground black pepper

In a blender or food processor, combine the oil, vinegar, water, basil, roasted peppers, sugar, garlic, salt, and pepper. Blend until smooth. Refrigerate until ready to serve. This dressing will keep 1 to 2 days in the refrigerator.

Chapter 4

Vegetables and Accompaniments

When you set down at de table,
Kin' o'weary lak an' sad,
An' youse jes' a little tiahed
An' perhaps a little mad;
How yo' gloom tu'ns into gladness
How yo' joy drives out de doubt
When de oven do' is opened
An' de smell comes po'in out;
When, de 'lectric light o'heaven
Seems to settle on de spot
When yo' mammy says de blessin'
An' de co'n pone's hot
—PAUL LAURENCE DUNBAR

"Some of the most positive impressions of Southern cooking—and at the same time, some of the most negative—come into sharp focus on vegetables," says historian John Egerton, in his immensely popular cookbook, *Southern Food.*

"Without question," he continues, "the traditional Southern way of cooking most vegetables leans to the heavy; bacon grease and chunks of seasoning meat have been used extensively, and so have other ingredients now thought to be unhealthy, such as salt, sugar, butter, and cream."

And so it is with the vegetables and side dishes we have enjoyed as African-Americans. Admittedly, vegetables have been, as critics complain, "cooked to death." But Paul Laurence Dunbar would agree that the overcooking process has been a beloved, multifunctional technique.

We can't forget that these are the foods that sustained our hard-working ancestors through some very tough times. "Beans and peas, cabbage and corn, grits, greens, potatoes and tomatoes and onions have often been as basic as bread and water and more important than meat to the survival and well-being of the people in the region," Egerton explains. Indeed, boiled turnips, rutabagas, and beets can be terribly boring and would have been difficult to consume in large quantities. On the other hand, slow-simmered collard greens and beans, with their smoky overtones, were immensely satisfying.

They are also easy to cook. Granny simply "put on" a pot of beans or greens and she was free to do something else. In her world, there was little demand for food prepared *a la minute.*

Contemporary chefs now rely on baby eggplant, young miniature squash, tender haricots verts, and wild mushrooms instead of sturdy starches. With their outstanding, potent flavor, they are ideal for the bistro style of cooking—a quick light sauté in butter or olive oil and they are done. And tender vegetables are a refreshing break from the traditional heavy fare.

Unfortunately, these beautiful bistro vegetables are often adorned with beurre blanc—a frighteningly rich butter sauce—cream sauces, flavored oils, and vinaigrettes that can make them as unhealthful as collards with bacon fat.

Tangled in the conflict between authentic Southern cooking and contemporary health concerns is a question for health-conscious cooks and for fans of vegetables prepared according to authentic Southern style: Is there a place for my cherished Old-World vegetables in the new style of cooking and eating? The answer is yes; it's simply a matter of moderation.

If you love the tang of collard greens, sticky-sweet candied yams, and creamy macaroni and cheese, you'll really love the offerings that follow. They depend upon bacon drippings, chopped ham, butter and cream for flavor because that's the way it was done in the old days. At the same time, for presentation's sake I've created a few modern interpretations.

If your health is a concern, you can choose these foods less often but still enjoy them as they were meant to be eaten, just in smaller quantities and with less frequency. You can skim the fat from your cooking broth and don't eat as much of the meat in your stockpot. If you enjoy fried foods as an occasional splurge, you will have plenty of room in your diet for an occasional indulgence in the vegetables and side dishes of our heritage, whether you choose side dishes prepared the old-fashioned way or in the contemporary style—or a mix of both.

Here's an example. Fried cornmeal mush still enjoys a significant following on Southern and Midwestern menus, but to give it new life and excitement as an appetizer on a contemporary bill of fare, we fried it and served it accented with sautéed wild mushrooms. Or consider white beans. They develop character as they rumble around the kettle with a hunk of ham and are great served as is with a wedge of buttered cornbread. But puree the beans, mix them with seasonings, and you quickly dismiss any notion that this is "survival food."

BARBECUED BAKED BEANS

No barbecue or picnic would be complete without a big pot of beans. With canned beans you don't need to worry about cooking and soaking.

6 slices smoked bacon

2 green onions, sliced

Four 16-ounce cans pork and beans, drained, with 1 cup liquid reserved

$^1/_2$ cup blackstrap molasses

1 cup Backyard Barbecue Sauce (see page 284)

Preheat the oven to 350°F.

In a large skillet over medium-high heat, cook 2 strips of bacon until crisp. Remove from the skillet and drain on paper towels. Dice and set aside. Add the green onions to the skillet and cook 1 minute. Stir in the drained pork and beans and cook 2 to 3 minutes. Stir in the reserved liquid, molasses, Backyard Barbecue Sauce, and diced bacon. Pour into a 13 × 9-inch baking pan.

Place the remaining 4 strips of bacon on top of the beans and bake until the bacon is brown and crisp, about 45 to 50 minutes. Serve hot.

EDNA LEWIS'S BAKED TOMATOES

MAKES 4 TO 6 SERVINGS

When the garden yields more plump, juicy tomatoes than your family can possibly eat, or when they look too beautiful to resist, try this luscious dish. Of course, you could always use canned stewed tomatoes, if time doesn't permit you to make your own.

1¹/₂ quarts (4–5 pounds) ripe tomatoes

¹/₃ cup cold water

2 tablespoons butter

1¹/₂ slices stale bread, trimmed and cut into 12 pieces

3¹/₂ tablespoons sugar

¹/₂ teaspoon freshly ground black pepper

Drop the tomatoes into a pot of boiling water, then turn off the heat and let stand for about 3 minutes. Remove the tomatoes to a colander to drain and cool. When cool enough to handle, remove the skin, which will peel off very easily when pierced with a knife. Quarter the tomatoes and remove the seeds. Place the tomatoes in an enameled, stainless steel, or glass saucepan with water, and cook over medium-high heat for 12 to 13 minutes, shaking the pan or stirring with a wooden spoon to prevent sticking. Set aside to cool until needed or can in sterilized jars and seal.

Preheat the oven to 375°F.

Butter a casserole with about 1 tablespoon of butter and line the sides of the pan with 8 pieces of the bread. Add the stewed tomatoes, sprinkle with sugar, and dot with some of the remaining butter. Grind fresh pepper overall and then place the remaining 4 pieces of bread on top, dotting each piece with the last of the butter. Bake about 35 minutes. Remove and cool slightly before serving.

CHEF'S TIP

You will need about 3 cups of fresh stewed tomatoes or three 8-ounce cans of commercially prepared stewed tomatoes for this dish.

John Harrison's Broccoli au Gratin

Some Americans still haven't acquired a taste for broccoli. A smidgen of cheese and a light cream sauce give the healthy vegetable a creamy taste, reminiscent of macaroni and cheese.

2 heads broccoli, trimmed
1 1/2 teaspoons salt
3 tablespoons butter
1/3 cup all-purpose flour, sifted
1 cup milk, scalded
1 cup half-and-half, scalded
1/2 teaspoon white pepper
1 cup shredded cheddar cheese
1/4 cup fresh unseasoned bread crumbs
1 tablespoon chopped fresh parsley

Preheat the oven to 350°F.

Wash the broccoli and cut it into florets. Place in a large pot with boiling water to cover and 1 teaspoon of the salt. Cook broccoli until tender but still firm, about 12 to 15 minutes. Drain well and shock in ice water to stop the cooking. Drain and place in a lightly buttered 9 × 12-inch baking pan.

In a heated saucepan, melt 2 tablespoons of the butter. Whisk in the flour and blend well. Add the milk and half-and-half and stir. Add the remaining salt, pepper, and cheese and continue to stir. Pour cheese sauce over the broccoli and sprinkle with the bread crumbs and parsley. Melt the remaining 1 tablespoon butter and sprinkle overall. Bake until brown, about 10 to 15 minutes.

Patrick Clark's Braised Greens and Rutabaga

The inspiration for these braised greens comes from Mom "all the way." She cooked them the traditional way, in a simmering stock, rich with smoked meat. This version adds one of Patrick's favorite vegetables: "I was the only kid in the family who liked rutabaga."

2 slices smoked bacon, cut into julienne
1 medium onion, peeled and sliced
1 clove garlic, crushed
1 teaspoon crushed red pepper flakes
4 pounds mixed mustard greens, collard greens, turnip greens, or kale, large stems removed and cut into wide chiffonade
1 teaspoon sugar
16 turns freshly ground black pepper
1 teaspoon salt
2 pounds rutabagas, cut into 2 × 2-inch dice
3 cups water
1 1/2 tablespoons butter
3/4 teaspoon chopped fresh thyme
1/2 teaspoon salt

In a large skillet over medium heat, sauté the bacon until just crisp. Add the onion, garlic, and red pepper and cook until the onion is transparent. Rinse the greens, allowing a small amount of water to cling to them. Add greens to the pot, cover, and cook until the greens are wilted. Uncover and add the sugar, 12 turns of the pepper mill, and salt. Reduce the heat to medium-high and partially cover. Cook the greens until just tender, about 15 minutes. Keep warm.

Place the rutabagas in pot large enough to hold them plus the water. Add the remaining ingredients and bring to a boil. Cook, covered, over high heat until glazed and tender.

To serve, drain the greens, reserving the pot liquor. Place the greens in a serving bowl and add the rutabagas and their juices. Toss to combine but do not break up the rutabaga. Reduce the pot liquor by half over high heat, then add back to the greens. Serve very hot.

HOPPIN' JOHN
(BLACK-EYED PEAS AND RICE)

MAKES 6 TO 8 SERVINGS

This is one of those good-luck foods that is as popular among African-American families as noodles are with the Chinese and sauerkraut and pork with the Germans on New Year's Day.

1 cup dried black-eyed peas
3¹/₂ cups water
3 ounces streak-of-lean and
  streak-of-fat, diced
1 small onion, diced
2 cloves garlic, minced
1 teaspoon salt
¹/₂ teaspoon freshly ground
  black pepper
¹/₂ teaspoon cayenne pepper
1¹/₂ tablespoons butter
1 cup long grain white rice

Carefully pick over the peas and rinse them in a bowl. Cover with the water and soak for 6 to 8 hours, then drain the peas, reserving the water.

In a soup kettle or Dutch oven, sauté the streak-of-lean 3 to 4 minutes. Sauté the onion and garlic 1 to 2 minutes, but do not brown. Add the reserved water, black-eyed peas, and salt and bring to a boil. Reduce the heat and add the peppers and butter. Cook, uncovered, for 30 minutes, adding water as needed. Stir in the rice and simmer, covered, for 20 to 25 minutes.

BLACK-EYED PEAS WITH HAM HOCKS

MAKES 6 TO 8 SERVINGS

Black-eyed peas have an earthy flavor that marries well with the smoky overtones of the ham hocks. Fresh black-eyes are best, but if you can't find them dried are fine.

2 smoked ham hocks, split
2 quarts water
2 pounds fresh black-eyed peas
1 small onion, chopped
¹/₂ tablespoon crushed red
  pepper flakes
1 tablespoon chopped fresh thyme
1 teaspoon salt
1 teaspoon freshly ground
  black pepper

In a saucepan, bring the ham hocks and water to a boil, making sure the hocks are covered. Reduce the heat and simmer, covered, until the meat can easily be removed from the bone and the stock is well flavored, about 1¹/₂ hours. Remove the ham hocks from the pan, discard the skin, dice the ham into small pieces and return it to the stock.

Add the black-eyed peas, onion, red pepper, and thyme. Bring to a boil, then reduce the heat and simmer 30 minutes. Adjust seasoning with salt and pepper and serve immediately.

BRAISED SAUERKRAUT

MAKES 6 TO 8 SERVINGS

Sauerkraut isn't a traditional part of the African-American food scene, but I learned this method of preparing it from Chef Robert W. Lee, with whom I trained at the Harrisburger Hotel in the 1960s. Bacon fat imparts a familiar smoky quality. For more pronounced flavor, don't rinse the sauerkraut.

2 pounds sauerkraut

$^1/_4$ cup bacon drippings

1 medium onion, finely chopped

2 cloves garlic, minced

3 cups water

2 teaspoons caraway seeds

2 cups sweetened applesauce

1 tablespoon sugar

Place the sauerkraut in a colander and rinse with hot water for 3 to 4 minutes, then drain well.

In a large sauté pan, heat the bacon fat over medium-high heat and cook the onion and garlic 3 to 4 minutes. Do not brown. Stir in the sauerkraut, $1^1/_2$ cups of the water, and the caraway seeds and simmer until the water has almost evaporated. Stir in the applesauce and sugar and cook 2 to 3 minutes. Add the remaining water, cover, and bring to a boil. Reduce the heat and simmer until the water has evaporated, about 30 to 45 minutes.

CORNMEAL CREPE POUCH
FILLED WITH MIXED GREENS

MAKES 6 TO 8 CREPES

*Wrapped in crepes, greens easily make the transition from casual
family supper to elegant dinner party fare.*

MIXED GREENS

2 quarts Smoked Ham Stock
(see page 281)

2 bunches mustard greens,
stems removed and washed

2 bunches turnip greens, stems
removed and washed

1/2 cup chopped onion

1/4 teaspoon crushed red pepper
flakes

1/2 teaspoon salt

1/2 teaspoon freshly ground
black pepper

CREPES

3 tablespoons yellow cornmeal

1 1/2 cups cooked yellow corn
kernels, drained

6 tablespoons flour

5 eggs, beaten

1/2 teaspoon salt

1/2 teaspoon white pepper

2/3 cup heavy cream

1/3 cup melted butter

1/4 cup clarified butter

1 large leek, green part only, cut
into long thin strips (8 to 10
inches long) and blanched

Bring the stock to a boil, add the greens, onion, and red pepper flakes and cook until the greens are tender, about 45 minutes to an hour. Season with salt and pepper and set aside.

In a bowl, combine cornmeal, corn, flour, eggs, salt, pepper, cream, and melted butter. Mix well. Heat a small nonstick sauté pan or crepe pan over medium-high heat and coat lightly with clarified butter. Pour just enough batter into the pan to cover the bottom. Cook until the crepe begins to brown, turn and cook 1 minute on the other side. Remove from the pan and place on a lightly oiled plate. Continue cooking the remaining batter, buttering the pan each time with clarified butter. Layer the cooked crepes between lightly buttered parchment paper. Set aside until ready to fill.

To serve, spoon about 1/4 cup of drained greens in the center of each crepe. Fold in each corner to form a pouch, then tie the pouch with a leek string and keep warm.

CORN FRITTERS

Dropped from a small measuring cup into hot oil, these fritters are a wonderful accompaniment to fried chicken. Make them even smaller and omit the powdered sugar and they are a fine alternative to croutons in a salad.

$3/4$ cup milk

1 tablespoon melted butter

3 eggs, lightly beaten

1 cup all-purpose flour

$1/2$ teaspoon salt

$1/8$ teaspoon white pepper

1 teaspoon baking powder

1 cup fresh corn kernels

Peanut oil

$1/2$ tablespoon powdered sugar

Beat the milk and butter into the eggs. Sift together the flour, salt, pepper, and baking powder and stir until smooth. Add the corn and continue stirring. In a heavy saucepan, heat the oil to 350°F. Spoon about $1/8$ cup batter into the hot oil and fry until golden brown. Drain on brown paper or paper towels and serve hot sprinkled with powdered sugar.

COUNTRY CORN PUDDING

MAKES 8 SERVINGS

This traditional dish is also attractive when cooked and served in individual timbales.
Cook the pudding in 4-ounce custard cups instead of a large casserole.

6 ears corn

3 eggs

1 cup milk

$^1/_2$ cup heavy cream

1 tablespoon sugar

$^1/_2$ teaspoon salt

$^1/_4$ teaspoon freshly ground
black pepper

2 tablespoons melted butter

$^1/_4$ cup cornmeal

Preheat the oven to 350°F.

With a sharp knife, scrape the corn kernels from each cob into a bowl. With the blunt edge of the knife blade, scrape the cobs all around to get all the corn pulp. You should have about 2 cups.

Combine the corn kernels and pulp, eggs, milk, cream, sugar, salt, pepper, butter, and cornmeal. Stir until thoroughly blended. Pour into a buttered $1^1/_2$-quart baking dish. Set the baking dish in a larger pan set on middle oven rack. Pour boiling water into the larger pan so it comes about two thirds of the way up the sides of the pudding pan. Bake until a wood pick inserted in center comes out clean, about $1^1/_4$ hours. Check for doneness after about 1 hour of cooking time.

COUNTRY FRIED APPLES

MAKES 6 SERVINGS

This was one of my mother's favorite dishes, whether she prepared them for breakfast with
fried Virginia ham or fresh pork sausage or scrapple and hot biscuits. It was one of her
final requests during her last days in the hospital.

$^1/_2$ cup (1 stick) butter

6 Rome apples, peeled, cored,
and cut into $^1/_2$-inch slices

$^1/_2$ cup sugar

$^1/_8$ teaspoon ground cinnamon

$^1/_2$ teaspoon fresh lemon juice

$^1/_4$ cup water

Heat the butter in a large sauté pan or skillet over medium-high heat. Add the apples and cook until just tender, about 3 to 4 minutes. Sprinkle with the sugar and cinnamon, toss, and cook for 1 minute. Add the lemon juice and water, stir, cover, and reduce the heat to low. Cook 2 minutes to form a glaze.

COUNTRY SUCCOTASH

My family took a different approach than most when it came to succotash. My mother
added homemade pork sausage to the buttery mixture of fresh corn and lima beans.
It added a taste of the country to the dish.

$^{1}/_{2}$ pound Country Sausage,
   crumbled (see page 204)
4 slices country bacon, finely
   diced
1 small onion, finely diced
1 small green pepper, finely diced
2 cups fresh corn kernels
2 tablespoons all-purpose flour
2 cups Chicken Stock
   (see page 279)
1 pound frozen Fordhook lima
   beans, thawed
2 teaspoons sugar
$^{1}/_{2}$ teaspoon salt
$^{1}/_{4}$ teaspoon freshly ground
   black pepper
1 teaspoon cayenne pepper
1 tablespoon butter

In a large skillet, brown the sausage and bacon over medium-high heat and pour off all of the fat except $^{1}/_{4}$ cup. Add onion, green pepper, and corn and cook for 3 to 4 minutes. Stir in the flour and cook 2 to 3 minutes. Stir in the chicken stock and lima beans. Bring to a boil, then reduce the heat and add the sugar, salt, and peppers. Simmer until the lima beans are tender, about 15 to 20 minutes. Stir in the butter and serve hot.

CREAMY GRITS

Stone-ground grits take much longer to cook than the quick variety and they are more difficult to find, but do look for them. They are worth it. Skip the individual serving-size packages of the instant kind that cook quickly but lack character.

4 cups water
1 teaspoon salt
$^1/_2$ teaspoon white pepper
$^1/_4$ cup ($^1/_2$ stick) butter
1 cup stone-ground or quick grits
1 cup heavy cream

Bring the water, salt, pepper, and butter to boil in a saucepan. Gradually stir in the grits, cover, and cook over medium heat for 35 to 40 minutes, stirring occasionally. Add the cream and cook for 5 to 6 minutes longer, being careful not to burn. Serve hot.

CREAMED POTATOES

MAKES 8 SERVINGS

This is an example of one of those home-style dishes that benefits from a minor modification of the way Mother cooked it. Simply slice the potatoes in $^1/_4$-inch slices, just as you would when making a gratin, to spruce up the presentation.

2 pounds new potatoes, peeled
  and cut into $^1/_2$-inch dice
1 quart water
$1^1/_2$ teaspoons salt
$^1/_4$ cup ($^1/_2$ stick) butter
1 small onion, finely diced
$^1/_4$ cup all-purpose flour
3 cups milk, warmed
$^1/_4$ teaspoon white pepper
1 tablespoon chopped fresh chives

Bring the potatoes, water, and 1 teaspoon of the salt to a boil in a saucepan. Reduce the heat to simmer and cook until the potatoes are tender when pierced with a fork. Drain well.

In a saucepan, heat the butter over medium-high heat, add the onion, and cook until transparent, about 2 to 3 minutes. Stir in the flour to make a roux and cook 1 to 2 minutes. Do not brown. Whisk in the warm milk until smooth. Season with the remaining salt and pepper. Combine with the potatoes and serve hot, sprinkled with fresh chives.

CUBAN BLACK BEANS AND RICE

MAKES 6 TO 8 SERVINGS

*African-Americans are descendants of people of assorted ethnicities, including the Spanish.
This adaptation of Moros y Cristianos (black beans and rice), takes a cue from the accompaniment
of the same name, a big part of Cuban menus.*

2 tablespoons olive oil

1 small onion, diced

2 cloves garlic, minced

$1/2$ green pepper, diced

$1/2$ red bell pepper, diced

2 cups dried black beans,
   cooked, or use canned

1 cup Chicken Stock
   (see page 279)

1 teaspoon chopped fresh thyme

$1/2$ teaspoon freshly ground
   black pepper

2 cups water

1 cup long grain white rice

$1/2$ teaspoon salt

Heat the olive oil in a saucepan over medium-high heat. Cook the onion, garlic, and green and red peppers 5 minutes. Add the black beans, chicken stock, thyme, and pepper and bring to a boil. Reduce the heat and simmer, stirring occasionally, until heated through. Stir in the water, rice, and salt, cover, and cook over low heat until the rice is tender, about 15 to 20 minutes. Correct the seasoning, if needed. Serve hot.

KYM GIBSON'S DHAL

Kym says when she sat down at the dinner table, it was a collaborative effort. "I had working parents and was raised in an extended family. Everybody gravitated toward the kitchen. If my grandfather was cooking you would get dhal and curried soups."

2 cups yellow split peas

2 tablespoons extra-virgin olive oil

3 tablespoons Madras curry powder

2 cloves garlic, minced

2 sprigs fresh thyme

1 large onion, diced

1 teaspoon marsala

5 cups Chicken Stock (see page 279)

1 teaspoon kosher salt

Soak the split peas for 30 minutes in hot water. Pour the olive oil into a 2-quart saucepan and heat for 1 minute. Add the curry powder, garlic, and thyme to the olive oil, then add the onion and cook until transparent. Add the marsala, split peas, chicken stock, and salt. Cook until the peas resemble mashed potatoes.

FRIED CORNMEAL MUSH

MAKES 8 SERVINGS

*Although this dish is deeply rooted in Southern cooking, you can still find it today
on the menus of country-style restaurants in the North.*

4 slices slab bacon

5 cups water

1 cup cornmeal

1 1/2 teaspoons salt

1 tablespoon chopped fresh
    parsley

2 eggs, beaten

1/2 cup all-purpose flour

In a heavy skillet over medium-high heat, cook the bacon until brown
and crisp. Drain on paper towels and crumble or chop fine. Set aside,
reserving 1/4 cup of the bacon drippings.

In a saucepan, bring the water to a boil, then reduce the heat and
gradually pour in the cornmeal, stirring vigorously. Stir in the salt and
parsley and cook 20 to 30 minutes. Pour into a greased 9 × 5-inch loaf
pan and refrigerate until set. It should be firm.

Turn the loaf out onto a cutting board, cut in slices about 3/4 inch
thick, then cut the slices in half diagonally. Heat the reserved bacon
drippings in a skillet over medium-high heat. Dip the cornmeal slices
in the eggs and dust with flour. Fry on each side until golden brown,
about 3 to 4 minutes per side. Drain on paper towels.

CHEF'S TIP

To insure the mush is heated through, place the mush in a baking pan
and finish in a preheated 400°F oven for 4 to 5 minutes.

Prince Akins's Fried Corn

MAKES 6 SERVINGS

Prince's mother provided the inspiration for this home-style dish, which over the years he has adapted for a more upscale presentation at Georgia.

9 ears fresh sweet corn

4 slices country bacon, finely diced

1 small green pepper, diced

3 tablespoons all-purpose flour

$1/2$ tablespoon sugar

1 cup water

1 teaspoon salt

$1/2$ teaspoon freshly ground black pepper

$1/4$ teaspoon cayenne pepper

$1/4$ cup half-and-half

With a sharp paring knife cut down the middle of the cob through each row of kernels and put them in a bowl. Scrape the milky juice from the cob into the bowl.

In a skillet over medium-high heat, fry the bacon until almost done, then stir in the green pepper and corn. Stir in the flour and sugar. Add the water while stirring and allow to cook for 10 to 12 minutes. Season with the salt, and black and cayenne peppers. Stir and cook until almost dry and brown. Add the half-and-half and simmer, stirring constantly, until almost dry.

Fried Plantains

MAKES 6 TO 8 SERVINGS

Plantains, eaten throughout Central America and the Caribbean with oxtails, grilled chicken, and pork, are a perfect substitute for candied sweet potatoes.

$1^1/2$ pounds ripe plantains

2 tablespoons butter

4 tablespoons peanut oil

1 tablespoon superfine sugar

Peel each plantain and make a series of even parallel cuts at an angle on each plantain, about $3/4$ inch wide.

In a cast-iron skillet, melt the butter over medium-high heat, then add the peanut oil and cook the plantains in batches on each side until golden brown and just starting to caramelize on the edges, about 2 minutes per side. Remove from the skillet, drain on paper towels, and sprinkle with sugar. Serve hot.

CHEF'S TIP

For the best taste, be sure your plantains are fully ripe, with black skin, and are slightly soft.

Clifton Williams's Garlicky Mashed Potatoes with Leeks

MAKES 6 SERVINGS

Garlic and leeks take mashed potatoes from down-home to uptown. Light cream and low-fat milk help keep an eye on fat. Parboiling the leeks brings out the flavor.

2 pounds russet potatoes
1 tablespoon plus 1 teaspoon salt
3 tablespoons butter
$1/4$ cup light cream, hot
$1/4$ cup low-fat (2%) milk, hot
1 tablespoon minced fresh garlic
$1/4$ cup finely sliced leeks, blanched
1 teaspoon white pepper

Peel and remove the eyes from the potatoes, cut them into quarters, and keep in cold water until ready to cook. Place the potatoes in a saucepan, cover with water, and add 1 tablespoon salt. Bring to a boil, then reduce the heat and simmer until the potatoes are tender, about 20 to 25 minutes. Drain well and place in the bowl of an electric mixer. Using the paddle, break up the potatoes well, then replace the paddle with a wire whip. Beat at slow speed until well mashed. Beat in the butter, cream, and milk, beating well after each addition. Beat until the potatoes reach the desired consistency. Blend in the garlic, leeks, remaining 1 teaspoon salt, and pepper and blend well. Beat at medium-high speed until the potatoes are light. Serve hot.

Edna Lewis's Whipped Potatoes

MAKES 6 TO 8 SERVINGS

6 medium Idaho potatoes, peeled and quartered
1 teaspoon salt
$1/4$ cup ($1/2$ stick) butter
$1/2$ teaspoon ground white pepper
Salt to taste
1 cup hot milk
2 teaspoons chopped fresh chives

Place the potatoes in a saucepan and pour in boiling water to cover. Add the salt and cook over medium-high heat for 20 minutes. Drain and mash with a potato masher or put them through a food mill. Add the butter, pepper, and salt. Pour in the hot milk and beat well by hand or with an electric mixer until the potatoes are light and fluffy. Spoon the mixture into a heated casserole, dot with additional butter, and set under the broiler to lightly brown the peaks. Sprinkle with chives and serve piping hot.

MOM PAN'S CANDIED SWEET POTATOES

MAKES 8 SERVINGS

*Virtually everyone has their favorite way of making candied sweet potatoes. This is
the way my mother, Mom Pan, made them, and frankly, they are hard to beat
and so sweet you will crave them like dessert.*

2 pounds sweet potatoes
$^1/_2$ cup (1 stick) butter
$^1/_4$ cup sugar
1 cup maple syrup

Preheat the oven to 350°F. Bake the sweet potatoes until tender, but
still a little firm, about 30 to 40 minutes. Set aside to cool. When cool,
peel them and cut into quarters.

In a large skillet, melt half the butter over medium-high heat and
sauté half the potato slices on both sides. Sprinkle with half the sugar
and cook until the edges are brown. Pour in half the maple syrup and
simmer 1 to 2 minutes. Repeat with the remaining sweet potatoes,
butter, sugar, and syrup.

KYM GIBSON'S SAUTÉED GREEN TOMATOES AND OLIVES

MAKES 8 SERVINGS

*Kym's grandmother was from Mississippi and she cooked with a heavy Southern style.
Quite naturally, says Kym, this menu, "Is a blend of all the things that made me."
This dish resonates Southern hospitality.*

4 green tomatoes
1 tablespoon Tabasco sauce
$^1/_4$ cup extra-virgin olive oil
$^1/_2$ cup sliced green olives
2 cloves garlic, minced
1 tablespoon minced cilantro
$^1/_4$ cup minced fresh chives

Cut the tomatoes into large chunks and mix in the Tabasco sauce.
Heat the olive oil in a sauté pan over medium-high heat, add the
tomatoes, green olives, garlic, and cilantro and sauté 2 to 3 minutes.
Remove from the heat, sprinkle with chives, and keep warm until
ready to serve.

MOM PAN'S GREEN BEANS

MAKES 8 SERVINGS

Fresh green beans are prized in the African-American community, whether simmered in a well-seasoned broth made with ham hocks or salt pork. Most matriarchs, like my mother, cooked a pot at least once a week.

3/4 pound salt pork fatback

2 1/2 quarts water

3 pounds fresh green beans, washed and snapped about 2 inches long

1 teaspoon salt (optional)

1 teaspoon freshly ground black pepper

Cut three slits in the salt pork. Bring the water to a boil in a saucepan, then reduce the heat to medium, add the salt pork and simmer, covered, for 1 hour. Stir in the green beans and cook until the beans are tender, about 40 to 45 minutes. Discard the salt pork. Season with salt and pepper. Serve hot.

CHEF'S TIP

Sprinkle these beans with toasted almonds, sautéed onions, chopped ham, or diced tomatoes, or any combination for a truly Southern experience.

PRINCE AKINS'S GREEN BEANS AND NEW POTATOES

MAKES 6 SERVINGS

By now you must have guessed that there are as many ways to prepare fresh green beans as there are good cooks. Here's another style.

3 pounds fresh green beans, snapped into 2-inch-long pieces

1/2 pound salt pork fatback

1 teaspoon salt

2 quarts water

1/2 teaspoon freshly ground black pepper

18 small new potatoes, scrubbed

In a saucepan, combine the green beans, salt pork, salt, water, and pepper. Bring to a boil and cover. Reduce the heat and simmer 10 to 15 minutes. Add the potatoes and cook 30 minutes. Remove the cover and continue to simmer until the potatoes are done. Serve hot.

Edna Lewis's Long-cooked Green Beans with Smoked Pork Shoulder

MAKES 8 TO 10 SERVINGS

1¹/₂ pounds dry cured pork
   picnic shoulder, ham, or bacon

2 quarts water

3 pounds whole fresh green
   beans, trimmed

1 teaspoon salt

¹/₂ teaspoon freshly ground
   black pepper

Finely chopped parsley, for garnish

Wash the pork well and place it in the water in a large saucepan. Bring to a boil and simmer over medium heat until the flavor has been extracted from the meat, at least 1 hour. Remove the cooked pork and add the beans to the stock. Bring to a boil, then reduce the heat and simmer over medium heat for at least 1¹/₂ hours. Season to taste with salt and pepper. When the beans are done, remove them from the heat and set aside until ready to serve. Reheat and serve hot, garnished with finely chopped parsley.

Copyright © 1988 by Edna Lewis. From *The Taste of Country Cooking*. Used by permission of Alfred A. Knopf.

Oven-roasted Potatoes

MAKES 6 TO 8 SERVINGS

A fresh option to accompany most any meat.

¹/₂ cup peanut oil

1 teaspoon salt

¹/₂ teaspoon freshly ground
   black pepper

1 teaspoon paprika

3 pounds Idaho potatoes, peeled,
   cut in half and then cut into
   diagonal slices

Preheat the oven to 350°F.

Combine the peanut oil, salt, pepper, and paprika in a bowl and mix well. Add the potatoes and stir to coat thoroughly. Place the potatoes in a lightly greased baking pan. Bake, stirring occasionally, until they are tender and brown, about 40 to 50 minutes.

John Harrison's Roasted Red Bliss Potatoes

MAKES 6 TO 8 SERVINGS

With a hint of rosemary and a splash of olive oil, potatoes are a favorite part of John's menu.

2$^1/_2$ pounds red new potatoes

$^1/_2$ cup extra-virgin olive oil

1 tablespoon chopped fresh rosemary

1 teaspoon salt

$^1/_2$ teaspoon freshly ground black pepper

$^1/_2$ teaspoon paprika

$^1/_2$ tablespoon chopped fresh parsley

Preheat the oven to 350°F.

Cut the potatoes into quarters. Combine the olive oil, rosemary, salt, pepper, and paprika in a bowl and mix well. Add the potatoes and toss to coat thoroughly. Place the potatoes on a baking sheet that has been sprayed with nonstick vegetable spray and bake, stirring occasionally, for 45 to 50 minutes. Garnish with parsley.

Pan-fried Green Tomatoes

MAKES 6 SERVINGS

Fanny Flagg popularized this Southern favorite in her novel and in the film "Fried Green Tomatoes." Previously the dish had been one of our best-kept secrets, as it is so handy when the season produces a bumper crop.

$^1/_4$ cup buttermilk

$^1/_4$ cup milk

1 egg, beaten

$^1/_2$ cup cornmeal

$^1/_4$ cup all-purpose flour

1 teaspoon salt

$^1/_2$ teaspoon freshly ground black pepper

$^1/_4$ teaspoon cayenne pepper

3 green tomatoes, sliced $^1/_4$ inch thick

Peanut oil

In a bowl, combine the buttermilk, milk, and egg. Mix well.

In a separate bowl, stir together the cornmeal, flour, salt, and black and cayenne peppers. Dip the tomato slices in the milk and egg mixture, then dredge in the cornmeal and flour mixture. Coat well. Heat the oil in a skillet over medium-high heat and cook the tomato slices on each side until golden brown, about 2 to 3 minutes per side. Drain on paper towels and serve hot.

Pan-fried Grits Triangles

MAKES 6 TO 8 SERVINGS

Italians like fried polenta as the basis for appetizers and first-course dishes. We think these, with their Southern accent, are equally terrific.

2 cups water
1 teaspoon salt
1 teaspoon white pepper
$^1/_2$ cup (1 stick) butter
$^1/_2$ cup stone-ground grits
$^1/_2$ cup heavy cream
2 eggs, beaten
1 cup all-purpose flour

Bring the water to a boil in a saucepan. Add the salt, pepper, and 2 tablespoons of the butter. Gradually stir in grits and cook, covered, for 5 to 6 minutes. Stir in the cream. Pour the cooked grits into a buttered 9 × 5-inch loaf pan and refrigerate until firm, 2 to 3 hours.

Remove the grits from the pan and cut into $^1/_2$-inch slices, then cut each slice in half diagonally, forming triangles. Dip each triangle in the eggs and then dredge in the flour. Heat the remaining butter in a skillet over medium heat, and cook the grits on both sides until golden brown. Keep warm until ready to serve.

Potato Pancakes

MAKES 8 SERVINGS

Serve these as dainty little accompaniments at brunch or as a hearty complement to braised meats. Either way, no one will be able to say, "No, thanks."

4 to 5 pounds russet potatoes, washed, peeled, and grated (about 6 large)
$^1/_2$ cup grated onion
$^1/_4$ cup all-purpose flour
1 teaspoon baking powder
1 teaspoon salt
$^1/_2$ teaspoon ground white pepper
1 tablespoon chopped fresh chives
2 teaspoons chopped fresh parsley
2 eggs, beaten
$^3/_4$ cup peanut oil

Place the potatoes and onion in a colander, rinse, and drain. In a large mixing bowl, combine the potatoes, onion, flour, baking powder, salt, pepper, chives, and parsley. Stir in the eggs and mix well. Heat the oil in a skillet over medium-high heat. Spoon in $^1/_2$ cupfuls of potato mixture into the skillet. Cook on each side until golden brown, about 3 to 4 minutes per side. Repeat with the remaining potato mixture. Drain on paper towels. Serve hot.

Rustic Baked Macaroni and Cheese

Everyone in the South makes this comfort food from scratch. One bite of this rich home-style casserole and you will wonder why you ever made macaroni and cheese from a package.

1 teaspoon salt

2 cups elbow macaroni

2 cups evaporated milk

2 eggs, beaten

$1/2$ teaspoon cayenne pepper

1 teaspoon salt

$1/4$ cup ($1/2$ stick) butter, melted

$2^1/2$ cups sharp cheddar cheese, grated

1 teaspoon paprika

Preheat the oven to 350°F.

Bring water to a boil in a large saucepan. Add the salt, then gradually stir in the macaroni. Cook over high heat for 10 to 12 minutes. Do not overcook. Drain and rinse with cold water. Drain again well and set aside.

Beat together the milk, eggs, pepper, salt, and butter. Layer one third of the macaroni in a buttered 2-quart casserole and top with a layer of grated cheese. Repeat the layering, ending with cheese. Pour the milk mixture overall, using a fork to lightly but thoroughly mix. Sprinkle the top with paprika. Bake, uncovered, until brown, about 40 to 45 minutes.

Sautéed Mustard Greens and Mushrooms

Unlike collards, which are significantly sturdier and require braising in a well-seasoned broth, mustard greens have a lighter leaf that lends itself well to brief cooking methods like this one.

4 bunches fresh mustard greens

$1/4$ cup extra-virgin olive oil

3 cloves garlic, minced

2 cups button mushrooms, sliced $1/4$ inch thick

$1/4$ cup water

$1/2$ teaspoon salt

$1/4$ teaspoon freshly ground black pepper

2 tablespoons cider vinegar

Thoroughly wash the greens, remove the stems, and drain well. Cut into broad strips.

In a large skillet, heat the oil over medium-high heat. Cook and stir the garlic and mushrooms for 2 to 3 minutes. Stir in the greens and continue to cook and stir until the greens are tender and limp, about 5 minutes. Reduce the heat to medium. Stir in the water, cover, and steam for 20 minutes. Season with the salt, pepper, and vinegar, toss, and serve hot.

Sautéed Wild Mushrooms

*Fans of today's quick-cooking methods will appreciate the ease
of preparation and potent flavor of this dish.*

$1/4$ cup ($1/2$ stick) butter

1 clove garlic, minced

1 large shallot, minced

$1/2$ pound shiitake mushrooms,
   diced

$1/4$ pound chanterelle mushrooms,
   diced

$1/4$ pound porcini mushrooms,
   diced

$1/4$ pound cremini mushrooms,
   diced

$1/4$ oyster mushrooms, diced

$1/2$ teaspoon salt

$1/4$ teaspoon freshly ground
   black pepper

$1/4$ cup dry sherry

1 tablespoon chopped fresh parsley

$1/2$ tablespoon chopped fresh
   chervil

Melt the butter in a sauté pan over medium-high heat. Cook the garlic for 2 minutes, then add the shallot and continue to cook 2 minutes more. Stir in the mushrooms and cook 3 to 5 minutes. Season with the salt and pepper. Stir in the sherry, parsley, and chervil and cook 2 minutes.

Sautéed Zucchini, Tomatoes, and Mushrooms

Zucchini and tomatoes have a natural affinity. Mushrooms and fresh basil add an Italian touch.

4 slices smoked bacon, diced

$1/4$ cup olive oil

$2^1/2$ cups zucchini, cut in half lengthwise, then cut into $1/2$-inch slices

1 pound button mushrooms

2 cloves garlic, minced

2 cups canned whole tomatoes, crushed and undrained

1 tablespoon chopped fresh basil

2 tablespoons cornstarch

$1/4$ cup water

Salt and freshly ground black pepper to taste

In a large heated skillet, cook the bacon over medium-high heat until crisp. Drain on paper towels and set aside. Discard the bacon drippings and heat the olive oil in the same pan over medium-high heat. Cook the zucchini for 3 to 4 minutes. Do not brown. Remove from the pan and set aside. Add the mushrooms and garlic and cook 3 to 4 minutes. Stir in the tomatoes and their juice and the basil and continue to cook for 3 minutes.

Mix the cornstarch with the water and pour into the pan. Cook and stir until mixture thickens, 3 to 4 minutes. Return the bacon and zucchini to the pan, stir, and correct the seasoning with salt and pepper. Reduce the heat to low and simmer 2 to 3 minutes. Serve at once.

SMOTHERED CABBAGE

MAKES 8 SERVINGS

With fresh, crisp heads of this cruciferous vegetable readily available all year long you no longer have to wait to take that nostalgic trip down Memory Lane to Mother's kitchen.

1/4 cup bacon drippings
2 heads green cabbage, cored and cut into 1/2-inch slices
1 medium onion, chopped
1 tablespoon cider vinegar
1 teaspoon sugar
1/2 teaspoon salt
1/2 teaspoon freshly ground black pepper

In a large saucepan, heat the bacon drippings over medium-high heat and stir in the cabbage. Cover and cook for 10 to 15 minutes, stirring occasionally. Add the onion and continue to cook until tender, about 10 to 15 minutes more. Stir in the vinegar, sugar, salt, and pepper and simmer 5 minutes. Serve hot.

SOUTHERN COLLARD GREENS

6 TO 8 SERVINGS

Ham hocks are simmered in an aromatic stock, which gives collards their palate-haunting flavor.

2 quarts water
2 pounds ham hocks, split
4 bunches collard greens
1/2 teaspoon crushed red pepper flakes
2 cloves garlic, minced
Salt and freshly ground black pepper

In a large stockpot, bring the water and ham hocks to a boil. Reduce the heat and simmer for 1 1/2 to 2 hours.

Wash the greens thoroughly, drain, and remove the stems. Cut into broad strips. Add greens, red pepper flakes, and garlic to pot. Return to a boil, then reduce the heat and simmer until the greens are tender, 1 1/2 hours. Remove the ham hocks from the pot. Discard the skin and bones and dice the meat. Return the meat to the pot. Season with salt and pepper to taste. Serve hot.

CHEF'S TIP

For a change of pace, try mixed greens, a combination of mustard greens or turnip greens, added to the pot.

STEWED OKRA AND TOMATOES

MAKES 6 TO 8 SERVINGS

You haven't begun to experience the versatility in our cuisine until you develop an appreciation for okra.

$^1/_4$ pound streak-of-lean and streak-of fat, sliced

1 medium onion, chopped

1 medium green pepper, diced

2 cloves garlic, minced

1 pound fresh whole okra

4 ripe tomatoes, roughly chopped

1 teaspoon salt

$^1/_2$ teaspoon sugar

$^1/_8$ teaspoon cayenne pepper

$^1/_2$ cup water

In a skillet or sauté pan, bring 1 cup of water to a boil. Cook the steak-of-lean 2 minutes on each side. Remove from the pan and wash the pan to remove any salt residue. Fry the streak-of-lean like bacon over medium heat until brown and crisp. Remove, drain, chop fine, and set aside. Pour off all but $2^1/_2$ tablespoons of drippings from the pan. Add the onion, green pepper, and garlic. Cook over medium heat for 3 minutes. Add the okra and continue to cook 15 minutes, stirring occasionally. Add the tomatoes, salt, sugar, cayenne, and water. Cover and simmer 10 to 12 minutes.

SWEET POTATO PANCAKES

MAKES 8 SERVINGS

Sweet potatoes turn up prepared in a host of delicious ways in traditional African-American cooking. Shredded and fried into pancakes, they are even more desirable.

1 pound fresh sweet potatoes

1 small onion

3 eggs

$^1/_4$ cup all-purpose flour

$^1/_2$ teaspoon baking powder

$^1/_4$ teaspoon ground nutmeg

$^1/_8$ teaspoon ground allspice

Salt and freshly ground black pepper to taste

$^1/_4$ cup peanut oil

Peel the sweet potatoes and shred either on a box shredder or in a food processor using the medium shredding disk. You should have about 3 cups. Shred the onion on the shredder or in a food processor using the medium shredding disk. Place the sweet potatoes and onions in a clean kitchen towel and twist to squeeze out as much liquid as possible. Place in a mixing bowl. Add the eggs, flour, baking powder, nutmeg, allspice, salt, and pepper and mix well.

Heat the peanut oil in cast-iron skillet over medium heat. Working in batches, spoon about $^1/_4$ cup of the mixture in the skillet forming pancakes. Cook the pancakes 2 to 3 minutes on each side.

Patrick Clark's Sweet Potato and Wild Mushroom Hash

MAKES 12 SERVINGS

This dish was originally created as an accompaniment to game, but since the sweet potatoes go so well with everything and they have been so popular in African-American culture, it just seems like a natural combination to other dishes as well.

3 tablespoons olive oil

2 tablespoons unsalted butter

2 pounds mixed shiitake, chanterelle, and cremini mushrooms, sliced

3 shallots, finely chopped

2 cloves garlic, minced

1 teaspoon chopped fresh thyme

3 large Yukon Gold potatoes, cut into 1/2-inch cubes

3 large sweet potatoes, cut into 1/2-inch cubes

1/4 cup peanut oil

1 cup peeled and diced red onion

Salt and freshly ground black pepper to taste

Pinch ground nutmeg

1/2 teaspoon grated orange zest

1/2 cup chopped walnuts, toasted

1 tablespoon chopped parsley

Heat half the oil and half the butter in a skillet. Divide the mushrooms into two batches and sauté each batch until light golden brown and all the liquid has evaporated. Toss mushrooms with the shallots and garlic and cook another 2 to 3 minutes. Toss in the thyme and set aside to drain.

Blanch the Yukon Gold and sweet potatoes in separate pots of boiling water until just tender. Heat 2 tablespoons of the peanut oil in a large nonstick skillet and sauté the onion until tender and transparent Add the Yukon Gold potatoes and the remaining oil and sauté until golden brown. Add the sweet potatoes and cook until all the potatoes are tender. Season with salt, pepper, and nutmeg. Toss in the orange zest and chopped nuts. Combine with the mushrooms and stir in the parsley. Place in a large serving dish and serve.

BLACK BEAN CAKES

MAKES 8 SERVINGS; ABOUT 16 CAKES

This dish is popular on the menus of some very trendy restaurants. For variety, substitute Great Northern beans for the black beans.

1 pound dried black beans, soaked overnight in water to cover and drained

2 quarts water

1 ham hock, split

1 sprig fresh parsley

1 sprig fresh thyme

1 teaspoon salt

2 tablespoons butter

1 medium onion, minced

4 cloves garlic, minced

$^1/_2$ cup all-purpose flour

1 tablespoon chopped fresh thyme

$^1/_2$ teaspoon cayenne pepper

2 egg yolks

Salt and freshly ground black pepper to taste

$^1/_2$ cup clarified butter

In a large saucepan, combine the beans, water, ham hock, herb sprigs, and salt. Bring to a boil, then reduce the heat to medium and cook until beans are tender, $1^1/_2$ to 2 hours. Drain and allow to cool. Discard the herbs and refrigerate the ham hock for another use.

In a skillet, heat the 2 tablespoons butter over medium-high heat and cook the onion and garlic 1 to 2 minutes. Add 2 tablespoons of the flour, season with the thyme and cayenne and cook, stirring, for 3 to 4 minutes. Do not brown. Remove from the heat and set aside.

Puree half the beans in a food processor or blender until roughly smooth. In a large bowl, mash the remaining beans against the sides of the bowl. Add the pureed beans to the mashed beans, stir in the onion mixture and the egg yolks, and season to taste with salt and pepper, mixing well.

Spoon about $^1/_4$ cup of the mixture on a parchment-lined baking pan. Cover and refrigerate for at least $1^1/_2$ hours.

In a large skillet, heat the clarified butter over medium-high heat, lightly dust the cakes with flour, and sauté on each side until brown and heated through, about 2 to 3 minutes per side.

WHITE BEAN CAKES

MAKES 8 SERVINGS

This dish is a slight variation of my popular Black Bean Cakes.

1 pound dried Great Northern
    beans, soaked overnight in
    water to cover
2 quarts water
1 ham hock, split
1 sprig fresh parsley
1 teaspoon salt
1/2 cup clarified butter
1 small onion, minced
4 cloves garlic, minced
Salt and freshly ground
    black pepper to taste
1/2 cup all-purpose flour
2 egg yolks
1 tablespoon chopped fresh sage
1/2 teaspoon cayenne pepper

Drain the beans and place them in a large saucepan with the water, ham hock, parsley, and salt. Bring to a boil, then reduce the heat to medium and cook until the beans are tender, $1\frac{1}{2}$ to 2 hours. Drain and allow to cool. Discard the parsley and refrigerate the ham hock for another use.

In a skillet, heat 2 tablespoons of the clarified butter over medium-high heat, add the onion and garlic and cook 1 to 2 minutes. Season with salt and pepper, add 2 tablespoons of the flour and cook, stirring, 3 to 4 minutes. Do not brown. Remove from the heat and set aside.

Puree half beans in a food processor or blender until roughly smooth. In a large bowl, mash the remaining beans on the side of the bowl. Add the pureed beans to the mashed beans. Stir in the onion mixture and egg yolks and season with sage and cayenne pepper. Mix well.

Using a $\frac{1}{4}$-cup measure, form cakes and place on a parchment-lined baking pan. Cover and refrigerate for at least $1\frac{1}{2}$ hours.

In a large skillet, heat the remaining clarified butter over medium-high heat and lightly dust the cakes with the remaining flour. Cook until brown and heated through, about 2 to 3 minutes on each side.

RICE PILAF

MAKES 8 SERVINGS

Quickly sautéing rice in butter coats the grains and prevents them from becoming sticky during cooking. Finishing the dish in the oven is the proper way to make a pilaf, but it can be cooked on top of the stove.

$1/4$ cup ($1/2$ stick) butter
1 small onion, finely chopped
2 cups long-grain rice
4 cups Chicken Stock
   (see page 279)
$1/2$ teaspoon salt
$1/2$ teaspoon white pepper
2 tablespoons melted butter
1 tablespoon chopped fresh
   parsley

Preheat the oven to 350°F.

In a saucepan over medium-high heat, melt the butter, add the onion, and cook until transparent, about 3 to 4 minutes. Add the rice and cook, stirring to coat the rice with the butter, about 2 minutes. Stir in the chicken stock, salt, and pepper, cover, and bring to a boil. Bake until the rice is tender and all the liquid is absorbed, about 15 to 20 minutes. Fluff with a fork and mix in the melted butter and parsley.

STEAMED BUTTERED RICE

MAKES 8 SERVINGS

Rice is one of those simple little dishes that sometimes frustrates the best of cooks. Some people boil it rapidly, then remove it from the heat and let it steam off the heat to prevent stickiness. I boil then simmer the rice over low heat. It's perfect every time.

$4^1/2$ cups water
2 cups long-grain white rice
1 teaspoon salt
$1/4$ cup ($1/2$ stick) butter

Combine the water, rice, salt, and butter in a saucepan. Cover and bring to a boil over high heat. Then reduce the heat to low and simmer undisturbed until the rice is tender, about 20 minutes.

SAFFRON RICE

MAKES 8 SERVINGS

Saffron gives this rice dish a special flavor very common in Spanish cooking. Sometimes cooks substitute turmeric, which costs less, but the flavor doesn't compare.

$^1/_4$ cup ($^1/_2$ stick) butter

2 cups long-grain white rice

$4^1/_2$ cups Chicken Stock (see page 279)

$^3/_4$ teaspoon saffron threads, crushed

$^1/_2$ teaspoon salt

Melt the butter in a saucepan over medium-high heat. Add the rice and cook, stirring to coat the rice well with butter. Stir in the chicken stock, saffron, and salt. Bring to a boil, cover, and reduce the heat to medium-low. Simmer undisturbed until the rice is tender, about 20 minutes.

KYM GIBSON'S RED MINT RICE

MAKES 8 SERVINGS

2 cups long-grain rice

3 cups tomato juice

$^1/_4$ cup ($^1/_2$ stick) butter

$^1/_2$ cup finely chopped onion

2 cups Chicken Stock (see page 279)

2 cups canned Italian plum tomatoes, diced

$^1/_2$ cup chopped fresh mint

Soak the rice in the tomato juice for 20 minutes. Melt 2 tablespoons of the butter in a saucepan over medium-high heat. Add the onion and sauté until tender. Add the rice mixture, 1 cup of the chicken stock, and the remaining butter. Bring to a boil. Stir in the remaining cup of chicken stock as needed to prevent sticking. Reduce the heat and let simmer for 10 minutes. Add the diced tomatoes and mint. Cover the pan and simmer for 5 minutes.

SAVANNAH RED RICE

As Southern traditions go Savannah Red Rice is wonderful, especially when served with grilled or fried fish, pork, and chicken. It can be enhanced by adding shrimp or smoked sausage.

$1/4$ pound salt pork, finely diced
1 small red pepper, diced
1 small green pepper, diced
1 rib celery, diced
1 medium onion, diced
2 cloves garlic, minced
2 cups long-grain white rice
2 cups crushed, canned whole
   tomatoes, undrained
2 tablespoons tomato paste
$1^1/_2$ cups water
$1/_2$ teaspoon salt
$1/_4$ teaspoon freshly ground
   black pepper
$1/_2$ teaspoon cayenne pepper

Heat a large heavy-bottomed saucepan and cook the salt pork over medium-high heat until crisp. Add the red and green peppers, celery, onion, and garlic and cook 3 to 4 minutes. Add the rice and stir, coating the rice with drippings. Stir in the tomatoes, tomato paste, water, salt, and black and cayenne peppers. Cover and simmer until the rice is tender and the liquid is absorbed, about 25 to 30 minutes.

Chapter 5

Breakfast and Lunch Dishes

HAS IT BEEN TOO LONG SINCE YOU AWAKENED TO THE PERFUME OF FRESHLY BREWED coffee accented by the crackle of bacon sizzling in a coal-black cast-iron skillet? Many of us seem to have forgotten that breakfast can be the best meal of the day. But nothing will make your family feel as warm and cozy on a lazy Sunday morning as the feast of Southern-style dishes that are gathered on the pages that follow.

There was a time when the morning meal was considered the most important of the day, designed to sustain our forefathers through long hours of hard labor in the hot sun. In many ways, breakfast almost seems synonymous with Southern living, a tradition that remains virtually unchanged. African-Americans, like Southerners, take the morning meal seriously. Quite seriously.

In Los Angeles, for example, a landmark breakfast-only restaurant, named Ray's Kitchen, was known for the long lines outside its doors. Roscoe's Chicken and Waffles, another hot Los Angeles spot, like Wells' in New York City, pleased diners exceedingly by serving early morning meals to folks on their way home after a long night of partying.

And don't even expect to get homemade biscuits after ten A.M. at the Beautiful Restaurant of the Perfect Church in Atlanta. By then, the table has been cleared and the dishes that served beaten biscuits, fried catfish, and scrambled eggs have been put away.

A very hearty affair, breakfast Southern-style includes: freshly baked rolls or biscuits with their pillowy centers; a mix of rustic meats, including fried fish, homemade sausage links, thick slices of country smoked bacon, fried or stewed chicken; crispy home-style potatoes fried with onions and colorful bell peppers, plus a wholesome array of grains and cereals.

While many of us think instantly of freshly brewed coffee as the quintessential breakfast aroma, there are others who are haunted by recollections of sausage made fragrant with just a hint of sage and red pepper; slow-cured country ham and jams or jellies put up as a way to preserve summer's bounty during the harsh months of winter.

• And who can forget Granny's pancakes and waffles baking on a griddle. Granny was a superb cook and her griddlecake repast, glistening with melted butter and Alaga or maple syrup, was no exception.

The poultry, meat, and seafood dishes take their cue from this era and will appeal to those with heartier appetites. The Country Sausage and Milk Gravy Over Cheese Biscuits is a truly satisfying entree for casual gatherings. Low Country Breakfast Shrimp served with Creamy Grits is wonderful for more dressy occasions. Round out your breakfast menu with plenty of cool, refreshing fruit to add natural sweetness and plan to offer an assortment of fresh juices and brewed teas. Few gifts will be as heart-warming and appreciated.

For those times when the occasion seems almost more important than the food, like when you're sharing a meal with family members who have come into town for a weekend visit, or you want slow down the hectic pace by sharing summer's bounty with a meal with the neighbors, plan to serve the meal around midday and call it brunch. A spontaneous gathering can be a wonderful opportunity to show off your family's favorite recipes.

To accommodate your hectic schedule, you may be tempted to take shortcuts with packaged and take-out foods. Don't be. When it comes to the morning meal, it should at least taste good. That doesn't mean your brunch menu has to be a complex one, although it can be, depending upon your time and inclination. But you do want to make sure the foods you serve are substantial enough to make everyone feel satisfied.

If you haven't been fond of grits, it is time to reacquaint yourself with them. The quick-cooking, processed variety you find packaged in individual envelopes simply pales when compared to the stone-ground variety that is so prevalent in the South. Most African-American cooks agree that grits benefit from slow, gentle cooking and a heaping splash of cream. The treatment they are given here will be pure, down-home satisfaction for your taste buds and will add a whole new dimension to your entertaining menu.

Perhaps the best part of this breakfast collection is that the recipes are both simple and delicious, not daunting, so you won't be exhausted by mealtime. You have nothing to lose. So what are you waiting for? Dust off the fine china and bring out the embroidered napkins and the linen tablecloth.

Or just pull up a chair.

COUNTRY HAM CROQUETTES AND EGG SAUCE

MAKES 6 SERVINGS

A garnish of fresh sage sprigs and a sprinkle of minced egg yolks are simple touches that enhance the appearance of this old-style breakfast that is steeped in Southern tradition.

1 cup (2 sticks) butter
$^3/_4$ cup all-purpose flour
$2^1/_2$ cups milk
$1^1/_2$ cups light cream
1 teaspoon salt
$^1/_2$ teaspoon freshly ground
    white pepper
$^1/_4$ cup finely diced onion
$^1/_4$ cup finely diced celery
$2^1/_2$ cups Smithfield ham,
    cooked and finely ground
$^1/_2$ teaspoon Worcestershire sauce
$^1/_2$ teaspoon dry mustard
4 eggs, lightly beaten
3 cups dried bread crumbs
Peanut oil
$^1/_2$ teaspoon fresh sage
6 hard-boiled eggs, peeled and
    chopped

In a saucepan, heat $^3/_4$ cup of the butter, then stir in the flour and make a roux. Gradually stir in the milk and 1 cup of the cream and season with salt and white pepper. Bring to a boil, cook and stir 3 to 4 minutes.

In a saute pan, heat the remaining $^1/_4$ cup butter. Add the onion and celery and sauté 3 to 4 minutes. Remove from the heat.

In a large bowl, combine the ground ham, Worcestershire sauce, mustard, and the celery and onion mixture and mix well. Add $1^1/_2$ cups of the white sauce mixed with two of the beaten eggs. Set the remaining white sauce aside over a hot water bath. Mix the ham mixture and the sauce and refrigerate until thoroughly chilled, about 2 hours.

Using a $^1/_4$-cup measure, form the chilled mixture into croquettes, dip in the remaining beaten eggs, and then in the bread crumbs, coating well. Heat the peanut oil in a heavy saucepan to 350°F. Place the croquettes in a frying basket and deep-fry until golden brown. Drain on paper towels.

Add the sage and chopped eggs to the reserved white sauce. Stir in the remaining $^1/_2$ cup of light cream to the desired consistency. Correct the seasoning and serve over the hot croquettes.

Country Sausage and Milk Gravy Over Cheese Biscuits

For a taste of Southern hospitality you can't beat the savory goodness of this dish.

$^3/_4$ pound Country Sausage
  (see page 204)
$^1/_3$ cup all-purpose flour
3 cups milk
$^1/_2$ teaspoon salt
$^1/_4$ teaspoon freshly ground pepper
12 Cheddar Cheese Biscuits
  (see page 230)

Brown the sausage in a skillet, cook through, and drain, reserving $^1/_3$ cup of the drippings. Return the skillet to the heat, heat the drippings, and add the flour. Stir until blond. Gradually add the milk and bring to a boil, stirring continuously until thickened. Reduce heat to simmer and season with salt and pepper. Add the crumbled sausage, stir, and serve hot over freshly baked Cheese Biscuits.

CREAMED CHICKEN AND OYSTER SHORTCAKE

MAKES 8 SERVINGS

This recipe is one of the ways my Uncle Dick used leftover chicken to make a wonderful, filling lunch.

1$^1/_2$ cups Chicken Stock
  (see page 279)
1$^1/_2$ cups milk
$^3/_4$ cup (1$^1/_2$ sticks) butter
Four 6-ounce boneless, skinless
  chicken thighs, cut into strips
$^1/_4$ cup all-purpose flour
2 pints Eastern oysters, shucked,
  with their liquor
1$^1/_2$ cups heavy cream
$^1/_2$ teaspoon salt
$^1/_8$ teaspoon white pepper
$^1/_8$ teaspoon cayenne pepper
One 9-inch pan Country
  Corn Bread, cut into three
  $^1/_4$-inch squares (see page 228)
8 sprigs fresh chervil

In two small saucepans, heat the chicken stock and milk.

In a sauté pan, heat $^1/_4$ cup of the butter and sauté chicken strips for 3 to 4 minutes. Add the flour and stir to make a roux. Do not brown. Add the hot chicken stock to the roux, then add the milk, whisking to make a smooth sauce. Bring to a boil, then reduce the heat and simmer until thick, about 10 minutes.

Heat the oysters in their own liquor and add $^1/_4$ cup of the butter. Heat the heavy cream separately and reduce by one third. Stir the oysters, liquor, and remaining butter into the chicken, then stir in the heavy cream. Season with the salt, and white and cayenne peppers.

Split the cornbread squares in half. Place the bottom half in the center of a soup plate, cover with some creamed chicken and oysters, and top with the other half of the bread. Add more creamed chicken and oyster mixture and garnish with a sprig of fresh chervil.

CREAMED CHIPPED BEEF ON BUTTERMILK BISCUITS

MAKES 8 SERVINGS

Mom Pan enjoyed creamed chipped beef and she made it often at our home with fresh chipped beef purchased from the Broad Street Farmers Market in Harrisburg, Pa. In some areas dried beef is a little salty. My mother's trick was to rinse it in hot water before cooking. As a child I learned to eat it on toast. Later while living in Sacramento, my family and I grew fond of the way it was prepared at the Stage Coach Restaurant. Al Stevens, the owner, made fresh buttermilk biscuits and poured it over. It is delicious served with the best home-fried potatoes.

$^1/_2$ pound dried chipped beef, thinly sliced

$^3/_8$ cup butter

$^3/_8$ cup all-purpose flour

1 quart half-and-half

Salt to taste

$^1/_4$ teaspoon ground white pepper

16 Southern Buttermilk Biscuits (see page 224)

Tear the dried beef into pieces and place in a colander. Rinse under hot water for 1 to 2 minutes and drain well. Heat the butter in a skillet, add the beef and sauté until the beef is coated well with butter, about 2 to 3 minutes. Add the flour, stirring constantly to make a roux, and cook 2 to 3 minutes. Do not brown. Add the half-and-half while continuing to stir. Reduce the heat and simmer until thickened. Season with salt to taste and pepper. Serve hot over split freshly baked Southern Buttermilk Biscuits.

FRIED PHILADELPHIA SCRAPPLE

I have eaten scrapple all my life. As a child I loved it with butter and maple syrup.
As I grew older, I learned to enjoy it plain, fried with home-fried potatoes and fried eggs.
Either way it tastes great. Scrapple keeps well in the refrigerator for up to 3 days.
It should be kept frozen if you want to store it longer.

1 pound boneless pork shoulder

1$^1/_2$ pounds pig's knuckles

2 quarts water

1 teaspoon salt

1 teaspoon crushed red pepper
flakes

$^1/_2$ teaspoon freshly ground pepper

1 teaspoon summer savory

$^1/_2$ teaspoon dried sage, crumbled

$^1/_4$ teaspoon ground thyme

$^1/_8$ teaspoon ground nutmeg

1$^3/_4$ cups yellow cornmeal

Maple or other syrup

Country Fried Apples
(see page 93)

Trim any excess fat from the pork and discard.

In a stockpot, bring the shoulder, knuckles, water, salt, and red pepper flakes to a boil. Reduce the heat and simmer until the pork is tender and the knuckle meat easily comes away from the bone, about 2 hours. Remove the pork from the broth, strain and skim off the fat. Pour the broth into a pot, reserving 2 cups.

Remove the meat from the knuckles and chop finely along with the pork shoulder. Add the chopped pork, pepper, summer savory, sage, thyme, and nutmeg to the pot and bring to a boil.

Place the cornmeal in a bowl. Gradually add the reserved liquid to the cornmeal, whisking gently. Stir the cornmeal mixture into the pork and broth and cook, stirring constantly, until the mixture is the consistency of mush, about 20 to 30 minutes. Pour the mixture into two lightly greased 9 × 5-inch loaf pans, cover, and refrigerate until set, at least 4 hours or overnight.

Turn out of the pan and slice into $^1/_2$-inch slices. Fry on each side until crusty and brown, about 3 minutes per side. Serve hot with your favorite syrup, and, if you like, with Country Fried Apples and eggs.

GRANNY'S CORNMEAL HOTCAKES WITH FRIED STREAK-OF-LEAN AND STREAK-OF-FAT

You can learn a lot from the old folks, like never compromise on taste. My grandmother never did. She would not eat pancakes unless they were crisp from a bit of cornmeal stirred into the batter. And she would not eat oleo, what her generation called margarine. So when we serve these hotcakes it's always with lots of rich, creamy butter.

9 slices streak-of-lean and
    streak-of-fat, cut in half
1 1/2 cups yellow cornmeal
1/2 cup all-purpose flour
2 teaspoons sugar
1/4 teaspoon baking soda
1/2 teaspoon baking powder
1/2 teaspoon salt
3/4 cup buttermilk
1/2 cup water
4 eggs, beaten
1/4 cup (1/2 stick) butter, melted

In a large skillet, blanch the streak-of-lean in boiling water to cover for 2 minutes to remove some of the salt. Drain and pat dry. Pour out the water, wipe out skillet, and heat over medium heat. Fry the streak-of-lean until crisp and golden brown, 2 to 3 minutes on each side. Drain on paper towels and keep warm.

In a bowl, sift cornmeal, flour, sugar, baking soda, baking powder, and salt. Add the buttermilk and water and stir. Add the eggs and continue to stir. Add the butter and stir thoroughly. Ladle the batter into a hot greased skillet or greased griddle. Cook until brown, about 1 to 2 minutes on each side. Serve hot topped with butter and your favorite syrup and 3 pieces of fried streak-of-lean for each serving.

CHEF'S TIP
Alaga (short for Alabama Georgia), a mixture of cane and corn syrup, or King corn syrup both taste delicious with these hotcakes.

GRANNY'S FRIED SALTED MACKEREL WITH BROWN BUTTER SAUCE

MAKES 4 SERVINGS

I never really thought of salt fish as a part of African-American heritage until I read that Africans came to this country and began to salt meats the way they had salted fish in Africa. In the 1950s my grandmother, Ada B. Lewis, used to fry salt mackerel and serve it with grits, eggs, fresh biscuits, coffee, and fruit. It was a breakfast ritual with her. Now I see the taste for salt fish among her generation and those that followed as an African-American tradition.

4 Cured Salted Mackerel fillets (see page 269) or use packaged
³/₄ cup all-purpose flour
1 teaspoon paprika
¹/₂ teaspoon freshly ground black pepper
¹/₂ cup peanut oil
¹/₄ cup (¹/₂ stick) butter
1 teaspoon fresh lemon juice
1 teaspoon chopped fresh parsley
Salt and pepper to taste
Creamy Grits (see page 95)

Open the package or crock and remove mackerel fillets from the brine. Rinse with cold water and place in a bowl. Cover with cold water and soak for 12 hours. Pour off the water and dry with paper towels.

In a bowl mix the flour, paprika, and pepper. Heat the oil in a skillet. Dust mackerel fillets with the seasoned flour and fry about 3 minutes on each side. Remove the mackerel from the pan and drain on paper towels. Add the butter to the pan and heat until brown. Add the lemon juice and parsley and season with salt and pepper to taste. Place fillets on a plate, nap with the sauce, and serve hot with Creamy Grits, eggs, and hot biscuits.

CHEF'S TIPS

Be sure to soak the mackerel at least 12 hours or it will be very salty. If you want to remove additional salt, soaking a few extra hours wouldn't hurt.

You can purchase cured salt mackerel two fillets to a package in brine.

Low Country Breakfast Shrimp with Creamy Grits

MAKES 4 TO 6 SERVINGS

This is a Charleston specialty that I discovered while traveling in the Low Country of South Carolina. It was prepared by Chef Frank Houston at Funderburk's at Middleborough, in Columbia. He and co-owner Bob Funderburk are two African-American entrepreneurs who really take pride in offering a unique experience and great hospitality in this quaint establishment.

$1/4$ pound streak-of-lean and streak-of-fat, sliced and finely diced

$1/2$ cup all-purpose flour

1 teaspoon salt

$1/2$ teaspoon freshly ground black pepper

1 teaspoon paprika

2 pounds large shrimp, peeled and deveined

$1/2$ cup diced onion

$1/4$ cup diced green pepper

2 cups tomato sauce or Pomi strained tomatoes

$1^1/2$ teaspoons Worcestershire sauce

$1/2$ teaspoon sugar

1 cup water

1 teaspoon Louisiana hot red pepper sauce

2 cups Creamy Grits (see page 95)

$1/2$ tablespoon chopped fresh parsley

Sauté the streak-of-lean in a heated heavy skillet or sauté pan until the fat has rendered. Remove from the pan and set aside.

Combine the flour, salt, pepper, and paprika. Lightly dust the shrimp in the seasoned flour, shaking to remove any excess. Add the shrimp to the rendered fat and cook over medium-high heat for 3 to 4 minutes. Stir in the onion and green pepper and continue to cook and stir 2 to 3 minutes. Add the tomato sauce, streak-of-lean, Worcestershire sauce, and sugar. Pour in the water and hot pepper sauce and continue stirring. Cover the pan, reduce the heat, and simmer 5 to 6 minutes, adding more water, if needed. Serve hot over Creamy Grits, sprinkled with chopped parsley to garnish.

Pan-fried Salmon Cakes
and Creamed Potatoes

MAKES 8 SERVINGS

Throughout our culinary history, canned food, particularly fish, has been an inexpensive ingredient that offered the added benefit of a long shelf life, making it practical for cooks to add lean protein to their diets even when the budget was limited. As a result, this recipe has appeared on the pages of virtually every African-American cookbook, from major publishing houses to smaller church publications. It tastes even better if you have some leftover fresh cooked salmon in the refrigerator.

Two 10-ounce cans pink
   salmon, drained
2 tablespoons butter
$2/_3$ cup minced onion
$1/_2$ cup minced green pepper
2 egg yolks
2 teaspoons Pommery mustard
1 cup mayonnaise
1 teaspoon fresh lemon juice
1 teaspoon Worcestershire sauce
1 tablespoon chopped fresh
   dill weed
1 teaspoon celery salt
$1/_2$ teaspoon salt
$1/_2$ teaspoon freshly ground
   black pepper
$1/_8$ teaspoon cayenne pepper
1 cup club cracker crumbs
$1/_2$ cup all-purpose flour
$1/_2$ cup clarified butter
Creamed Potatoes (see page 95)

Drain the salmon in a colander and remove the bones and any skin. Using a fork, flake the salmon and set aside.

In a small sauté pan or skillet, heat the butter and sauté the onion and green pepper for 2 to 3 minutes. Place them in a bowl with the egg yolks and beat with a wire whisk. Whisk in the mustard, mayonnaise, lemon juice, Worcestershire sauce, dill, celery salt, salt, black and cayenne peppers, and cracker crumbs and mix well. Add the salmon and continue to stir until mixed well. Form into $2^{1}/_2$-inch patties, using a $1/_4$-cup measure. Dust the cakes with flour.

Heat the clarified butter in a skillet and fry the cakes until golden brown, about 4 to 5 minutes on each side. Serve hot with the creamed potatoes.

PECAN WAFFLES WITH COUNTRY SAUSAGE

MAKES 6 SERVINGS

People who already love the crispy-crunch of fresh, hot waffles fresh will find it hard to resist these with cornmeal and pecans stirred into the mix.

2¹/₂ cups all-purpose flour
¹/₂ cup yellow cornmeal
3 teaspoons baking powder
3 tablespoons sugar
1 teaspoon salt
3 eggs, separated
1¹/₄ cups milk
¹/₄ cup butter, melted
¹/₄ cup finely chopped pecans
2¹/₄ pounds Country Sausage, cooked, in twelve 3-ounce patties (see page 204)
Syrup

In a large bowl, sift together the flour, cornmeal, baking powder, sugar, and salt.

In another bowl, beat together the egg yolks and milk. Blend in the butter. Pour the liquid ingredients over the dry ingredients and stir well. Beat the egg whites to stiff peaks and gently fold into the batter. Add the pecans and stir again. Cook on a preheated greased waffle iron until golden brown. Serve with warm Country Sausage patties and your favorite syrup.

POACHED EGGS AND HAM ON BUTTERMILK BISCUITS WITH OYSTER SAUCE

MAKES 8 SERVINGS

*I developed this recipe for brunch and breakfast menus while operating
Rent-A-Chef Catering Service in northern California.*

16 slices Smithfield Virginia
　　ham, cut in half, then into
　　3-inch squares
$^1/_2$ teaspoon salt
1 tablespoon cider vinegar
16 eggs
8 Southern Buttermilk Biscuits
　　(see page 224)
2 cups Oyster Sauce
　　(see page 288)
1 tablespoon chopped fresh chives

In a skillet, fry the ham over low heat 3 to 4 minutes on each side. Drain and set aside. Keep warm.

In a saucepan, bring a quart of water to a boil, add the salt and vinegar, then reduce the heat to a simmer. Break the eggs one at a time into a small bowl, then slide each egg into the simmering water. Simmer until the whites are set and the yolks are still spongy, about 3 to 5 minutes. Remove the eggs from the water with a slotted spoon, drain well on paper towels, and trim the edges.

Place a hot split buttermilk biscuit on a warm plate. Arrange a piece of country ham on each biscuit half. Place a poached egg on top of each and nap with Oyster Sauce. Garnish with chopped chives. Serve immediately.

Sautéed Chicken Livers Smothered in Mushroom Gravy

Granny used to think of the midday meal as dinner so she made it heavy enough to sustain the family through an afternoon of chores. She planned a lighter meal for supper, maybe a soup and some cornbread. For a stick-to-your ribs lunch, serve this with hot buttered cornbread and collard greens.

2 pounds chicken livers
1 1/2 cups all-purpose flour
1 teaspoon salt
1 teaspoon ground white pepper
1/2 teaspoon cayenne pepper
1/2 cup (1 stick) butter
1 bunch green onions, including green tops, thinly sliced
3/4 pound button mushrooms, sliced
2 cups water
Steamed Buttered Rice (see page 114)

Wash the chicken livers, drain on paper towels, and pat dry. Cut any large livers in half. Season the flour with 1/2 teaspoon salt, 1/2 teaspoon white pepper, and 1/4 teaspoon cayenne pepper. Dredge the livers in the seasoned flour, shaking off any excess.

In a large skillet, heat the butter and sauté the onions and mushrooms until lightly brown. Remove from the skillet and set aside. In the same pan, sauté the chicken livers in batches until brown. Remove from the skillet and set aside. Add 1/4 cup of the flour to the skillet and stir to make a roux. Cook until brown, about 4 minutes. Add the water, stirring constantly to make a smooth gravy. Add the remaining 1/2 teaspoon salt, 1/2 teaspoon white pepper, and 1/4 teaspoon cayenne pepper. Return the onions and mushrooms to the pan, stir, and add the chicken livers. Simmer until the chicken livers are tender, about 10 to 15 minutes, adding more water if needed. Serve hot over Steamed Buttered Rice.

Scrambled Eggs and Pork Brains with Creamy Grits

MAKES 4 SERVINGS

Mom Pan was fond of scrambled eggs and brains. She would go to the Broad Street Farmer's Market on Saturday morning and get them as fresh as possible. She served them with grits and hot biscuits.

2 tablespoons butter

1 pound pork brains (available fresh at meat markets)

4 eggs, beaten

$1/_2$ teaspoon salt

$1/_2$ teaspoon freshly ground black pepper

2 cups Creamy Grits (see page 95)

Southern Buttermilk Biscuits (see page 224)

Melt 1 tablespoon of the butter in a skillet over medium heat. Add the brains and fry until brown, stirring occasionally. Add the remaining 1 tablespoon butter and melt. Beat eggs with salt and pepper and add to the brains. Cook the eggs until they become firm around the edges, then stir, bringing the cooked edges to the center of the pan. Continue to quickly cook and stir until the eggs are cooked. Serve immediately with Creamy Grits and hot buttermilk biscuits.

SIMMERED BEEF TONGUE
WITH RAISIN SAUCE

Tongue has been revered throughout the ages, prized by French and Italian gastronomes for its rich flavor and wholesome goodness. It has been served pickled, spiced—even spit-roasted in some cultures. On menus reflecting the new bistro style of cooking you could expect to find cooked tongue dressed with mayonnaise and served in a salad like chicken or ham, tossed with a vinaigrette with baby greens, or as it appears here, in a fanciful sauce that makes it charming fare for a luncheon or Sunday brunch.

One 2^1/$_2$- to 3-pound beef
   tongue
2^1/$_2$ quarts boiling water
1 sprig parsley
2 whole cloves
1 teaspoon salt
1 bay leaf

RAISIN SAUCE
3 cups Smoked Ham Stock
   (see page 281)
^{1}/$_4$ cup seedless black raisins
^{1}/$_4$ cup sugar
^{1}/$_8$ teaspoon ground nutmeg
2 tablespoons cornstarch
1 tablespoon water
Salt to taste

Rinse the tongue and set aside.

In a large stockpot, bring the water to a boil, add the tongue, parsley, cloves, salt, and bay leaf. Return to a boil, then reduce the heat and simmer until the meat is tender when pierced with a fork, about 1^1/$_2$ hours. Shock in an ice water bath to cool. Peel tongue and store in the hot broth until ready to serve.

For the Raisin Sauce, place the Smoked Ham Stock, raisins, sugar, and nutmeg in a large saucepan and bring to a boil. Reduce the heat and simmer 15 to 20 minutes. Mix the cornstarch with the water and stir into the sauce. Cook over medium heat until thickened. Season to taste with salt, stir, and continue to cook 5 minutes. Cut the tongue into ^{1}/$_4$-inch slices across the grain, then cut on a bias to make slices broader. Serve hot on a plate napped with the raisin sauce.

Sweet Potato Waffles

MAKES 6 SERVINGS

These waffles are a perfect side dish, suitable for serving with almost any meat. For a refreshing change of pace, enjoy them at breakfast with fresh sausage. There is no better way to take the chill off a cold Sunday morning in winter.

1 cup mashed baked sweet
    potatoes
3 eggs, separated
$1/4$ cup packed brown sugar
1 teaspoon vanilla
$1/4$ teaspoon ground nutmeg
$1/2$ cup (1 stick) butter, melted
$1^1/_2$ cups milk
2 cups all-purpose flour
1 tablespoon baking powder
$1/2$ teaspoon salt
$1/4$ cup granulated sugar

Puree the sweet potatoes in a food processor, then combine in a mixing bowl with the egg yolks, brown sugar, vanilla, and nutmeg. Stir, then slowly pour in the melted butter, alternating with the milk and continuing to stir.

Sift together the flour, baking powder, and salt. Add to the mix to make a thick batter.

In a separate bowl, beat the egg whites until they form soft peaks. Beat in the sugar, continuing to beat until stiff peaks are formed. Fold the egg whites into the sweet potato mixture, but do not overmix.

Pour enough batter to almost cover the surface of a preheated greased waffle iron with a thin layer. Close the iron and bake according to the manufacturer's instructions or until iron is no longer steaming.

Chapter 6

··········

Fish
and
Shellfish

REMEMBER WHEN WE DIDN'T HAVE TO PAY FOR THE FISH AND SHELLFISH ON OUR DINING tables? When we depended upon the ocean, gulfs, bays, inlets, lakes, streams, marshes, ponds, and rivers for our endless supply?

Never mind the source, African-American cooks again demonstrated their culinary prowess: They reached for their trusty coal-black skillet and then pan-fried the catch, even when it was merely a bottom-feeding garbage fish like crappie and catfish.

That is, happily, no longer so.

African-American fish cookery does have its roots in ruralism, but it is not limited to the poor country cooking of the South nor does it depend solely upon the generosity and good fortune of fisherman.

Instead, the influences on today's seafood dishes are mostly regional, the kind of nuances that evolve when Aunt Bessie from Oklahoma quibbles with Aunt Louise from Pennsylvania about whether fried catfish should be dipped in batter or breaded in bread crumbs.

It is almost funny to think of all the ways African-American fish dishes have been embellished over the years into what we consider traditions today. The influence was simple: Folks in various regions of the country each devised their preferred cooking technique—whether the fish is baked, broiled, grilled, fried, poached, or steamed and sauced—depending upon what was available in the fisherman's bucket.

The variety and combinations seemed almost endless: In the coastal regions, there was nothing quite like heralding spring with pan-fried tender, juicy young blue crabs caught just as they shed their skin. In the South, shellfish was plentiful and fried catfish with hushpuppies was about as true a Southern experience as one could ever have.

Yankees up North pulled porgies and all sorts of flounder out of their lakes and streams. African-Americans who are descendants of Caribbean Islanders, where tropical warm breezes, island vegetation, exotic fruits, and sweet sea creatures provide the colorful backdrop, spice their seafood chowders and specialties with a powerful, pepper punch.

In Louisiana, there are the French-style dishes created by Creoles, such as poisson en papillote (fish cooked in parchment paper), étouffée, and the myriad uses for oysters. Crispy po'boys (Louisiana's hero sandwich) and barbecued shrimp are a quintessential N'Awlins experience.

Black Cubans and Spanish contribute a funky salsa beat with their fondness for crab, lobster, snapper, shrimp, and salt fish. Atlantic dwellers, from the shores of the Chesapeake to the swampy marshes of the Carolina Low Country, inject an affinity for sea scallops, flounder, crabs, oysters, shrimp, and whiting. A real low-country seafood boil, the kind where you gather dozens of your friends and neighbors and enjoy each other's company—that is one of the real splendors of life.

With such a kaleidoscope and more for inspiration, it's no wonder chefs in the 1990s have invented such distinctive fish and shellfish dishes, some of them not just pleasing to the palate, but purely elegant in their presentation as well. Some of them will seem familiar because they don't require any unusual or hard to find ingredients and they jump off where their plain home-style cousins left off.

BAKED FLOUNDER FILLETS
STUFFED WITH CRAB

In the early 1970s, I was executive chef at the Cloister Restaurant in Buffalo, New York. I developed this recipe, which immediately became a favorite of the owners, James and Angel Di Lapo.

$^{1}/_{2}$ cup clarified butter

1 small onion, diced

$^{1}/_{2}$ green pepper, diced

$^{1}/_{2}$ red pepper, diced

$^{1}/_{2}$ cup dry white wine, plus a
little more to finish the dish

2 egg yolks

$^{1}/_{2}$ teaspoon Coleman's dry
mustard

$^{1}/_{2}$ cup mayonnaise

2 teaspoons fresh lemon juice

1 teaspoon celery salt

$^{1}/_{4}$ teaspoon ground white pepper

$^{1}/_{8}$ teaspoon cayenne pepper

$^{1}/_{2}$ cup dry bread crumbs

1 tablespoon chopped fresh parsley

1 pound fresh lump crabmeat,
picked over for cartilage and
bits of shell

Sixteen 3-ounce flounder fillets

1 teaspoon paprika

Preheat the oven to 400°F.

In a sauté pan or skillet, heat 3 tablespoons of the clarified butter and cook the onion, green and red peppers 2 to 3 minutes. Add the wine and simmer until most of the wine has evaporated. Remove from the heat and stir in the egg yolks, mustard, mayonnaise, lemon juice, celery salt, white and cayenne peppers, bread crumbs, and parsley. Mix well. Carefully fold the crabmeat into the mixture.

Place 8 fish fillets in a buttered baking pan. Place about $^{1}/_{4}$ cup of crab dressing in the center of each fillet. Cut the remaining 8 fillets in half lengthwise. Arrange a fillet half on both sides of the dressing so that some of the filling is exposed in the center. Press along the edges to seal the filling to the bottom fillets. Spoon on the remaining clarified butter and sprinkle with paprika.

Bake until the flounder is flaky and brown on top, about 15 to 20 minutes. Sprinkle with about 1 tablespoon of white wine during the last 2 minutes of cooking time.

BAKED TROUT WITH OYSTER STUFFING AND PECAN-LEMON BUTTER SAUCE

This is a purely elegant treatment for trout. It also works well with chicken.

$^1/_4$ cup ($^1/_2$ stick) butter

2 green onions, minced

2 ribs celery, minced

1 tablespoon chopped fresh parsley

2 teaspoons minced fresh dill weed

1 pint Eastern oysters, shucked, drained, and coarsely chopped, with liquor reserved

$^1/_2$ tablespoon fresh lemon juice

$^1/_2$ cup half-and-half

1 teaspoon salt

$^1/_2$ teaspoon cayenne pepper

$^1/_2$ teaspoon freshly ground black pepper

4 cups stale bread cubes, crust removed

Eight 8-ounce boneless rainbow trout

2 tablespoons clarified butter

2 teaspoons paprika

Pecan-Lemon Butter Sauce (recipe follows)

Preheat the oven to 400°F.

In a sauté pan, heat the butter and cook the green onions and celery 2 to 3 minutes. Stir in the parsley, dill, oysters, and lemon juice and simmer 1 to 2 minutes. Stir in the half-and-half and season with salt and cayenne and black peppers. Add the bread cubes, stir, and remove from the heat.

Divide the stuffing evenly among the fish, packing it loosely in the fish. Fold the fish to cover the stuffing and place the trout on a buttered baking pan. Brush each trout with the clarified butter. Bake until skin is brown and crisp, about 15 to 20 minutes. Sprinkle with paprika during the last 5 minutes of cooking. Nap with Pecan-Lemon Butter Sauce before serving.

Pecan-Lemon Butter Sauce

MAKES 2 3/4 CUPS

1/2 cup (1 stick) butter
1 cup pecan halves
1 cup chardonnay
2 tablespoons fresh lemon juice
1 tablespoon chopped fresh dill weed

In a sauté pan, heat 1/4 cup of the butter and cook the pecans until lightly toasted, about 3 to 4 minutes. Remove the nuts from the pan. Add the chardonnay and lemon juice and cook over high heat until reduced by one third. Whisk in the remaining 1/4 cup butter, bit by bit, until sauce is silky. Return the pecans to the pan and add the dill.

Deep-fried Lake Trout

MAKES 6 SERVINGS

It may surprise you to find that the sweet, delicate lake trout for which Baltimore is famous, is really whiting from the sea. You'll love it by any name.

6 fresh, boneless lake trout, heads removed and cleaned, or 6 whiting
1 teaspoon salt
1/2 teaspoon freshly ground black pepper
1 teaspoon fresh lemon juice
1 cup milk
1 egg, beaten
3 cups peanut oil
1 cup all-purpose flour

Season the fish lightly with salt and pepper. Drizzle with lemon juice.

Combine the milk and beaten egg. Heat the peanut oil to medium-high heat in a large cast-iron skillet or frying pan. Dredge the fish in flour, then fry until golden brown, about 4 to 5 minutes. Turn and cook the other side. Drain on paper towels and serve immediately.

GRILLED SALMON FILLETS WITH CILANTRO VINAIGRETTE

MAKES 6 SERVINGS

While living in Washington State I used to spend time with some friends who were members of the Qaunalt Indian tribe. They lived on a private island, bordered by the Pacific Ocean. They were allowed to fish for salmon using gill nets. We created wonderful recipes to use up the unlimited supply.

This dish, created while I was on the faculty of the School of Hotel and Restaurant Management at California State Polytechnic University, Pomona, was inspired by that memory. In opening the Restaurant at Kellogg Ranch, a student-operated restaurant, I added this dish to the menu as an example of Asian influence on California cuisine.

Six 6-ounce salmon fillets

MARINADE
3 tablespoons sesame oil
1 cup vegetable oil
$^1/_2$ teaspoon salt
$^1/_8$ teaspoon freshly ground
  black pepper
1 teaspoon coriander seed, cracked
2 teaspoons minced fresh
  gingerroot
1 teaspoon grated lime zest
$^1/_3$ cup white wine

2 tablespoons peanut oil
3 large shallots, thinly sliced
1 cup Cilantro Vinaigrette
  (see page 80)
6 sprigs fresh cilantro

In a mixing bowl, combine the sesame and vegetable oils, salt, pepper, coriander seed, ginger, lime zest, and wine. Mix well, then cover the salmon fillets with the marinade and refrigerate for 1 hour. Remove the fish and drain the excess marinade. Grill the fish over hot coals to medium doneness.

In a sauté pan, heat the peanut oil, add the sliced shallots, and sauté 2 minutes then set aside until ready to serve. Do not brown the shallots.

To serve, place the salmon on a warm plate, nap Cilantro Vinaigrette over it and sprinkle with sautéed shallots. Place a sprig of fresh cilantro on top. Serve with Fried Cornmeal Mush (page 98) and Country Succotash (page 94), if desired.

Darryl Evans's Smoked, Grilled Salmon Fillets on Couscous with Balsamic Vinaigrette and Caramelized Vidalia Onions

MAKES 4 SERVINGS

Most people know that couscous is indigenous to Africa and they assume that means North Africa. What they don't know is that it has been enjoyed all over the continent as well, not just Morocco and Tunisia. Middle Eastern cookery has made couscous popular among American diners but it is welcome on African-American dinner tables, too.

6 cups cold water

2 tablespoons kosher salt

4 center-cut salmon fillets, about $2^{1}/_{4}$ pounds

2 Vidalia onions, cut into julienne

1 cup chardonnay

$^{1}/_{4}$ cup seasoned rice vinegar

2 tablespoons honey

Balsamic Vinaigrette (see page 79)

TO FINISH THE DISH

2 cups Chicken Stock (see page 279)

1 cup couscous

2 teaspoons finely minced chives

1 tomato, peeled and chopped

$^{1}/_{4}$ cup aromatic hardwood chips, soaked

4 sprigs cilantro

2 teaspoons freshly cracked black peppercorns

Make a brine with the water and salt and place the salmon in it for 30 minutes. Remove the fish from the brine and pat dry. Place in the refrigerator to dry for 30 minutes.

Sweat the onions until golden brown or until caramelization begins. Deglaze the pan over medium-high heat with the wine, then add the vinegar and honey and simmer 2 minutes. Set aside.

To finish the dish, bring the chicken stock to a boil. Place the couscous in a small bowl and pour the stock over it. Cover with plastic wrap and let steam for 10 minutes. Pour 2 tablespoons of the vinaigrette over the couscous and mix until the grains start to stick together. Add a few chopped chives and some of the chopped tomato and stir.

Heat a grill and place the soaked wood chips on the coals. Spray the grill rack with nonstick spray. When the wood starts to smoke, add the salmon and grill 3 minutes on each side for medium doneness. Place couscous in the center of a serving plate, then place a piece of grilled salmon on top and spoon caramelized onions on top. Garnish with a cilantro sprig, remaining chopped tomatoes, chopped chives, and fresh cracked black peppercorns.

MARYLAND CRAB CAKES

MAKES 8 SERVINGS

*I learned to make crab cakes while training under Chef Robert W. Lee at the
Harrisburger Hotel in the mid-1960s. I created this version for the Baltimore fish
market, which sold 500 pounds of the delicacy a week.*

1/4 cup (1/2 stick) butter

1 small onion, minced

4 egg yolks

2 teaspoons Coleman's dry
  mustard

8 slices white bread, crusts
  trimmed, flattened, and
  finely diced

1/4 teaspoon cayenne pepper

2 teaspoons Old Bay seasoning

1/2 cup mayonnaise

2 tablespoons chopped fresh
  parsley

3 dashes Tabasco sauce

2 teaspoons Worcestershire sauce

1 teaspoon fresh lemon juice

1 teaspoon salt

1/2 teaspoon white pepper

3 pounds jumbo lump crabmeat,
  picked over for cartilage and
  bits of shell

Peanut oil

2 eggs, beaten

1 cup milk

1 cup all-purpose flour

1 cup fresh bread crumbs

8 lemon wedges

2 cups Tartar Sauce
  (see page 290)

Heat the butter in a small sauté pan and cook the onion until transparent. Set aside.

In a large bowl, combine the onion, egg yolks, and mustard. Stir in the bread, cayenne, Old Bay seasoning, mayonnaise, parsley, Tabasco sauce, Worcestershire sauce, lemon juice, salt, and pepper. Gently fold in the crabmeat, being careful not to break up the lumps.

Form into sixteen cakes (using about 1/3 cup for each cake). Heat the oil in a deep-fryer to 350°F.

In a small bowl, combine the beaten eggs and milk. Dip the crab cakes in flour and then using a slotted spoon dip in the egg wash. Sprinkle with fresh bread crumbs, coating well. Deep-fry until golden brown, about 5 minutes. Serve with lemon wedges and tartar sauce.

CHEF'S TIP

For a lighter dish, dust the crab cakes with flour and sauté in peanut oil or butter over medium-high heat for 3 to 4 minutes on each side. You can also bake unbreaded crab cakes without the flour. Sprinkle lightly with melted butter and paprika and bake in a preheated 350°F oven until brown on top, about 6 to 8 minutes.

MARYLAND FRIED OYSTERS

MAKES 6 SERVINGS

Fresh oysters are delicious cooked in this fashion and served just as they are. For a Creole touch, serve them in a hollowed-out toasted submarine sandwich roll with shredded lettuce and tartar sauce. Pass plenty of hot sauce on the side.

36 large Eastern oysters, shucked and drained
2 eggs, beaten
$1/4$ cup water
2 cups yellow cornmeal
1 tablespoon Old Bay seasoning
1 teaspoon salt
1 teaspoon freshly ground black pepper
Peanut oil
6 lemon wedges

Drain the oysters in a colander and pat dry with paper towels. Beat the eggs and water together.

In a bowl, combine the cornmeal, Old Bay seasoning, salt, and pepper. Dip the oysters one at a time in the egg wash, then in the seasoned cornmeal. Dip in the egg wash and dust with cornmeal again, then refrigerate at least 30 minutes.

Heat the oil in a deep-fryer to 350°F. Fry the oysters until they are golden brown. Serve with lemon wedges and your favorite sauce—cocktail or tartar.

New Orleans Shrimp Creole

Unlike many classic Creole dishes, this dish doesn't set a fire on the palate, making it ideal to serve to children. I often serve this to my kids for breakfast with grits and fried catfish. They love it.

1/4 cup (1/2 stick) butter

2 pounds large shrimp, peeled and deveined

1 medium onion, cut into 1-inch dice

3 cloves garlic, minced

1 medium green pepper, cut into 1-inch dice

1/4 cup all-purpose flour

2 cups canned Italian plum tomatoes, mashed

1/2 cup chardonnay

1 1/2 cups water

1 tablespoon chopped fresh thyme

1 bay leaf

1/2 teaspoon sugar

1 teaspoon salt

1/2 teaspoon freshly ground black pepper

1/2 teaspoon cayenne pepper

1 tablespoon chopped fresh parsley

2 cups Steamed Buttered Rice (see page 114)

In a large skillet, heat 2 tablespoons of the butter and cook the shrimp until they turn pink, about 3 to 4 minutes. Remove from the pan and set aside.

Wipe the pan dry and heat the remaining 2 tablespoons butter in it. Cook the onion and garlic 2 to 3 minutes. Add the green pepper and continue to cook 1 minute. Stir in the flour to make a roux and cook 2 to 3 minutes. Do not brown. Stir in the tomatoes, then stir in the wine and cook 2 to 3 minutes. Stir in the water, thyme, bay leaf, sugar, salt, and black and cayenne peppers. Bring to a boil, then reduce the heat and simmer for 20 minutes, stirring occasionally.

Return the shrimp to the sauce, stir, and simmer 3 to 4 minutes. Stir in the parsley and serve hot over Steamed Buttered Rice.

OYSTERS EN BROCHETTE

MAKES 6 SERVINGS

In some parts of the country, oysters are such a common, everyday ingredient, it's easy to forget that they can be the centerpiece when a more dramatic presentation is in order. For a light luncheon, grilled oysters crown a bed of fluffy Rice Pilaf.

48 medium Eastern oysters,
  shucked and drained
1 teaspoon salt
1 teaspoon freshly ground pepper
8 slices country bacon, cut into
  6 pieces each
1/4 cup (1/2 stick) butter, melted
1 tablespoon fresh lemon juice
2 tablespoons chopped fresh
  parsley
4 dashes Tabasco sauce
3 cups Rice Pilaf (see page 114)

Season the oysters with salt and pepper. Arrange the oysters on 6 skewers, alternating with the bacon pieces. Brush the skewers with half the melted butter. Grill over hot coals or broil under a preheated broiler until the bacon browns and the oysters curl at the edges. Add the lemon juice, chopped parsley, and Tabasco sauce to the remaining butter. Brush over skewers and serve at once on a bed of Rice Pilaf.

PAN-FRIED PORGIES

MAKES 8 SERVINGS

For those of us who grew up in the city, the closest we could expect to come to a fishing hole was the local fish market. In Harrisburg, Pennsylvania, that was located in the Broad Street Market and a kind-hearted woman named Miss Millie cooked shrimp, oysters, and all kinds of fish including porgies, which we took to go. Unfortunately for the rest of the family, by the time the kids got home there was no more fish for supper. With this recipe, you can make sure there's always some left over.

8 medium porgies
2 tablespoons fresh lemon juice
1^1/$_2$ cups all-purpose flour
1 teaspoon salt
1 teaspoon freshly ground
  black pepper
^{1}/$_8$ teaspoon cayenne pepper
^{1}/$_2$ teaspoon garlic powder
1 teaspoon paprika
1 cup peanut oil

Ask your fish man to clean, split, and remove the backbone from the porgies. Rinse them thoroughly, then sprinkle with lemon juice.

In a bowl combine the flour, salt, black and cayenne peppers, garlic powder, and paprika. Heat the oil in a large skillet over medium-high heat. Dredge the fish in the seasoned flour, shaking off any excess and fry in the hot oil until crisp and brown, about 3 to 4 minutes on each side. Drain on paper towels and serve hot with Savannah Red Rice (page 116) and Creamy Coleslaw (page 59).

Pan-roasted Whitefish with Pecan Crust

MAKES 8 SERVINGS

African-Americans who live near the Great Lakes appease their appetite for fish with Lake Superior whitefish, known as walleye, because it cooks up so tender and flaky, but you can use any firm-fleshed whitefish in this dish.

4 large whitefish fillets, cut in half on a diagonal
1 tablespoon fresh lemon juice
1 egg, beaten
1 tablespoon water
$1/4$ cup all-purpose flour
$1/2$ teaspoon salt
$1/2$ teaspoon freshly ground black pepper
$1/2$ cup pecans, finely chopped
$1/2$ tablespoon chopped fresh parsley
$1/4$ cup clarified butter
8 Black Bean Cakes (see page 112)
2 cups Roasted Red Pepper Sauce (see page 290)

Preheat the oven to 350°F.

Wash the fish and pat dry. Sprinkle with lemon juice and set aside.

In a small bowl, beat together the egg and water. In a separate bowl, combine the flour, salt, pepper, pecans, and parsley. Coat the belly side of the fillet with the egg wash, then dredge in the pecan mixture, covering one side only. Place on a baking sheet lined with greased parchment paper.

Heat the butter in a nonstick skillet over medium-high heat and sauté the fillets crust side down, until brown, about 3 to 4 minutes. Remove from the pan, pour out the fat and return them to the skillet, skin side down, sautéing 1 to 2 minutes. Finish cooking in the oven until the fillets are firm, about 10 minutes.

To serve, arrange a fish fillet on top of each black bean cake and nap with Roasted Red Pepper Sauce.

Timothy Dean's Poached Lobster with Black-eyed Peas and Sweet Yellow Corn

Timothy's mother's black-eyed peas were exquisite; lobster is majestic.
For Timothy, this dish combines the "elite of the elite."

Two 2-pound Maine lobsters
1 sprig fresh rosemary
3 cups red wine
$1/2$ tablespoon butter
$1/2$ tablespoon all-purpose flour
1 pound fresh black-eyed peas, cooked (see page 112 for procedure)
4 cups fresh corn kernels, cooked
Chopped chives
$1/8$ teaspoon freshly cracked pepper

Place the lobsters in a stockpot with boiling water and rosemary and cook until shell is bright red, about 6 to 8 minutes. Remove from the pot and shock in ice water to stop the cooking. Crack the shells, remove the tails and claws, and set aside.

In a saucepan, reduce the red wine by a quarter. Make a beurre manié by blending the butter and flour together to form a paste. Add the beurre manié to the red wine in small pieces, whisking well until thickened. Add the black-eyed peas and corn and cook 2 to 3 minutes. Remove from the heat, add the lobster and stir.

Serve on a heated plate, garnished with chopped chives and cracked pepper.

KYM GIBSON'S SALMON CROQUETTES

MAKES 8 SERVINGS

Fond memories of food richly and lovingly prepared have always provided the inspiration for a chef's creative dishes. One bite and you, too, will think of home.

2 cloves garlic, minced
1 small onion, finely chopped
1 rib celery, finely chopped
$^1/_4$ cup extra-virgin olive oil
1 large potato
2 tablespoons chopped fresh dill
One 14$^3/_4$-ounce can salmon
$^1/_2$ teaspoon white pepper
1 tablespoon baking powder
2 eggs, beaten
$^1/_2$ cup all-purpose flour
$^1/_2$ cup fine bread crumbs

Sauté the garlic, onion, and celery in 2 tablespoons of the oil. Set aside.

Dice the potato and boil until tender. Drain. Mash the potato, add the garlic, onion, celery, and dill. Drain the salmon and combine with the mashed potato. Add the white pepper and baking powder to the beaten eggs and mix thoroughly with the potato and salmon mixture. Refrigerate and allow to cool.

Remove the mixture from the refrigerator and form small oval croquettes. Mix the flour and bread crumbs and coat the croquettes with it. Heat the olive oil in a sauté pan-fry the croquettes until golden brown on each side, 2 to 3 minutes per side. Serve on a bed of Sautéed Green Tomatoes and Olives (page 101).

Sautéed Calypso Shrimp with Caribbean Sauce

My friend Gary Miller loved this dish so much that he put it on the menu of his restaurant, Patrice's, located in Montego Bay, Jamaica. It captures the essence of island magic.

$^1/_4$ cup plus 2 teaspoons clarified butter

1$^1/_2$ red peppers, cut into julienne

1$^1/_2$ orange peppers, cut into julienne

1$^1/_2$ yellow peppers, cut into julienne

1$^1/_2$ green peppers, cut into julienne

48 large shrimp (16 to 20 per pound), peeled and deveined

$^1/_4$ cup Frangelico liqueur

2 cups Caribbean Sauce (see page 286)

In a large skillet, heat 2 tablespoons of the butter and sauté the peppers 2 to 3 minutes. Set aside.

In the same skillet, heat the remaining butter and cook the shrimp in two batches 2 to 3 minutes on each side. Stir in the liqueur and cook 1 minute. Add 1 cup Caribbean Sauce. Repeat with the remaining shrimp, liqueur, and sauce.

To serve, arrange the shrimp on a serving plate and sprinkle the peppers over them. Serve hot with Hoppin' John (see page 89) and Fried Plantains (see page 99).

SAUTÉED SOFT-SHELL CRABS
WITH CHORON SAUCE

MAKES 8 SERVINGS

I enjoy eating soft-shell crab in so many ways including sushi, but I created this dish for sentimental reasons. After dining at my dear friend Rudy Lombard's restaurant in Oakland, California, in the early 1980s, I wanted to capture the unique flavors myself.

I tried to dine there often when Stanley Jackson was the executive chef because he made the food taste so wonderful. It also was an opportunity to share a favorite meal with an old friend like Dr. Owen Ellington, who was living in Oakland at the same time.

8 large soft-shell crabs, dressed
1 1/2 cups milk
1 cup all-purpose flour
1/2 teaspoon salt
1/4 teaspoon freshly ground
    black pepper
1/8 teaspoon cayenne pepper
1/2 teaspoon celery salt
1 teaspoon paprika
1/4 cup clarified butter
8 lemon wedges
Choron Sauce (recipe follows)

Place the crabs in a shallow baking pan, add the milk and turn to coat well. Set aside.

In a bowl, combine the flour, salt, black and cayenne peppers, celery salt, and paprika. Dredge the crabs in the flour mixture, shaking off any excess.

Heat the butter in a large skillet and sauté the crabs until golden brown, about 3 to 4 minutes on each side. Squeeze the juice of 1 lemon wedge over each crab and remove them from the pan. Serve on a warm plate napped with Choron Sauce.

CHORON SAUCE

This wonderful sauce begins with a rich hollandaise and has tangy tomato puree incorporated into it with lots of herbs.

2 tablespoons shallots, minced
1/2 cup white wine vinegar
1 teaspoon dried tarragon
4 black peppercorns, crushed
6 egg yolks
2 cups clarified butter
2 tablespoons fresh lemon juice
1 tablespoon warm water
2 tablespoons tomato puree
Salt and cayenne pepper to taste
1 tablespoon chopped fresh
   parsley
1/2 teaspoon chopped fresh
   tarragon

In a small saucepan, combine the shallots, vinegar, dried tarragon, and peppercorns. Bring to a boil, then reduce the heat and simmer until reduced by three quarters, about 2 to 3 minutes. Remove from the heat and cool. Transfer the sauce to a stainless-steel bowl and whisk in the egg yolks, beating well. Hold the bowl over a hot water bath and continue to beat until the yolks have thickened and become creamy. Remove from the heat and gradually whisk in the butter, whisking constantly. Whisk in the lemon juice, warm water, and tomato puree and season with salt and cayenne pepper to taste. Stir in the fresh herbs, cover, and keep warm until ready to serve. Do not overheat.

SOUTHERN FRIED CATFISH FILLETS

MAKES 4 TO 6 SERVINGS

African-Americans have always loved catfish. Now that farm-raised catfish is so readily available, others have acquired a taste for its sweet, juicy meat. Whether you like it pan- or deep-fried, one thing is certain: You'll always want it with hushpuppies.

1 cup peanut oil
3 pounds catfish fillets, rinsed,
   trimmed of any fat, and
   patted dry
1 teaspoon salt
1 tablespoon freshly ground
   black pepper
2 cups yellow cornmeal

Heat the oil to medium in a large cast-iron skillet. Cut the fillets into 3- to 4-ounce pieces. Lightly season the fish with salt and pepper. Season the cornmeal with the remaining salt and pepper and dredge the fish in it. Fry in the hot oil until golden brown, about 3 to 5 minutes. Turn and cook on the other side until done, about 3 minutes longer. Drain on paper towels and serve immediately with Southern Hushpuppies (page 227), Tartar Sauce (page 290), or Hot Pepper Butter Sauce (page 23).

Spanish Rice al Domingo (Chef Randall's Paella)

MAKES 6 TO 8 SERVINGS

Rice has been an important staple for human existence dating back to antiquity, although it didn't arrive in Europe until the eighth or ninth century when it was introduced by the Moors. This dish, created in the 1940s by Chef Domingo of the Penn Harris Hotel, Harrisburg, Pennsylvania, is a tribute to those black pioneers and to the Spaniards who devised the saffron-infused dish.

One 2$^1/_2$- to 3-pound frying chicken, cut into 10 pieces

$^1/_4$ cup all-purpose flour

1 teaspoon salt

$^1/_2$ teaspoon freshly ground black pepper

$^1/_2$ cup olive oil

1 cup smoked ham, diced

$^1/_2$ cup Portuguese linguiça sausage, diced

1 medium onion, diced

4 cloves garlic, minced

$^1/_2$ green pepper, diced

3 green onions, thinly sliced

$^1/_2$ cup diced pimento

2 cups long-grain white rice

2 cups chopped, canned whole tomatoes

2 cups boiling Chicken Stock (see page 279)

$^1/_2$ cup clam juice

1 teaspoon saffron threads, crushed

Salt and white pepper to taste

24 topneck clams, scrubbed

3 fresh or thawed frozen lobster tails, split in half lengthwise

1$^1/_2$ pounds large shrimp, peeled and deveined

1 cup frozen peas, cooked

Preheat the oven to 325°F.

Rinse the chicken pieces and pat dry. Combine the flour, salt, and pepper in a bowl and lightly dust the chicken pieces with it.

In a large skillet or paella pan, heat the olive oil and fry the chicken until crispy and brown, about 6 to 8 minutes on each side. Remove from the pan, drain, and set aside. Add the ham and linguiça to the skillet and cook 3 to 4 minutes. Stir in the onion, garlic, green pepper, green onions, and pimento and cook 2 to 3 minutes, scraping up the browned bits in the bottom of the pan. Stir in the rice and cook 1 minute, coating the rice well with oil. Stir in the tomatoes, hot stock, clam juice, and saffron. Adjust the seasoning with salt and white pepper.

Arrange the chicken, clams, lobster, and shrimp in the pan, cover, and cook in the oven until all the liquid is absorbed, about 20 to 30 minutes.

Attractively arrange the paella on a serving platter, or serve from the paella pan. Sprinkle the peas over the paella before serving.

EARLEST BELL'S TWICE-COOKED
FISH CAKES

MAKES 12 SERVINGS

This dish is a marvelous way to use up leftover fish or any extra garlic mashed potatoes that may be lurking in the refrigerator. If you don't have garlic mashed potatoes, start from scratch and add the garlic to the mixture. No fish? Poach some.

3 cups cooked cod

2 cups mashed potatoes

1 teaspoon minced garlic

Salt and freshly ground
    black pepper to taste

1 teaspoon chopped fresh parsley

1 tablespoon butter, melted

1 egg, beaten

$^1/_2$ teaspoon seasoned salt

$^1/_2$ cup all-purpose flour

Vegetable oil

Preheat the oven to 350°F.

Flake the fish and mix with the potatoes and garlic. Season with salt, pepper, and parsley. Mix in the butter and as much of the egg as needed to moisten the mixture. Mix thoroughly. Divide into 12 to 14 portions, roll each into a ball, then flatten. Combine the seasoned salt and flour and coat the fish lightly with it.

Heat enough vegetable oil to coat the bottom of a skillet to medium-high heat and pan-fry the fish cakes until golden brown, 2 to 3 minutes on each side. Place in the oven until completely heated, about 5 minutes.

CHEF'S TIP
These cakes are delicious served with Pan-fried Green Tomatoes (page 104) and Tartar (page 290) or Remoulade Sauce (page 289).

Chapter 7

Poultry
and
Wild Game

Just as the drumbeat of our ancestors communicated with the ears and minds
of the slaves that traveled against their will to a new land to work the plantations
so did their ability to season the limited staples they were given for preparation divulge
to their taste buds and their souls insuring their physical and spiritual survival.
The planters and their families also ate and grew very fond of these African flavors.

—UNKNOWN AUTHOR

Remember the perfume that lingered in the house when chicken with fresh herbs and corn bread dressing was roasting? It meant someone very, very special was coming to dinner.

Poultry is just one of those foods that African-Americans have savored throughout our rich culinary history, whether we stewed it in an aromatic broth, baked it to succulent goodness, smothered it in a creamy gravy of natural juices, barbecued it to feed a crowd, or fried it for Sunday supper, chicken has been served gloriously at every meal of the day. African-American cooks find even chicken livers and gizzards intriguing.

When you think about it, there really are precious few foods that have such broad appeal and are quite as satisfying as chicken cooked to juicy perfection. It has been that way for what seems like a millennium.

Half a century ago, we ate chicken from our own chicken coops that tasted like chicken. Many of the dishes you are about to experience will take you back to that era, a time when Granny cooked effortlessly with recipes that were uncomplicated and straight-foward, when barnyard fowl filled every pot.

When we lived in the country, hunting wild birds like geese, turkey, pheasant, partridge, quail, and duck and small animals like possum, squirrel, raccoon, and rabbit was something we depended upon, a way to put meat on the table. The cookbook, *Kentucky Hospitality, A 200-Year Tradition*, even presents a recipe for preparing bear's paws, considered to be a great delicacy near the turn of the century.

Then we migrated to the cities and there was no way to hunt or raise our own birds. We traded the coop for the supermarket. What presented a convenience for some cooks, created a quandary. As city dwellers, we lost our enthusiasm for the squirrels running around in our neighborhoods; they were somehow less appetizing.

Domesticated fowl and game, however, refused to be plucked from the menu. Chicken also endeared itself to America, largely because it takes fabulously to the whim of the chef. Consider the age-old dispute over fried chicken: Soak the bird in buttermilk? Let the coating sit an hour or so, then coat with flour again? Cook over high heat? Cover the pan?

Health-conscious cooks will treasure the broiled and roasted poultry specialties in this section for those times when they want something without a lot of added fat.

Removing the skin at serving time also spares fat calories. Grilled chicken occupies a special place in the collection as well, because it is so versatile. You can make it dance to the rhythm of a funky salsa beat just by seasoning it with Caribbean spices and serving with plantains and Cuban black beans and rice. Or, you can make it the centerpiece for casual back-yard entertaining with a simple marinade and a dip in a barbecue sauce you make yourself.

Adding little touches like fresh sage in the pan gravy and minced fresh herbs in the dumplings are just two of the ways you can turn yesterday's favorites into something fabulous today, as you will see in Oven-roasted Garlic-Rosemary Chicken with Corn Bread Dressing and Giblet Gravy or Pan-fried Chicken Smothered in Sage Gravy. You can vary this dish to suit your own style of cooking: Stuff the bird with the dressing or bake it in a separate baking pan.

Though some people shy away from rabbit, those familiar with the texture can vary some of the dishes calling for chicken by tossing rabbit into the kettle. And, though I am a purist and don't subscribe to the practice, some African-American cooks are looking to turkey parts as leaner alternatives to smoked meats for seasoning vegetables.

Finally, don't despair if there isn't someone in your family who enjoys hunting and could share some of his game with you. Fresh quail, rabbit, and pheasant are just some of the game that is as close as the local farmer's market. In fact, you will find cuts of meat and choices of game you never knew existed.

I hope the trip will excite your spirit of adventure and will encourage you to experiment with all the dishes that follow.

KYM GIBSON'S CURRIED CHICKEN

MAKES 8 SERVINGS

You can feel Kym's grandfather's Guyanese roots all over this dish.

Eight 6-ounce boneless, skinless
   chicken breasts
$1/_4$ cup lime juice
2 tablespoons extra-virgin
   olive oil
3 tablespoons Madras curry
   powder
2 cloves garlic, minced
2 sprigs fresh thyme
1 medium onion, diced
1 teaspoon marsala
$1^1/_2$ cups Chicken Stock
   (see page 279)
2 teaspoons seasoned salt

Slice the chicken breasts into strips and soak in the lime juice. Pour the olive oil into 2-quart saucepan and heat over medium-high heat for 1 minute. Sauté the curry powder, garlic, and thyme for 1 minute. Add onion and cook until transparent. Stir in the marsala and add the chicken strips. Sauté over high heat for 2 to 3 minutes. Reduce the heat, pour the stock into the pan, cover, and simmer for 20 to 30 minutes. Season with salt and serve on a bed of Red Mint Rice (page 115).

GRILLED CHICKEN CARIBBEAN WITH FRIED PLANTAINS AND CUBAN BLACK BEANS AND RICE

MAKES 8 SERVINGS

This chicken recipe was the star at a dinner I prepared for the Black Faculty and Staff Association honoring Dr. Hugh La Bounty, former president of Cal-Poly, Pomona, upon his retirement. The theme for the event was A Caribbean Evening. The menu's first course was a callaloo soup, with a salad course of spring greens with mango vinaigrette, a main course of this Grilled Caribbean Chicken with a wonderful sauce, hoppin' John, sautéed zucchini and yellow squash and for dessert tropical fruit strudel with rum custard sauce.

1 cup peanut oil
1 cup cider vinegar
$^1/_4$ cup soy sauce
1 Scotch bonnet pepper, seeded and finely diced
1 medium onion, finely diced
2 green onions, finely sliced
2 teaspoons salt
1 tablespoon sugar
2 teaspoons ground allspice
1 teaspoon ground cinnamon
1 teaspoon ground nutmeg
2 teaspoons crushed dried thyme
3 teaspoons chopped fresh thyme
2 teaspoons freshly ground pepper
Two 2$^1/_2$- to 3-pound fryers, quartered
3 cups Cuban Black Beans and Rice (see page 96)
1$^1/_2$ pounds Fried Plantains (see page 99)
2 cups Caribbean Sauce (see page 286)

In a blender or food processor, combine the oil, vinegar, soy sauce, Scotch bonnet pepper, onion, green onions, salt, sugar, allspice, cinnamon, nutmeg, dried and fresh thyme, and pepper. Blend until smooth.

Wash the chicken and pat dry. Place in a large plastic bag or covered container and pour the marinade over it, turning to coat all sides. Seal and refrigerate for at least 4 hours or overnight. Remove the chicken from the marinade and drain well, reserving the marinade.

Cook chicken, skin side up, on a lightly greased grill 6 inches above the heat source. Cook turning and basting often with the marinade, until the chicken is done, about 20 minutes on each side. Serve with Cuban Black Beans and Rice and Fried Plantains. Nap the Caribbean Sauce over the chicken.

John Harrison's Grilled Breast of Chicken with Grilled Fruit

Toss boneless, skinless chicken breasts with garlic and oil, then seal in airtight zippered bags or a covered container, pop it into the cooler, and head for the family reunion. Grill with your favorite fruits if you want it to dress it up.

Four 8-ounce boneless, skinless
   chicken breasts
1 teaspoon salt
1 teaspoon freshly ground
   black pepper
1/4 cup extra-virgin olive oil
4 thick slices pineapple
4 thick slices orange
4 thick slices apple
4 sprigs fresh mint

Season the chicken breasts with salt and pepper, rub with olive oil, and grill over a hot fire for 6 to 8 minutes. Turn and cook 6 to 8 minutes longer. Grill the fruit just enough to heat through when the chicken is just about done, being careful not to burn. Arrange the fruit and chicken on a plate garnished with fresh mint.

GRILLED CHICKEN WITH BACKYARD BARBECUE SAUCE

MAKES 8 SERVINGS

If you are one of those backyard barbecuers who always makes the mistake of lathering your grilled meats with the sauce too early in the cooking, here's a piece of advice: Wait until the meat is almost done so the sugar in the sauce doesn't burn and ruin the meat.

$^1/_2$ cup peanut oil

$^1/_2$ cup cider vinegar

3 cloves garlic, minced

1 teaspoon salt

1 teaspoon freshly ground
  black pepper

$^1/_2$ teaspoon cayenne pepper

1 teaspoon paprika

$^1/_4$ cup packed dark brown
  sugar

2 teaspoons prepared mustard

2 teaspoons Worcestershire
  sauce

1 teaspoon lemon juice

Two $2^1/_2$- to 3-pound fryers,
  quartered

3 cups Backyard Barbecue Sauce
  (see page 284)

In a large bowl, whisk together the peanut oil, vinegar, garlic, salt, black and cayenne peppers, paprika, brown sugar, mustard, Worcestershire sauce, and lemon juice.

Wash the chicken and pat dry. Add to the marinade and turn to coat well. Cover and refrigerate for at least 3 hours or overnight, turning occasionally. Remove the chicken from the marinade and drain, reserving the marinade. Place the chicken quarters skin side up on a lightly greased grill about 6 inches above medium-hot coals. Cook, turning and basting often with the reserved marinade, until the meat is done, about 35 to 40 minutes. Nap with Backyard Barbecue Sauce and serve hot.

Oven-roasted Garlic-Rosemary Chicken with Corn Bread Dressing and Giblet Gravy

MAKES 4 TO 6 SERVINGS

With the exception of fried chicken, nothing said Sunday dinner like this hearty menu.
With a pot of greens or string beans and peach cobbler, you had a meal fit to serve the preacher.
To keep the bird moist, I recommend cooking it breast side down for the first 50 or 60 minutes,
then turning it over and basting it with the fat in the roasting pan until it is done.

One 4-pound roasting chicken
2 tablespoons butter, melted
1 teaspoon salt
$^1/_2$ teaspoon ground white pepper
4 cloves garlic
2 tablespoons butter, softened
1 teaspoon freshly chopped
  rosemary

CORN BREAD DRESSING
$^1/_4$ cup ($^1/_2$ stick) butter
2 small onions, finely diced
2 ribs celery, finely diced
1 teaspoon poultry seasoning
1 cup Chicken Stock
  (see page 279)
$1^1/_2$ cups stale bread, cut into
  $^1/_4$-inch cubes
$1^1/_2$ cups crumbled Country
  Corn Bread (see page 228)
$^1/_8$ teaspoon cayenne pepper
Salt and freshly ground black
  pepper to taste

1 medium carrot, diced
2 cups Giblet Gravy
  (see page 292)

Preheat the oven to 450°F.

Wash the chicken and pat dry. Brush with the melted butter and sprinkle with salt and pepper. Blanch the garlic in boiling water for 5 minutes, shock in an ice water bath, dry, and mince. Cream together the softened butter, garlic, and rosemary. Rub under the skin of the chicken.

For the Corn Bread Dressing, in a skillet over medium-high heat, melt the butter and sauté 1 diced onion, 1 diced celery rib, and the poultry seasoning 3 to 4 minutes. Add the stock and simmer 2 minutes.

In a large bowl, combine the bread cubes, corn bread, vegetable mixture, cayenne pepper, salt, and pepper to taste. Mix lightly, but well.

Stuff the chicken with the dressing and truss. Place the diced carrot and the remaining celery and onion in a roasting pan. Place the chicken breast side down on the rack over the vegetables. Roast for 15 minutes. Reduce the heat to 325°F and continue to roast for 40 to 45 minutes. Turn the chicken breast side up, baste with the pan juices, and roast, basting every 10 minutes, until the juices run clear when pierced in the leg joint with a fork, about 30 minutes more. Remove the chicken from the pan, remove and discard the strings, and keep warm until serving time.

Drain the vegetables from the pan stock and degrease it for use in making the gravy. Slice the chicken and serve hot with the dressing and giblet gravy.

PAN-FRIED CHICKEN SMOTHERED IN SAGE GRAVY

MAKES 6 TO 8 SERVINGS

Here's another rendition of the fried chicken theme. This time, fresh sage from the garden adds another dimension to the gravy.

Two 2$^1/_2$- to 3-pound frying chickens, quartered

1$^1/_2$ cups all-purpose flour

1 teaspoon salt

1 teaspoon ground white pepper

$^1/_2$ teaspoon cayenne pepper

$^1/_2$ cup peanut oil

$^1/_2$ medium onion, finely diced

4 cups water

2 tablespoons chopped fresh sage

Salt and freshly ground black pepper to taste

Steamed Buttered Rice (see page 114)

Wash the chicken pieces and pat dry with paper towels.

Combine the flour, salt, and white and cayenne peppers in a bowl. Dredge chicken in seasoned flour, shaking off and reserving the excess.

In a large skillet, heat the peanut oil over medium-high heat and fry the chicken until browned, about 5 to 6 minutes on each side. Remove from the skillet and set aside. Add onion and sauté 1 minute, then add $^1/_2$ cup of the flour mixture and stir until brown to make a roux. Add the water, stirring constantly, to make a smooth gravy. Season with sage and salt and black pepper to taste. Return the chicken to the skillet, cover well with gravy, and simmer until the chicken is tender, about 20 to 30 minutes, adding more water if needed. Serve hot over Steamed Buttered Rice.

Darryl Evans's Pan-fried Almond- and Pecan-crusted Breast of Chicken with Honey Glaze

MAKES 4 SERVINGS

Pecans are a Georgia staple and they give chicken a crispy coating without the usual dip in a deep-fat fryer. The honey glaze adds to the mellow flair of this dish.

2 cups pecans, finely chopped

1 cup almonds, finely chopped

1 cup all-purpose flour

3 cloves garlic, minced

1 small onion, finely diced

Four 6-ounce boneless, skinless
  chicken breast halves

Salt, white pepper, and freshly
  ground black pepper to taste

2 eggs, beaten

$^1/_2$ cup water

$^1/_4$ cup extra-virgin olive oil

$^1/_2$ cup honey

1 cup Chicken Stock
  (see page 279)

2 tablespoons rice vinegar

$^1/_4$ cup ($^1/_2$ stick) butter

$1^1/_2$ cups Rice Pilaf
  (see page 114)

Preheat the oven to 350°F.

Combine the nuts, $^3/_4$ cup of the flour, garlic, and onion. Season the chicken with salt and white and black pepper. Combine the eggs and water in a shallow bowl. Dust the chicken in the remaining $^1/_4$ cup of flour, then dip in the egg wash and dredge in the nut crumbs. Heat the olive oil in a sauté pan and sauté the chicken over medium-high heat on both sides until golden brown. Finish in the oven for 2 to 3 minutes. Place on a napkin-covered plate to drain any liquid that accumulates.

Heat the honey, stock, and vinegar in a saucepan. Bring to a boil over medium-high heat and reduce by half. Gradually whisk in the butter to make a smooth sauce. Serve the chicken on a bed of Rice Pilaf napped with the honey glaze.

ROAST BREASTS OF CHICKEN WITH CHAMPAGNE SAUCE

MAKES 8 SERVINGS

This is a recipe I developed while operating Rent-A-Chef Catering Service in California. It is simple but elegant. With its sweet and tangy flavor it works well for small parties or large weddings.

8 boneless chicken breasts left
   with the last wing joint still
   attached
1 teaspoon salt
1 teaspoon ground white pepper
$^1/_2$ cup (1 stick) melted butter
2 cups champagne
2 cups Chicken Stock
   (see page 279)
$1^1/_2$ cups red currant jelly
$^1/_4$ cup sugar
3 drops red food color
2 tablespoons cornstarch
$1^1/_2$ tablespoons water
Salt and white pepper to taste

Preheat the oven to 350°F.

Rinse the chicken breasts and pat dry with paper towels. Season with salt and pepper. Place in a roasting pan and coat well with melted butter. Roast the breasts skin side down for 15 minutes. Turn and roast 25 minutes on the other side. Remove the pan from oven, transfer the breasts to a warm platter and keep warm. Do not turn off the oven.

Drain the juices into a saucepan and degrease. Add the champagne and bring to a boil, then reduce over high heat by half. Deglaze the roasting pan with the stock, reduce by half, then add the reduced stock to the juices, along with the red currant jelly and sugar. Whisk, bring to a boil, then reduce the heat to simmer. Stir in the food color and allow to simmer for 20 minutes.

Combine the cornstarch and water, whisk into the sauce, and continue to simmer until the sauce thickens, about 10 minutes. Correct the seasoning with salt and pepper to taste. Return the chicken breasts to the roasting pan, coat well with sauce, and return to the oven for 10 minutes to heat through. Serve hot napped with champagne sauce.

STEWED CHICKEN AND HERB DUMPLINGS

MAKES 4 TO 6 SERVINGS

Stewed chicken is another one of those homey, classic dishes that benefits from a slight update. Aromatic herbs stirred into the dumplings gives the dish a new boost of fresh flavor.

One 3- to 3^1/$_2$-pound frying chicken

3 quarts plus ^{1}/$_2$ cup water

1 small onion, chopped

2 ribs celery, chopped

1 medium carrot, chopped

1 bay leaf

^{1}/$_2$ tablespoon chopped fresh parsley

1 teaspoon salt

^{1}/$_2$ teaspoon white pepper

Salt and freshly ground black pepper to taste

HERB DUMPLINGS

1 egg

3 tablespoons milk

1 tablespoon cold water

^{1}/$_2$ teaspoon chopped fresh sage

^{1}/$_2$ teaspoon chopped fresh thyme

1^1/$_2$ cups all-purpose flour

^{1}/$_4$ teaspoon salt

1 teaspoon baking powder

Place the chicken in a large stockpot and cover with 3 quarts water. Add the onion, celery, carrot, bay leaf, parsley, salt, and white pepper. Cover and bring to a boil, then reduce the heat to simmer and cook until chicken is tender, about 1^1/$_2$ hours. Remove the chicken from the pot and allow to cool, reserving the stock. Remove meat from the bones, cut up and set aside. Stain the stock into a saucepan, removing the fat, and bring to a boil.

For the dumplings, beat the egg until light. Add the milk, water, sage, and thyme and mix. Sift 1 cup of the flour, salt, and baking powder together. Mix with the egg mixture to form a light dough.

In a mixing bowl, combine the remaining ^{1}/$_2$ cup flour and ^{1}/$_2$ cup water, then add it to the boiling stock. Stir and allow to simmer until the sauce is thickened. Adjust the seasoning with salt and pepper to taste. Return the diced chicken pieces to the sauce. Drop dumplings from a tablespoon into the rapidly boiling sauce. Reduce the heat to a simmer, cover tightly, and simmer for 10 to 12 minutes. Serve in a soup plate over a mound of creamy whipped potatoes, if you wish.

STEWED CHICKEN AND
SWEET POTATO WAFFLES

MAKES 6 SERVINGS

We were fond of waffles in my house when I was growing up. Later, when I lived in New York City, I loved to eat at Wells on 7th Avenue and 135th Street. Folks went there after a late night of partying for the best chicken and waffles. It was a wonderful way to end an evening. I put together this recipe because I really like the sweet taste of sweet potato in the waffles. The creamy rich chicken over the crispy crunchy waffles is a nice match. Serve it for lunch, dinner, or something extra for breakfast.

One 2¹/₂- to 3-pound frying
   chicken
1 small onion, chopped
2 ribs celery, chopped
1 medium carrot, chopped
1 bay leaf
1 sprig parsley
1 teaspoon salt
¹/₄ teaspoon ground white pepper
¹/₂ cup all-purpose flour
¹/₂ cup water
Salt and freshly ground
   black pepper to taste
6 Sweet Potato Waffles
   (see page 133)
2 teaspoons chopped fresh
   parsley

Place the chicken in a large stockpot and cover with water. Add the onion, celery, carrot, bay leaf, parsley sprig, salt, and pepper. Cover and bring to a boil. Reduce the heat to simmer and cook until the chicken is tender, about 1¹/₂ hours. Remove the chicken from the pot and allow to cool, reserving the stock. Remove the meat from the bones, cut up, and set aside. Strain the reserved stock into a saucepan and bring to a boil.

In a mixing bowl, combine the flour and water, then add it to the stock. Stir and simmer until the sauce is thickened. Adjust the seasoning with salt and pepper to taste. Return the diced chicken to the sauce and heat through.

Place a hot sweet potato waffle on a plate, cover with stewed chicken, and garnish with chopped parsley.

UNCLE DICK'S DEEP-FRIED CHICKEN WITH CORN FRITTERS

MAKES 4 SERVINGS

Richard Ross represents many things to me. First, he was my uncle, a large man—6 feet 5 inches and well over 240 pounds. He had a deep voice and we learned at a very early age to pay attention. Second, from the 1940s to the 1950s, he owned and operated the Hotel Large in Large, Pennsylvania, outside Pittsburgh, with his wife, my aunt Dolly.

Although they both cooked well, he was the first man I ever heard addressed by the title chef. And he earned it. He operated the hotel, restaurant, and lounge and at the same time, did off-premises catering through Ross's Catering Company, in and around the Pittsburgh area. He trained the late Hank Wilson of Wilson's Catering in East Liberty, Pennsylvania.

But the memory that I recall most vividly is the sound of chicken frying in the deep-fryer and the savory bouquet of corn fritters frying in the other basket. I have eaten a lot of chicken in my travels, in many places, but there is only one that can compete with Uncle Dick's, at 23rd Street and Griffith in Los Angeles, named Poor Red's.

1 whole chicken, quartered
1 cup all-purpose flour
2 teaspoons salt
1 teaspoon freshly ground
   black pepper
1 teaspoon cayenne pepper
$1/2$ tablespoon paprika
$1/2$ teaspoon garlic powder
1 teaspoon poultry seasoning
Peanut oil
12 Corn Fritters (see page 92)
$1/2$ tablespoon powdered sugar

Rinse the chicken, drain, and pat dry. In a bowl or brown paper bag, mix the flour, salt, black and cayenne peppers, paprika, garlic powder, and poultry seasoning. Dredge the chicken in the seasoned flour and shake to remove any excess flour. Heat the oil a deep-fryer to 350°F. Place the chicken in the deep-fryer basket and fry until golden brown and crisp, about 18 to 20 minutes). Drain on paper towels. Serve immediately with hot Corn Fritters sprinkled with powdered sugar.

EDNA LEWIS'S VIRGINIA FRIED CHICKEN WITH BROWN GRAVY

There are as many ways to cook fried chicken as there are cooks. Edna prefers a heavy-bottomed aluminum pan most often, but likes a black cast-iron skillet on a wood stove that has a wider heating surface. Feel free to turn the chicken a number of times during the cooking time to get the desired brown color, but avoid cooking longer than 25 minutes. Because chickens today are reared mostly in confinement, they are very tender and don't need the long cooking they once did.

1 cup all-purpose flour
1 cup whole wheat flour
3 teaspoons salt
1 teaspoon freshly ground
  black pepper
Two $2^1/_4$- to $2^1/_2$-pound chickens,
  cut into 8 pieces each
$^1/_2$ cup lard, at room temperature
$^1/_2$ cup (1 stick) butter, at room
  temperature
1 slice Virginia smoked ham
  (optional)
2 cups Brown Gravy
  (see page 291)

Combine the two flours and add the salt and pepper. Mix well. Rinse the chicken pieces and pat dry. Reserve the backs and wing tips for the stock used in the gravy. Roll each piece of chicken in the seasoned flour and place the coated pieces on a wide platter or a sheet of waxed paper. Let rest for about 1 hour so that loose flour doesn't fall into the frying pan and burn before the chicken pieces are properly browned.

Heat a large skillet until hot and add the lard. When it is near the smoking point, add the chicken pieces, butter, and ham. The cooking fat should cover the chicken by about half. Do not crowd the pan. Cover and cook on medium-high heat, watching closely to prevent burning, until the chicken is golden brown, about 10 to 12 minutes on each side. Remove the cooked pieces from the skillet, drain on paper towels, and serve piping hot with Brown Gravy.

ROASTED CAPON STUFFED WITH SWEET POTATO DRESSING

MAKES 8 TO 10 SERVINGS

Capon is one of the yard birds most families reserved for special occasions. The intense flavor of our favorite tuber, the sweet potato, takes an otherwise ordinary stuffing to new heights.

One 7- to 8-pound capon
$^1/_4$ cup clarified butter
1 teaspoon salt
$^1/_2$ teaspoon freshly ground
   black pepper

SWEET POTATO DRESSING
$^1/_4$ cup clarified butter
$^1/_4$ cup finely diced celery
$^1/_4$ cup finely diced onion
$^1/_2$ cup Chicken Stock
   (see page 279)
$^1/_4$ teaspoon dried sage,
   crumbled
$1^1/_2$ medium sweet potatoes,
   baked, peeled, and mashed
   (about 1 cup)
1 cup $^1/_4$-inch stale bread cubes
$^1/_2$ teaspoon salt
$^1/_4$ teaspoon freshly ground
   black pepper

TO FINISH THE DISH
$^1/_4$ cup diced carrot
$^1/_4$ cup diced celery
$^1/_4$ cup diced onion
2 cups Chicken Stock
   (see page 279)

Preheat the oven to 425°F.

Rinse the capon and pat dry with a towel. Brush with the butter and season with salt and pepper.

For the dressing, heat $^1/_2$ cup butter in a sauté pan or skillet over medium-high heat, add the celery and onion and sauté 2 to 3 minutes. Add $^1/_2$ cup chicken stock, sage, and mashed sweet potatoes. Mix well, add the bread cubes, and mix again. Season with salt and pepper. Stuff the capon with the dressing and truss the bird.

Place the bird on a rack in a roasting pan with along with the diced carrot, celery, and onion. Roast skin side up for 45 to 50 minutes. Reduce the heat to 350°F and continue roasting, basting every 15 to 20 minutes, until the juices run clear when the leg joint is pierced with a fork, $1^1/_2$ to 2 hours. Remove the capon to a warm platter and keep warm. Drain the fat from the roasting pan, place over high heat. Deglaze the pan with the chicken stock, reducing by half, scraping up the browned bits and mashing the vegetables. Strain the sauce, carve and slice the capon. Serve napped with sauce.

Roast Goose Stuffed with Apple and Chestnut Dressing

MAKES 8 SERVINGS

When roasted properly, goose is delicious.

One 5-pound roasting goose
1 teaspoon salt
$^1/_2$ teaspoon freshly ground pepper

APPLE AND CHESTNUT DRESSING
$^1/_2$ cup (1 stick) butter
1 small onion, diced
1 rib celery, diced
2 cups $^1/_2$-inch stale bread cubes
$1^1/_2$ cups peeled, cored, and diced Granny Smith apples
$^3/_4$ cup chestnuts, roasted, peeled, and coarsely chopped
2 teaspoons chopped fresh thyme
1 tablespoon chopped fresh sage
$^1/_2$ cup apple cider
$^1/_2$ teaspoon salt
$^1/_4$ teaspoon freshly ground pepper

TO FINISH THE DISH
1 small onion, coarsely chopped
2 ribs celery, coarsely chopped
1 medium carrot, chopped
1 goose neck
1 goose gizzard
1 goose liver
4 cups water
2 teaspoons salt
$^1/_4$ cup all-purpose flour
Freshly ground pepper to taste

Preheat the oven to 400°F.

Wash the goose and pat it dry. Sprinkle the cavity and rub the skin with salt and pepper. Puncture lightly all over the skin with a fork.

For the dressing, heat the butter in a skillet over medium-high heat and sauté the onion and celery, until tender, about 2 to 3 minutes. In a large bowl, combine the bread cubes, apples, chestnuts, thyme, sage, and sautéed vegetables and mix well. Moisten with the apple cider and season with salt and pepper.

Stuff the goose with the dressing and truss. Place the goose breast side up on a rack over the onion, celery, and carrot surrounded by the goose neck and giblets in a roasting pan. Add the water and salt to help the goose retain its juices. Roast for 30 minutes. Reduce the heat to 350°F and continue to roast, basting every 20 minutes, until a thermometer inserted into the thigh joint registers 180°F, 2 to $2^1/_2$ hours.

Remove the goose to a warm platter and set aside. Remove the giblets from the pan. Set aside to cool; discard the neck. Finely dice the giblets. Strain the pan juices and skim the fat, reserving 3 tablespoons fat.

In a skillet over medium-high heat, heat the reserved fat, add the chopped giblets, and sauté 2 to 3 minutes. Add the flour to make a roux and cook until brown. Stir in pan juices, bring to a boil, then reduce the heat and simmer until the gravy thickens, about 10 to 15 minutes. Correct the seasoning with salt and pepper to taste. Serve the hot gravy over sliced goose and dressing.

CHEF'S TIP

To roast chestnuts, cut an X in the flat side of each chestnut and place in a roasting pan. Toss lightly with vegetable oil. Roast in a preheated 400°F oven for 10 to 15 minutes. Set aside until cool enough to handle. Peel.

Roast Pheasant with Port Wine Sauce

MAKES 4 SERVINGS

I celebrated my thirtieth birthday at The Other Place, a well-known restaurant in Seattle, Washington. The owner, Bobby Rossellini, was one of the first chefs I encountered who truly was interested in locally grown products. In fact, he established his own game and veal farm and a fishing company so he would always have the freshest ingredients on hand. This recipe comes close to the wonderful pheasant dinner I had on my birthday.

Two 2- to 2¹/₂-pound pheasants, cleaned
1 teaspoon salt
1 teaspoon freshly ground black pepper
2 small pieces celery, with leaves
2 sprigs parsley
2 cloves garlic
8 slices bacon
¹/₂ cup ruby port
1 tablespoon minced shallots
1 cup pheasant stock or rich Chicken Stock (see page 279)
3 tablespoons red currant jelly
Salt and freshly ground black pepper to taste
1 tablespoon butter

Preheat the oven to 400°F.

Wash the pheasants, season inside and out with salt and pepper. Place a piece of celery, a sprig of parsley, and a clove of garlic inside each bird. Wrap each bird all over with overlapping bacon slices; truss (tie). Place the pheasants breast side down on a rack in a roasting pan and roast for 30 minutes. Turn the pheasants breast side up and continue to roast, basting frequently with the pan juices, for an additional 25 minutes. Remove the bacon and baste thoroughly with the pan juices. Roast for 5 minutes more. Transfer the birds to a platter and keep warm.

Strain and degrease the pan juices, deglaze the roasting pan with the port. Stir in the shallots and stock. Stir in the red currant jelly and bring to a boil, then reduce the heat to simmer and cook until reduced by half. Taste and adjust the seasoning with salt and pepper. Strain and finish by stirring in the butter. Carve the pheasants, place on warm plates, and nap with port wine sauce.

CHEF'S TIP
You can use the pheasant neck and wing tips to make pheasant stock following the chicken stock instructions.

Pan-broiled Quail with Virginia Ham

MAKES 8 SERVINGS

In the old days, quail could be had easily and it was a nice alternative to chicken. Today, it is still easy to get, but what you will find in the supermarket is usually frozen. If you have a specialty grocer nearby, have him get it for you fresh. It may cost a bit more, but it's worth it. The breastbone will already be removed.

4 slices Smithfield ham, sliced
  $1/8$ inch thick and cut in half
8 quail, split up the backbone,
  breastbone removed
1 teaspoon salt
$1/4$ teaspoon freshly ground
  black pepper
$1/4$ teaspoon red pepper flakes
2 teaspoons brown sugar
1 tablespoon cider vinegar
1 cup peanut oil

If the ham is salty, soak the slices in water for 30 minutes to 1 hour. Drain and pat dry and cut the fat around the edges to keep it from curling during cooking. Cook the ham on both sides in a heated heavy skillet over low heat until brown and tender, about 20 minutes. Set aside on a warm platter.

Wash the quail and flatten them. In a bowl, combine the salt, black pepper, red pepper flakes, sugar, vinegar, and oil. Place the quail in the marinade, cover, and marinate in the refrigerator for at least 1 hour. Heat a large skillet. Drain the quail to remove the excess marinade and pan broil until tender and golden, about 6 to 8 minutes on each side. Place on top of a slice of ham and serve hot.

Southern Fried Quail, Wild Mushroom Sauce, and Spoon Bread

MAKES 6 SERVINGS

Wild mushrooms have a rich taste that nicely accents the rustic flavor of the birds in this dish.

6 whole quail, split

1 cup all-purpose flour

1 teaspoon salt

$^1/_2$ teaspoon freshly ground black pepper

$^1/_2$ teaspoon cayenne pepper

$^1/_4$ cup bacon drippings

2 tablespoons butter

$1^1/_2$ cups Wild Mushroom Sauce (see page 190)

Granny's Spoon Bread (see page 225)

Rinse the quail and pat dry with paper towels. Combine the flour, salt, and black and cayenne peppers in a bowl. Dredge the quail in the seasoned flour, coating well. Shake to remove any excess flour. Heat the bacon drippings and butter in a skillet over medium-high heat and fry the quail until brown, about 5 to 6 minutes on each side. Serve hot on a pool of Wild Mushroom Sauce with Spoon Bread alongside.

BRAISED FRICASSEE OF SQUIRREL

Hunting small game was one of the joys of being near the woods when I was young. Rabbits, squirrels, and groundhogs were plentiful. Today, it's best to know someone who can hunt them for you. Egg yolks and cream make a luxurious sauce.

2 squirrels, washed and cut into 8 pieces each
$1/2$ teaspoon salt
$1/4$ teaspoon freshly ground black pepper
$1/4$ teaspoon cayenne pepper
$1/2$ cup peanut oil
1 small onion, finely diced
1 clove garlic, minced
$1/2$ cup all-purpose flour
1 quart Chicken Stock (see page 279)
1 bay leaf
1 sprig thyme
1 sprig sage
2 egg yolks, beaten
$2/3$ cup heavy cream
2 teaspoons cider vinegar
$1/8$ teaspoon ground nutmeg
Salt and freshly ground black pepper to taste

Preheat the oven to 325°F.

Season the squirrel with salt, black and cayenne peppers.

In a large skillet, heat the oil over medium heat and add the squirrel pieces, onion, and garlic. Cook lightly on all sides, but do not brown. Remove the meat from the pan. Add the flour and stir to make a roux. Cook $1^{1}/_{2}$ to 2 minutes, stir in half the stock, return the meat to the pan, and add enough of the remaining stock to cover the squirrel. Bring to a boil, stir, then reduce the heat and simmer until the sauce thickens. Add the bay leaf, thyme, and sage. Cover the pan and braise in the oven until the squirrel is tender, 1 to $1^{1}/_{2}$ hours. Remove the squirrel from the sauce, set aside, and keep warm.

Degrease the sauce. Reduce over high heat until the desired consistency is reached. Strain.

In a small bowl, combine the egg yolks and heavy cream. Temper this by stirring a little of the sauce into the mixture, then stirring it back into the sauce. Bring to just below a simmer. Do not boil. Season with the vinegar, nutmeg, and salt and pepper to taste. Pour the sauce over the squirrel. Serve hot with Steamed Buttered Rice (page 114).

GRILLED RABBIT SAUSAGE WITH SWEET POTATO PANCAKES

MAKES 8 SERVINGS

Rabbit usually comes to the table fried or fricasseed in traditional African-American cookery. This recipe accentuates the subtle, chickenlike flavor of rabbit. You don't need fancy equipment, although a sturdy mixer with a sausage-making attachment does the job in half the time. A food processor and an inexpensive stuffing horn are all that's needed. The sausage freezes well.

2 rabbits
2 tablespoons peanut oil
1 small onion, roughly chopped
6 cloves garlic, chopped
2 ounces Smithfield ham, thinly
    sliced and chopped
$1/2$ bunch parsley
$1/2$ bunch thyme
$1/2$ bunch sage
$1/2$ bunch mustard greens, stems
    removed and blanched
2 tablespoons red pepper flakes
$3/4$ pound ice cubes
$1/2$ pound pork fat, diced
2 teaspoons coarse sea salt
1 teaspoon freshly ground
    black pepper
$1/4$ package (4 ounces) pork
    casings
$1/4$ cup extra-virgin olive oil
Sweet Potato Pancakes
    (see page 110)

Remove all the bones from the rabbits or have your local butcher do it. Cut the meat into chunks.

In a skillet or sauté pan, heat the oil over medium-high heat and cook the onion and garlic until tender; do not brown. Place the vegetables and the rabbit in the freezer until ice cold, then refrigerate until ready to use.

Combine the rabbit, ham, onion mixture, parsley, thyme, sage, mustard greens, red pepper flakes, and ice cubes in a meat grinder. Process using small holes or chop finely in a food processor. Refrigerate until ready to mix.

Place the mixture in a mixer with the pork fat and blend well. Season to taste with salt and pepper. To test for flavor, cook a small amount of the sausage in a skillet, then correct the seasoning, if necessary.

Moisten the stuffing horn and slide a casing onto it. Tie a knot at the end. Pierce the casing with a fork to let air escape while stuffing. Feed in the sausage mixture, filling the casing loosely. Pinch the sausage at about 5-inch lengths, then twist to make a link. Repeat until the entire casing and rabbit mixture is used. Tie a knot at the end. You should have about 16 to 18 links or about 5 pounds sausage.

Poach the links in water for 20 minutes. Remove from the liquid. Cook on a medium-hot grill until golden brown on all sides, basting with olive oil. Serve hot with Sweet Potato Pancakes.

CHEF'S TIP
Chill the meat thoroughly to prevent overheating during grinding.

Pan-fried Rabbit Smothered in Natural Gravy

MAKES 6 TO 8 SERVINGS

Browning the vegetables gives the gravy a rich quality that shows off the flavor of the rabbit. All that is needed is crusty bread, salad, and rice.

1 cup all-purpose flour

$^1/_2$ teaspoon salt

$^1/_4$ teaspoon freshly ground pepper

2 rabbits, rinsed and each cut into 8 pieces

$^3/_4$ cup ($1^1/_2$ sticks) butter

1 medium onion, diced

3 cloves garlic, minced

1 medium carrot, diced

2 ribs celery, diced

$1^1/_4$ quarts Veal (Brown) Stock (see page 281)

2 teaspoons cider vinegar

1 tablespoon chopped fresh thyme

Salt and freshly ground black pepper to taste

Steamed Buttered Rice (see page 114)

In a bowl, combine the flour, salt, and pepper. Dredge the rabbit in the seasoned flour and shake off any excess.

In a skillet, melt the butter over medium-high heat and fry the rabbit until brown, about 6 to 8 minutes per side. Remove from the skillet and set aside. Add the onion, garlic, carrot, and celery to skillet and sauté until brown, about 5 to 6 minutes. Stir in the stock, vinegar, and thyme. Bring to a boil, then reduce the heat and simmer until the gravy thickens, about 10 to 15 minutes. Return the rabbit to the skillet, stir, and adjust the seasoning with salt and pepper to taste. Cover and allow to simmer until the rabbit is tender, $1^1/_2$ hours. Correct the seasoning and consistency, if needed. Serve hot with Steamed Buttered Rice.

Venison Patties with Wild Mushroom Sauce

Jimmy Jackson was my bother-in-law and the hunter in our family. Although deer meat is a little too lean for my taste and it dries out very fast, I find that adding a little pork fat makes the patties juicy. If there is a hunter in your family, ask him for a ration so you can see for yourself. Hunters always have more meat than they need.

$2^{1}/_{2}$ pounds ground venison

$^{1}/_{4}$ pound ground pork fat

3 cloves garlic, minced

1 teaspoon crushed red pepper flakes

2 tablespoons dried sage, crumbled

1 tablespoon salt

1 teaspoon freshly ground black pepper

$^{1}/_{4}$ cup peanut oil

2 cups Wild Mushroom Sauce (see page 190)

In a mixing bowl, combine the venison, pork fat, garlic, red pepper flakes, sage, salt, and pepper. Use your hands to mix thoroughly. Shape into sixteen $2^{1}/_{2}$-ounce patties. Heat the oil in a skillet and fry patties over medium-high heat until brown, about 3 to 4 minutes on each side. Serve in a pool of Wild Mushroom Sauce with a little sauce napped on top.

Chapter 8

Beef, Lamb, Veal, and Pork

"The men and the women slaves on Colonel Lloyd's farm received, as their monthly allowance of food, eight pounds of pickled pork, or its equivalent in fish. The pork was often tainted and the fish were of the poorest quality. With their pork or fish, they had given them one bushel of Indian meal, unbolted, of which quite fifteen percent was more fit for pigs than for men."

—FREDERICK DOUGLASS, *LIFE AND TIMES OF FREDERICK DOUGLASS*, 1892.

Let's face it, some African-Americans are no longer eating chitterlings and other pig's offal because of painful memories like this depiction by Frederick Douglass. They appreciate their culinary heritage, but they refuse to be defined by it.

There are just as many others who refuse to eschew the historic accomplishments of slaves who smuggled in the foods of their native land and labored furiously for generations to perfect ways to cook discarded organ meats. The foods of our roots, including those of the fifth quarter, are being reclaimed as a way of celebrating African-American heritage.

That caldron of pork parts bubbling away on the stove in a tiny, crowded kitchen is no longer the static image of African-American cuisine. Today, the seasoned brew survives because it spices up the flavor of collard greens in upscale restaurants, as well as maybe keeping us in touch with the past.

It is quite natural that it would.

Slave cooks were reconciled to the fact that meat from whatever the source was a blessing, not to be missed. It was with much fortitude and creativity that these pioneers, like contemporary chefs working with new and unusual ingredients, turned their monotonous existence—based upon a few rib bones, some pork knuckles and entrails—into something that not only provided them with nourishment, but tasted good, too.

They are the originators of Southern Cuisine as we know it today, says historian John Egerton. Prior to their influence, well before the plantation days, the colonists' diet was comprised of "the same boring, bland food they still know in Britain today," he says.

The slave cook's influence can't be overemphasized. They brought to the New World their expertise on cultivation techniques and carried okra, sesame and watermelon seeds, black-eyed peas, African yams, and an affinity for spices and seasonings from Africa. Though they received very little meat—and what they did get was the toughest and least desirable—they devised a diet that was filled with healthful grains, vegetables, fruits, and legumes, which they seasoned with onions, celery, and herbs from their gardens, with spices they either brought with them or learned about from the American Indians, and with smoked meats, which were plentiful.

The slave cook was able to do so much with so little that it seems important to show you examples of our superb cookery of fifth quarter foods and wild meats. I don't tamper with many of these, like Simmered Chitterlings Country Style with Hog Maws or Fried Liver and Onions, for sentimental reasons. I wanted to remind you of all the magnificent dishes that evolved from these modest beginnings, food that just got better and better as African-American cooks honed their skills and expanded their inventory. Roux has many uses and it shows up here again in smothered short ribs and pork chops, pot roast and oxtails braised to succulent tenderness. Plus, I have preserved legendary cooking styles, including barbecue.

At the same time I want to delight you with dishes that begin with finer cuts like tenderloin and veal, created to grace any modern dinner table.

I hope that by the time you reach the end of the collection, you'll want to embrace and be proud of our ancestor's achievements. And, you may be surprised when you realize just how much you have missed by the way food this good tastes.

Beef

BARBECUED BEEF BRISKET WITH PLANTATION SAUCE

MAKES 6 TO 8 SERVINGS

Don't make the mistake of trying to hurry this brisket along by cooking it quickly over a hot fire. The key to truly great barbecue is slow cooking over a moderate fire. You can also stop worrying about preparing a special rub for this cut. The sauce that is suggested as an accompaniment is all the spice you really need.

One 3-pound beef brisket, trimmed
1 teaspoon salt
1 teaspoon freshly ground black pepper
3 cups Plantation Sauce, warmed (see page 285)

Place a covered drip pan in the center of the coals. Rub the brisket with salt and pepper. When the coals are hot and turn white, place the brisket fat side down on the grill and close the top. Set the dampers so you maintain a slow burning fire, adding more wood or charcoal if needed. Cook the brisket, turning occasionally so it browns all over, until the brisket reaches an internal temperature of 150 degrees, $4^1/_2$ to 5 hours.

Remove the meat from the grill and let rest 10 to 15 minutes before carving. Trim some of the fat and slice the meat thinly across the grain. Nap with heated Plantation Sauce and serve.

CHEF'S TIP
This recipe works best in a grill that is covered. A smoker is even better.

Braised Short Ribs of Beef in Natural Gravy with Fresh Horseradish

Feel free to serve these ribs the traditional way, over hot, buttered wide noodles.
The fresh horseradish gives an extra zing to the gravy.

Eight 10-ounce beef shorts ribs, trimmed

1 cup all-purpose flour

$^1/_2$ teaspoon salt

$^1/_2$ teaspoon freshly ground black pepper

$^1/_2$ cup peanut oil

1 rib celery, diced

1 medium carrot, diced

1 small onion, diced

$1^1/_2$ quarts Veal (Brown) Stock (see page 281)

$^1/_3$ cup tomato puree

1 bay leaf

Salt and freshly ground black pepper to taste

$^1/_4$ cup grated fresh horseradish

Pat the ribs dry. Preheat the oven to 350°F.

In a bowl, combine the flour, salt, and pepper. Dredge the short ribs in the seasoned flour, shaking off any excess. Reserve $^1/_4$ cup flour. Heat the oil in a large skillet over high heat and brown the ribs evenly on all sides. Remove from skillet to a heatproof casserole. Add the celery, carrot, and onion to the skillet and sauté until lightly brown. Stir in the reserved flour to make a roux. Reduce the heat to medium and cook and stir until the roux is brown, about 3 to 4 minutes. Stir in the stock and allow to simmer until the gravy thickens, about 10 to 15 minutes. Add the tomato puree and bay leaf and season with additional salt and pepper to taste. Stir in the horseradish.

Pour the gravy over the short ribs, cover, and braise until the ribs are tender, about 2 hours. Remove the ribs from the gravy and set aside, keeping warm. Strain the gravy, degrease, correct the seasoning with salt and pepper and add more stock, if you think the gravy is too thick.

To serve, place a short rib in the center of each plate and nap with gravy. Serve hot with Steamed Buttered Rice (page 114) and Sautéed Zucchini, Tomatoes, and Mushrooms (page 108).

GRILLED LONDON BROIL
WITH MUSHROOM SAUCE

*A basic French dressing or vinaigrette, which is used to marinate tough cuts of meat, is nothing
more than a simple mix of oil, vinegar, and seasonings. American cooks also add tomatoes
to the list. Chef Robert W. Lee taught me this shortcut for London broil, using bottled
Kraft French Dressing when I was training under him at the Harrisburger Hotel
in the early 1960s. I still enjoy it today.*

3 pounds flank steak, trimmed
(about 2 steaks)
3 cups Kraft French Dressing or
your favorite French dressing
1 teaspoon salt
1 teaspoon freshly ground
black pepper

MUSHROOM SAUCE
3 tablespoons butter
1 small onion, minced
1$^1/_2$ pounds button mushrooms,
sliced
3 tablespoons all-purpose flour
2 cups Veal (Brown) Stock
(see page 281)
$^1/_2$ cup canned whole tomatoes,
crushed
$^1/_4$ cup dry sherry
Salt and freshly ground
black pepper to taste

Place the steaks in a large, shallow baking dish. Cover with the French
dressing, turning to coat well on both sides. Marinate for at least 30
to 45 minutes at room temperature or overnight in the refrigerator.

For the sauce, in a skillet, melt the butter and sauté the onion until
golden, 3 to 4 minutes. Add the mushrooms and continue to sauté for
3 to 4 minutes. Stir in the flour to make a roux and cook over medium
heat until brown. Stir in the stock, tomatoes, and sherry. Bring to a
boil, then reduce the heat and simmer, stirring, until the sauce thickens and is smooth, about 15 to 20 minutes. Correct the seasoning
with salt and pepper to taste.

Remove the steak from the marinade and season with salt and pepper.
Grill 6 to 8 minutes on each side over hot coals or under a preheated
broiler to medium-rare or desired doneness. Slice across the grain.
Serve 2 to 3 slices per person napped with the mushroom sauce.

LEAH CHASE'S POT ROAST WITH GARDEN VEGETABLES

MAKES 8 TO 10 SERVINGS

There are two types of Creole cooks: Those who do things home-style and those with an uptown flair. At Dooky Chase, you get a little bit of both as this dish demonstrates.

5 pounds beef chuck roast

4 cloves garlic

2 tablespoons salt

2 tablespoons freshly ground black pepper

$1/2$ cup all-purpose flour

$1/2$ cup vegetable oil

1 medium onion, chopped

2 cups water, or more if needed

6 whole new potatoes, scrubbed

4 medium carrots, peeled and cut into 1-inch pieces

1 pound fresh green beans, trimmed and cut into halves

1 medium green pepper, cut into strips

1 medium red pepper, cut into strips

2 tablespoons chopped fresh parsley

Steamed Buttered Rice (see page 114)

Cut eight 1-inch slits all over the roast. Cut each garlic clove in half lengthwise and stuff each slit with garlic, salt, and pepper. Rub any remaining salt and pepper over the entire roast and pat flour on all sides. Heat the oil over high heat in a Dutch oven or small deep roasting pan. Place the roast in the hot oil and brown on all sides. Add the onion and water. Reduce the heat and cook, covered, for about 45 minutes. Uncover about halfway through the cooking time and turn the roast over. Add more water, if needed. Add the potatoes and carrots and cook until the potatoes are tender. Add the beans and peppers, cover, and cook until all the vegetables are tender. Sprinkle with the parsley. To serve, place 3 slices of pot roast on some rice in the center of a plate, spoon gravy and a few vegetables over the meat.

Oven-braised Pot Roast with Potato Pancakes

MAKES 6 TO 8 SERVINGS

If you are one of those people who prefer your meat well-done so there isn't even a trace of pink, then the tender juiciness of this recipe will put a smile on your face.

3 pounds beef eye round
   pot roast, trimmed
$^1/_8$ cup peanut oil
1 medium carrot, diced
1 rib celery, diced
1 medium onion, diced
1 clove garlic, minced
$^1/_2$ cup tomato puree
1 bay leaf
1 sprig parsley
$^1/_4$ cup all-purpose flour
Salt and freshly ground
   black pepper to taste
16 Potato Pancakes
   (see page 105)
Sautéed Mustard Greens and
   Mushrooms (see page 106)

Preheat the oven to 325°F.

Pat the meat dry with paper towels so it will brown well. In a heat-proof casserole or braising pan, heat the oil over high heat and brown the meat evenly on all sides. Remove from the pan and set aside. Stir the carrot, celery, onion, and garlic into the pan. Cook over medium-high heat until brown. Stir in the tomato puree, bay leaf, and parsley and bring to a boil. Return the roast to the pan, cover, and cook in the oven for $2^1/_2$ to 3 hours. Remove the pot roast from the pan and keep warm.

Skim the fat from the cooking juices, reserving $^1/_3$ cup fat. Heat reserved fat in a saucepan over medium heat, stir in the flour to make a roux, and cook 5 to 6 minutes. Return the casserole with the cooking juices to high heat and bring to a boil. Whisk in the roux, then reduce heat to simmer, and cook until the gravy thickens and reduces a little, about 20 minutes. Strain the gravy and correct the seasoning with salt and pepper. Cut roast into $^1/_4$-inch slices across the grain. Serve hot with gravy napped over pot roast slices, 2 Potato Pancakes, and Sautéed Mustard Greens and Mushrooms.

Pan-broiled Baby Steer Liver
with Sautéed Onions

MAKES 6 SERVINGS

Just about every ethnic cuisine includes a liver specialty and African-American cookery is no exception. Liver requires little preparation, just don't make the mistake of overcooking it. A quick sauté and you're done.

1/4 cup (1/2 stick) butter
2 medium onions, thinly sliced
2 pounds baby beef liver in
   1/4-inch-thick slices, cut into
   3-inch pieces
1 teaspoon salt
1 teaspoon freshly ground
   black pepper
2 tablespoons peanut oil

In a sauté pan, heat the butter over medium-high heat until hot. Add the onions and sauté until golden brown, about 4 to 5 minutes. Set aside and keep warm. Season the liver with salt and pepper and pan-broil in a heated heavy skillet that has been greased with peanut oil until brown, about 3 to 4 minutes on each side. Do not overcook. Serve smothered with sautéed onions.

Smothered Swiss Steak Hunter-Style

MAKES 8 SERVINGS

Braising in a tomato-rich sauce adds flavor and tenderizes the meat. Smothered in this tasty sauce, it is a model of African-American food.

8 pounds beef round steak,
   cut into 5-ounce pieces
1/4 cup peanut oil
1/4 cup diced onion
3/4 cup sliced button mushrooms
3 cloves garlic, minced
1/4 cup all-purpose flour
2 cups Veal (Brown) Stock
   (see page 281)
1 1/4 cups tomato puree
1 3/4 cups canned whole
   tomatoes, chopped
1/2 tablespoon chopped fresh
   basil
1/2 tablespoon chopped fresh
   oregano
1 bay leaf
Salt and freshly ground
   black pepper to taste

Preheat the oven to 325°.

Pat the steak pieces dry. In a large skillet, heat the oil over high heat and cook the steaks until brown, about 1 minute per side. Remove the steaks from the skillet and place in a baking pan. Add the onion, mushrooms, and garlic to the skillet and sauté until lightly brown. Stir in the flour to make a roux. Cook and stir until the roux is brown, about 3 to 4 minutes. Stir in the stock, tomato puree, and chopped tomatoes. Allow to simmer until the sauce thickens. Add the basil, oregano, bay leaf, and salt and pepper to taste. Pour the sauce over the steak, cover, and cook until the steaks are tender, 1 1/2 to 2 hours. Strain off any fat and serve hot with sauce napped over the steaks.

SOUTHERN BRAISED OXTAILS

MAKES 8 SERVINGS

In France, boned, stuffed oxtails are a way to turn a thrifty meat into superlative eating. Oxtail ragout is another treatment. But if you are looking for something more home-style and simple, braised oxtails are just the thing. It's another variation on the smothered theme.

5 pounds oxtails, trimmed

1 cup all-purpose flour

$1/2$ teaspoon salt

$1/2$ teaspoon freshly ground
   black pepper

$1/4$ cup peanut oil

1 small onion, diced

4 cloves garlic, minced

1 medium carrot, diced

1 rib celery, diced

$1^1/2$ quarts Veal (Brown) Stock
   (see page 281)

$3/4$ cup tomato puree

1 bay leaf

1 sprig fresh thyme

Salt and freshly ground
   black pepper to taste

Preheat the oven to 350°F.

Cut the oxtails into 2-inch pieces or have the butcher do it for you.

In a bowl, combine the flour, salt, and pepper. Dredge the oxtails in the seasoned flour, reserving $1/4$ cup. Heat the oil in a large skillet over high heat and brown the oxtails evenly on all sides. Remove from skillet to a heatproof casserole. Stir the onion, garlic, carrot, and celery into the skillet and cook over medium-high heat until lightly brown. Stir in the $1/4$ cup reserved flour to make a roux. Reduce the heat and cook until the roux is brown, about 3 to 4 minutes. Add the stock, stir, and simmer until the gravy thickens, 10 to 15 minutes. Add the tomato puree, bay leaf, and thyme, and season with salt and pepper to taste.

Pour the gravy over the oxtails, cover, and braise in until the oxtails are tender, about 3 hours. Remove from the gravy and keep warm in the residual heat of the oven. Strain the gravy and remove any fat. Correct the seasoning and reduce to the desired consistency, if necessary. Place equal portions of oxtails on each plate and nap with gravy. Serve hot with Hoppin' John (page 89) and Stewed Okra and Tomatoes (page 110).

John Harrison's Grilled Sirloin Steak à la Johnny

Sometimes our menus cry out for steak smothered in a rich gravy, served with favorite vegetables that have been cooked Southern style. Other times, a steak with the sauce served on the side is even better.

Four 10-ounce sirloin steaks
1 teaspoon salt
1 teaspoon freshly ground
   black pepper
1 tablespoon butter
1 tablespoon olive oil
1 small onion, sliced
$^1/_2$ cup sliced button mushrooms
$^1/_4$ cup sliced red peppers
$^1/_4$ cup sliced green peppers

Season the steaks with salt and pepper and grill over hot coals to the desired doneness, 4 to 5 minutes per side for rare.

In a sauté pan, heat the butter and olive oil, add the onion, mushrooms, and red and green peppers. Sauté until tender. Place the steak on plates and garnish with the sautéed vegetables.

STUFFED SIRLOIN OF BEEF
WITH WILD MUSHROOM SAUCE

This dish made quite an impression at the American Academy of Chefs dinner at Town and Gown, on the campus of the University of Southern California.

4 pounds sirloin strip loin, completely trimmed, tip removed

STUFFING
1 tablespoon butter
2 large shallots, minced
1 clove garlic, minced
1 pound cremini mushrooms, diced
1 teaspoon chopped fresh tarragon leaves
2 cups fresh bread crumbs
$^1/_2$ cup Veal (Brown) Stock (see page 281)
Salt and freshly ground pepper
8 slices country bacon

WILD MUSHROOM SAUCE
2 tablespoons butter
1 large shallot, minced
$^1/_4$ pound porcini mushrooms, sliced
$^1/_4$ pound chanterelle mushrooms, sliced
$^1/_2$ pound cremini mushrooms, sliced
Salt and freshly ground pepper
2 tablespoons all-purpose flour
2 cups Veal (Brown) Stock (see page 281)
$^1/_4$ cup dry sherry
$^1/_2$ tablespoon chopped parsley

Preheat the broiler.

Remove all the fat from the piece of sirloin strip and cut into it into eight 8-ounce pieces. Place one piece at a time between two pieces of plastic wrap. With a cleaver or mallet, flatten each piece evenly and set aside.

For the stuffing, heat the butter in a skillet and sauté the shallots and garlic 1 minute. Add the mushrooms and continue to sauté 4 to 5 minutes. Add the chopped tarragon and bread crumbs, stir, and remove from the heat. Stir in the stock, season with salt and pepper to taste, and mix well. Spoon the mushroom filling over each steak piece. Roll tightly and wrap each with a slice of bacon. Broil 2 to 3 minutes on all sides under on a hot broiler. Reduce the oven heat to 350°F. Place the steaks in a baking pan and finish cooking in the oven for 3 to 4 minutes. Slice each stuffed steak across the grain on a cutting board.

For the sauce, heat the butter in a saucepan over medium-high heat and sauté the shallots 1 minute. Add the mushrooms, season with salt and pepper, and sauté 3 to 4 minutes. Stir in the flour and then the stock. Bring to a boil, reduce the heat to simmer, and cook for 30 minutes. Add the sherry and chopped fresh parsley. Adjust the seasoning with salt and pepper to taste and simmer 4 to 5 minutes. Keep warm until serving time.

Spoon some wild mushroom sauce on a heated dinner plate and arrange the sliced steak on the sauce. Serve hot.

Prince Akins's Carpetbagger Steak

If you like oysters, you'll love the surprise tucked in these steaks. They are sublime.

Six 10-ounce center-cut filet
    mignon steaks
18 Eastern oysters, shucked,
    with their liquor
$^1/_2$ teaspoon salt
$^1/_4$ teaspoon freshly ground
    black pepper
1 tablespoon fresh lemon juice
$^1/_8$ teaspoon cayenne pepper
$^1/_4$ teaspoon celery salt
2 dashes hot red pepper sauce
1 tablespoon chopped fresh
    parsley
2 tablespoons butter
Splash chardonnay, about
    2 tablespoons

Cut a horizontal slit in each filet to make a pocket. Place the oysters in a bowl and season with salt, black pepper, lemon juice, cayenne pepper, celery salt, hot red pepper sauce, and parsley. Set aside 6 oysters, then insert 2 oysters into each filet.

On a hot grill or under a heated broiler, cook the filets to the desired doneness, about 4 to 6 minutes on each side.

Heat the butter in a sauté pan and sauté the reserved oysters 1 to 2 minutes. Add the oyster liquor and chardonnay and cook until the oysters begin to curl at the edges. Remove from the heat. Place a sautéed oyster and a little sauce on top of each filet and serve with Mom Pan's Green Beans (page 102) and Fried Corn (page 99).

Lamb

BRAISED LAMB SHANKS WITH RAGOUT OF WHITE BEANS, SWEET CORN, AND BABY CARROTS

MAKES 8 SERVINGS

Here's another example of a simple, inexpensive meat that is transformed into something so flavorful and tender you would expect to pay a fortune for it in a restaurant. Serve it at a lunch or supper for friends. All that's needed is a crisp salad and crusty bread.

1 cup all-purpose flour
$^1/_2$ teaspoon salt
$^1/_2$ teaspoon freshly ground
   black pepper
$^1/_4$ teaspoon cayenne pepper
8 lamb shanks, trimmed
$^1/_4$ cup olive oil
1 rib celery, diced
1 medium carrot, diced
1 medium onion, diced
2 cloves garlic, chopped
1 quart Veal (Brown) Stock
   (see page 281)
1 cup burgundy
1 cup canned whole tomatoes,
   chopped
2 teaspoons dried Greek
   oregano, crumbled
1 bay leaf
Salt and freshly ground black
   pepper to taste

Preheat the oven to 325°F.

In a bowl combine the flour, salt, and black and cayenne peppers. Dredge the lamb shanks in the seasoned flour, reserving $^1/_4$ cup. Heat the oil in a large skillet over high heat and brown the shanks evenly on all sides. Remove from the skillet to a heatproof casserole. Add the celery, carrot, onion, and garlic to the skillet and sauté until lightly brown. Stir in the reserved flour to make a roux. Reduce the heat and cook until the roux is brown, about 3 to 4 minutes. Stir in the stock and wine and simmer until the gravy thickens, about 10 to 15 minutes. Add the tomatoes, oregano, and bay leaf and season with salt and pepper to taste. Pour the gravy over the lamb shanks, cover, and braise in the oven until the shanks are tender, about $2^1/_2$ hours.

When the shanks are almost done make the ragout. Melt the butter in a skillet and sauté the onion 1 to 2 minutes. Stir in the corn, carrots, and beans, and heat through.

RAGOUT

1 tablespoon butter

1 small onion, minced

1 cup fresh sweet corn kernels, cooked (about 3 ears)

24 baby carrots, cooked

2 cups dried white beans, cooked (see page 113 for procedure)

Salt and freshly ground black pepper to taste

Remove the shanks from the gravy and keep warm. Strain the gravy removing any fat, correct the seasoning with salt and pepper, and add more stock if the sauce is too thick. Spoon some ragout in the center of each serving plate, top with a lamb shank, and nap gravy over the shank. Serve hot.

Pan-broiled Lamb Chops
with Roasted Garlic Sauce

MAKES 6 SERVINGS

As a very young man I learned to enjoy the taste of lamb. It has always been one of my favorite meats.

24 cloves garlic

1 tablespoon olive oil

12 lamb loin chops cut $1/2$ inch thick, trimmed, fat reserved

1 teaspoon salt

1 teaspoon freshly ground black pepper

$1/4$ cup water

$1^1/_2$ cups burgundy

1 large shallot, chopped

1 sprig rosemary

Salt and freshly ground black pepper to taste

1 tablespoon butter, softened

Preheat the oven to 350°F.

Coat the garlic cloves with olive oil, place in a baking pan, and roast in the oven for 8 to 10 minutes. Remove and puree; set aside.

Thoroughly heat a large skillet over high heat and melt enough lamb fat from the chops to coat the bottom of the skillet. Sear the lamb chops quickly until they are brown on both sides and season with salt and pepper to taste. Reduce the heat to medium and continue to cook to the desired doneness. Transfer to a warm platter and keep warm.

Pour off any fat, deglaze the skillet with the water, add the burgundy, shallot, pureed garlic, and rosemary. Bring to a boil, then cook over medium heat until reduced by half. Season with salt and pepper to taste. Just before serving, finish the sauce by stirring in butter until it melts. Place 2 lamb chops warmed dinner plates in a pool of sauce.

Roasted Leg of Lamb with Garlic, Rosemary, and Natural Gravy

MAKES 6 TO 8 SERVINGS

This dish is one of my sister Mary Francis's favorites. She cooked roast lamb often and I enjoyed it as much as she did. Now my children request it too.

One 6- to 7-pound leg of lamb, trimmed, boned, and trussed
6 cloves garlic, sliced into slivers
1 teaspoon salt
1 teaspoon freshly ground black pepper
$^1/_4$ cup olive oil
1 tablespoon chopped fresh rosemary
$^1/_4$ cup all-purpose flour
2 cups Lamb Stock (see page 280)
Salt and freshly ground black pepper to taste

Preheat the oven to 375°F.

With a sharp knife, make thin slits in the leg of lamb. Insert pieces of garlic in the slits. Season the lamb with salt and pepper and rub all over with the olive oil and rosemary. Place the lamb on a rack and roast in the oven until it reaches an internal temperature of 140°F for medium-rare, about $1^1/_4$ to $1^1/_2$ hours. Transfer to a warm platter and let rest 8 to 10 minutes before carving.

Strain the pan juices, skimming off the fat, and reserve $^1/_4$ cup of the fat. In a saucepan, heat the reserved fat over medium heat and stir in reserved flour to make a roux. Cook until brown, then gradually stir in the pan juices and stock and stir until smooth. Adjust the seasoning with salt and pepper to taste. Serve hot over slices of roast lamb.

Veal

PAN-BROILED VEAL CHOPS
WITH SAUTÉED WILD MUSHROOMS

MAKES 6 SERVINGS

The tender white flesh of young calves needs very little preparation, as you will see from this dish.
Wild mushrooms are a richly flavored accompaniment.

2 tablespoons olive oil

6 veal loin chops

1 teaspoon salt

1 teaspoon freshly ground pepper

1½ cups Sautéed Wild
Mushrooms (see page 107)

Heat a large skillet over high heat until hot, then coat the bottom of the skillet with olive oil. Sear the veal chops quickly until they are brown on both sides. Season with salt and pepper to taste. Reduce the heat and continue to cook to the desired doneness. Transfer to a warm platter. Serve hot with Sautéed Wild Mushrooms.

VEAL SWEETBREADS ON VIRGINIA HAM WITH MUSHROOM CREAM SAUCE

MAKES 6 SERVINGS

One pair of sweetbreads is all you'll need to serve two guests. Sweetbreads are the tender and tasty thymus gland of a cow.

3 pairs veal sweetbreads
4 cups Chicken Stock
   (see page 279)
3 slices Smithfield ham, cut
   in half
5 tablespoons butter
2 tablespoons olive oil
2 eggs, lightly beaten
1 cup all-purpose flour
$^1/_2$ teaspoon salt
$^1/_2$ teaspoon freshly ground
   black pepper

MUSHROOM CREAM SAUCE

1 tablespoon minced shallots
1 pound button mushrooms,
   sliced
$^1/_3$ cup dry sherry
$1^1/_2$ cups heavy cream
2 teaspoons chopped fresh parsley
Salt and freshly ground
   black pepper to taste

In a bowl, soak the sweetbreads in cold water to cover for 1 hour. Drain well and remove the pink membrane from them.

In a saucepan, heat the chicken stock to a simmer. Place the sweetbreads in the stock and cook for 20 minutes. Remove from the stock and shock in an ice water bath to stop the cooking. Trim the sweetbreads of any tubes, remaining membrane, and any discolored sections. Drain the cooled sweetbreads well. Cut into serving portions.

If the ham is salty, soak the slice in water for 30 minutes to 1 hour. Drain and pat dry. Cut the fat around the edges to keep it from curling. Cook the slices on both sides in a heavy skillet over low heat until brown and tender, about 20 minutes. Set aside on a warm platter.

Heat the butter and oil in a skillet. Dip the sweetbreads in the beaten eggs, then in the flour, and sauté on both sides until evenly brown, about 4 to 5 minutes. Season with salt and pepper and transfer to a heated platter.

To make the sauce, remove all but 3 tablespoons of the butter and oil mixture from the skillet. Add the shallots and sauté 2 to 3 minutes. Add the mushrooms and continue to cook until the moisture has evaporated from the skillet. Add the sherry and cook over high heat until reduced by half. Add the cream and parsley and simmer until the sauce thickens. Season with salt and pepper to taste.

Place a slice of ham on a warmed serving plate and arrange half a pair of sweetbreads on top of the ham. Nap with mushroom sauce and serve hot.

Sautéed Calf's Liver with Slab Bacon and Country Fried Apples

One bite of liver garnished with chewy bacon and sweet apples and you will have plenty of reason to indulge in this dish again and again.

16 slices slab bacon, thickly sliced

2 pounds calf's liver in $^1/_2$-inch-thick slices, cut in half

1 teaspoon salt

1 teaspoon freshly ground black pepper

$1^1/_2$ cups all-purpose flour

$^1/_4$ cup ($^1/_2$ stick) butter

2 cups Country Fried Apples (see page 93)

In a heated skillet over medium-high heat, fry the bacon until brown and crisp, drain on paper towels, and set aside. Pour off all but $^1/_4$ cup of bacon drippings. Season the liver with salt and pepper. Dredge in the flour and shake off any excess. Add the butter to the pan with the drippings and sauté the liver until brown, about 2 minutes on each side, being careful not to overcook. Serve hot, sprinkled with bacon and with Country Fried Apples.

CHEF'S TIP
Creamed Potatoes (page 95) go well with this dish.

Pork

AUNT DOLLY'S STUFFED PORK CHOPS

MAKES 8 SERVINGS

Aunt Dolly used to make this dish for people she loved. It's one you will remember.

$^1/_4$ cup ($^1/_2$ stick) butter

1 medium onion, minced

2 ribs celery, minced

2 cups $^1/_2$-inch stale bread cubes

1 tablespoon chopped fresh
    parsley

1 teaspoon dried sage, crumbled

1 teaspoon salt

$^1/_4$ teaspoon ground white pepper

$^1/_8$ teaspoon cayenne pepper

1 cup Smoked Ham Stock
    (see page 281)

Eight $^3/_4$-inch-thick center cut
    loin pork chops, with pocket

Salt and freshly ground
    black pepper to taste

2 teaspoons paprika

MADEIRA SAUCE

$^1/_4$ cup all-purpose flour

3 cups Smoked Ham Stock
    (see page 281)

$^1/_4$ cup Madeira

$^1/_4$ teaspoon salt

$^1/_4$ teaspoon ground white pepper

Preheat the oven to 350°F.

In a skillet or sauté pan, melt the butter and sauté the onion and celery until tender-crisp, about 3 to 4 minutes. In a bowl, combine the bread cubes and sautéed onion and celery, tossing to mix. Add the parsley, sage, salt, and white and cayenne pepper and continue to toss. Add the stock to the stuffing, a little at a time, mixing well to moisten.

Season the pork chops with salt and pepper. Fill the pockets with stuffing and place the chops stuffing side down in a well-greased baking pan. Sprinkle with paprika and bake in the oven until cooked through, about 30 to 40 minutes. Remove the chops from the pan and keep warm.

For the sauce, add the flour to the pan, stirring to make a roux, and cook over medium heat until brown. Stir in the stock, then add the Madeira and bring to a boil. Reduce the heat, simmer 15 to 20 minutes, season with salt and pepper, strain, and serve over pork chops.

BAKED SPARERIBS AND SAUERKRAUT

MAKES 6 TO 8 SERVINGS

*Growing up in central Pennsylvania you learn to enjoy Pennsylvania Dutch cooking.
Sauerkraut is a big part of that cuisine, served in many ways—on hot dogs, with sausage,
with pork—and my favorite, with baked spareribs.*

4 pounds spareribs, cut into
   pieces
1 teaspoon salt
1 teaspoon freshly ground
   black pepper
8 cups Braised Sauerkraut
   (see page 90)

Preheat the oven to 350°F.

Season the spareribs with salt and pepper on both sides. Place on a
rack in a roasting pan and roast in the oven until the meat is tender,
$1^1/_2$ to 2 hours, turning when half the cooking time has passed.

When the spareribs are done, place them in a large casserole, cover
with Braised Sauerkraut, and bake for 30 minutes. Serve hot with
Creamed Potatoes (page 95) and Country Fried Apples (page 93).

BARBECUED BONELESS PIG'S FEET

MAKES 4 TO 6 SERVINGS

*I love pig's feet but I do not like having to work so hard to eat them. That is the
beauty of this dish: All you have to do is slice and eat.*

6 pig's feet, washed and split
3 quarts cold water
1 teaspoon salt
$^1/_4$ cup cider vinegar
1 bay leaf
1 small onion, quartered
2 ribs celery, coarsely chopped
4 cups Backyard Barbecue Sauce
   (see page 284)

Wash the pig's feet and place in a large stockpot. Cover with the water
and bring to a boil. Reduce the heat and simmer for 1 hour, skimming
as needed. Add the salt, vinegar, bay leaf, onion, and celery. Add more
water if needed to make sure that pig's feet are covered. Return to a
boil, then reduce the heat to simmer and continue to cook until the
feet are tender, 1 to $1^1/_2$ hours. Remove the feet from the broth and
set aside to cool.

Preheat the oven to 350°F.

Remove the bones from the feet and arrange the meat in the shape of a
log, place in a baking pan, and cover with warmed Backyard Barbecue
Sauce. Bake in the oven until thoroughly heated, about 20 to 30 minutes. Serve hot with Down-home Potato Salad (page 60), Southern
Collard Greens (page 109), and Country Corn Bread (page 228).

Chaurice Sausage
(Louisiana Hot Sausage)

MAKES 3 1/2 TO 4 POUNDS

The best chaurice I have found outside of Louisiana is made at a little place called Pete's Hot Links on Jefferson Boulevard in Los Angeles. Most of the barbecue houses either buy from Pete or they make their own. This one tastes similar to Pete's.

2¹/₂ pounds pork butt, cut into strips

1 pound pork fatback, cut into strips

5 teaspoons coarse sea salt

1 medium onion, minced

6 cloves garlic, minced

2 tablespoons paprika

1 tablespoon chili powder

3 teaspoons cayenne pepper

2 teaspoons red pepper flakes

1 teaspoon freshly ground black pepper

1 teaspoon ground allspice

2 teaspoons chopped fresh thyme

¹/₂ cup minced fresh flat-leaf parsley

1 package pork casings, rinsed (about ¹/₄ pound)

Pass the pork and fatback strips through a meat grinder using the medium holes. Place the pork and fat mixture in a large bowl with the salt, onion, garlic, paprika, chili powder, cayenne pepper, red pepper flakes, black pepper, allspice, thyme, and parsley. Mix well. Cook a small amount of the mixture in a skillet to test the flavor. Adjust the seasoning, if needed.

Pass this mixture through the grinder set on medium, cover, and refrigerate for 2 hours. Tie a knot in one end of the casings. Use a stuffing horn to pack the mixture into the casings by hand. If your mixer has a sausage attachment, remove the hole attachment from the grinder and attach the special sausage horn to it. Slide a casing onto the horn and tie the end. Pass the sausage through the grinder, holding the casing as it is filled. When 8 inches of the casing have been filled, twist to form a link. Continue filling and twisting every 8 inches until done. Refrigerate until ready to cook.

Prick the sausage all over with a fork so it does not burst. Chaurice may be fried for breakfast; cut into pieces, fried, and added to gumbo or jambalaya; or served with red bean and rice. In California it is grilled and napped with barbecue sauce.

CHAURICE SAUSAGE WITH
LOUISIANA RED BEANS AND RICE

MAKES 8 SERVINGS

One of my favorite Creole recipes is red beans and rice. I love it with chaurice sausage.
It also goes well with pan-broiled pork chops.

1 pound dried red beans

2 ham hocks, split

2 quarts Smoked Ham Stock
    (see page 281)

2 bay leaves

1 teaspoon chopped fresh thyme

1 teaspoon cayenne pepper

1 teaspoon fresh ground
    black pepper

2 tablespoons bacon drippings

1 pound smoked hot sausage,
    diced

1 cup finely diced onions

$^1/_2$ cup finely diced celery

2 tablespoons minced garlic

$^1/_2$ cup minced green pepper

1 bunch green onions, minced

2 tablespoons chopped fresh
    parsley

2 pounds (eight 4-ounce links)
    Chaurice Sausage (see page
    201)

Salt and freshly ground black
    pepper to taste

4 cups Steamed Buttered Rice
    (see page 114)

Wash the red beans and soak overnight in water. Drain and place the red beans and ham hocks in a large stockpot. Cover completely with stock. Bring the pot to a boil, cover, and reduce the heat to simmer. Add the bay leaves, thyme, and cayenne and black pepper and allow to simmer for about 1 hour to form a concentrated flavor or until ham hock meat easily pulls away from the bone. Remove the ham hocks from the pot, remove and discard skin, dice the ham into small pieces, and return the pieces to the pot.

Heat the bacon drippings in a skillet and sauté the diced sausage for 3 to 4 minutes. Add the onions, celery, and garlic and continue to sauté for 5 to 6 minutes. Add the green pepper, green onions, and parsley and sauté 3 minutes. Add to the pot of red beans and continue to cook the seasoned beans until they are tender, about 1 hour.

Place the Chaurice Sausage links in a skillet and cook over medium heat for 15 to 20 minutes, turning to brown evenly on all sides. Correct the seasoning with salt and black pepper to taste. Place $^1/_2$ cup hot Steamed Buttered Rice on a warm plate. Spoon some red beans over the rice. Arrange a sausage on a plate with Mom Pan's Candied Sweet Potatoes (page 101).

CHITTERLING SAUSAGE

MAKES 5 POUNDS; ABOUT TWENTY 4$^1/_2$-OUNCE LINKS

Most people are surprised to find chit'lins are popular in so many other cultures. When my wife, Barbara, and I were in Hawaii, we dined on kalua pig, lomi salmon, and poi at Uno's Hawaiian food in Honolulu. The owner, upon discovering I was a chef, quickly emerged from the kitchen with a bowl of chitterlings cooked with taro leaves, a tradition only the family ate. This dish is from the Normandy region of France where it is called andouillettes and is served grilled.

5 pounds Simmered Chitterlings Country Style with Hog Maws (see page 214)

$^1/_4$ cup ($^1/_2$ stick) butter

1 medium onion, diced

3 cloves garlic, minced

1 cup diced Roasted Red Peppers (see page 272)

1 cup cider vinegar

1 teaspoon red pepper flakes

1 teaspoon salt

1 teaspoon freshly ground black pepper

1 package pork casings, rinsed (about $^1/_4$ pound)

Grind the chitterlings and hog maws through the large holes in a meat grinder. Melt 2 tablespoons of the butter in a large sauté pan over medium high heat. Add onion and sauté 2 to 3 minutes, but do not brown. Stir in the garlic and roasted red peppers and remove from the heat and mix with the chitterlings. Combine $^1/_2$ cup of the cider vinegar and the red pepper flakes, stir, then add the chitterlings mixture, salt, and pepper and mix well. Cook a small amount of the mixture in a hot skillet to check the flavor. Adjust the seasoning if needed. Refrigerate for 2 hours, then stuff into casings by hand or using a sausage-making attachment for the mixer (see Chaurice Sausage, page 201, or Rabbit Sausage, page 175).

Prick the sausage with a fork to prevent it from bursting while poaching. In a large saucepan, bring water to a boil, reduce the heat to simmer, and add the remaining vinegar and salt and pepper. Poach the sausage for 15 minutes. Remove from the heat and let the sausage cool in the liquid, then remove and refrigerate.

To serve, melt the remaining 2 tablespoons of butter in a skillet over medium heat and brown the sausage on all sides until heated through, or grill evenly over medium coals.

Serve with Fried Cornmeal Mush (page 98) and Smothered Cabbage (page 109).

COUNTRY SAUSAGE

MAKES 6 SERVINGS

You just can't beat sausage you make yourself. Your entire family will enjoy this sausage at breakfast or stirred into vegetables as a seasoning.

2$^1/_4$ pounds lean ground pork
2 teaspoons dried sage, crumbled
3 cloves garlic, minced
1 tablespoon minced fresh parsley
2 teaspoons salt
1 teaspoon freshly ground
   black pepper
1 teaspoon cayenne pepper

In a large bowl, combine the pork, sage, garlic, parsley, salt, and black and cayenne peppers, mixing thoroughly with your hands. Shape the sausage into 3-ounce patties or stuff the sausage into casings, twisting or tieing into 3-inch links.

GRILLED SPARERIBS
WITH BACKYARD BARBECUE SAUCE

MAKES 6 TO 8 SERVINGS

If you want to start a debate, just ask two cooks what is the best way to achieve the tastiest ribs. Some people think it's in the spice; others say a marinade makes them their moist, delicious best. That's what makes the difference between rib joints.

One of the best, K. C. Barbecue in Berkeley, California, uses a dry rub like this one. If you're ever in the neighborhood, stop in and tell them Chef Randall suggested you give them a try.

3 slabs spareribs, about 7 to
   9 pounds
3 tablespoons salt
1 tablespoon sugar
2 teaspoons freshly ground
   black pepper
2 teaspoons dried thyme leaves,
   crumbled
1 teaspoon allspice
2 teaspoons chili powder
1 teaspoon cayenne pepper
2 teaspoons onion powder
2 teaspoons garlic powder
6 cups Backyard Barbecue Sauce
   (see page 284)

Trim the excess fat from the ribs.

In a bowl, combine salt, sugar, black pepper, thyme, allspice, chili powder, cayenne pepper, and onion and garlic powders. Rub evenly over the spareribs. Place the ribs in a shallow pan, cover, and refrigerate for at least 2 hours or overnight.

Place the grill rack about 6 inches above the coals. Place ribs meat side down on the rack. Cover the grill but open the vents to allow some heat to escape so the ribs will cook slowly. Grill the ribs for 30 to 45 minutes, then turn and continue to cook on the other side until the meat is tender, about 30 to 45 minutes. Turn the ribs and brush on a heavy coating of Backyard Barbecue Sauce, cover, and cook 2 to 3 minutes. Turn and coat the other side. Cover again and cook 2 to 3 minutes more. Remove from the heat, cut the ribs into serving pieces and serve hot, piled on a plate napped with sauce.

Mom Pan's Baked Ham

MAKES 10 TO 14 SERVINGS

This was a family tradition in the Randall household. The ham would grace Easter tables and Sunday and birthday dinners—in fact, almost any holiday or special dinner. There was always enough left over for a big, juicy sandwich or for ham and eggs and biscuits the next morning.

3 cups ginger ale
$^1/_2$ teaspoon ground cloves
$^3/_4$ cup packed dark brown sugar
One 8- to 10-pound bone-in smoked ham

Preheat the oven to 350°F.

Bring the ginger ale, cloves, and brown sugar to a boil in a saucepan. Reduce the heat and simmer 4 to 5 minutes. Remove from the heat and set aside.

Trim the excess fat from the ham and score the ham with a knife. Place it on a rack in a roasting pan and pour the ginger-ale mixture over the ham. Bake in the oven for $1^1/_2$ to 2 hours, basting often. Remove the ham from the roasting pan and place on a cutting board to rest for 5 minutes before carving.

CHEF'S TIP
If you line your roasting pan with foil, it will make clean up easier.

Patrick Yves Pierre-Jerome's Medallions of Pork Tenderloin with Black Bean Sauce

Pierre accepted an invitation to participate in the third An Elegant Taste of Heritage benefit dinner, held in Washington, D.C., at the Grand Hyatt Hotel. This dish was his contribution to the menu. If you don't have a hinged basket, just spoon a tablespoon of the onions on top of the pork.

2 tablespoons olive oil

$^1/_8$ teaspoon salt

$^1/_8$ teaspoon freshly ground black pepper

Twelve 2-ounce pork tenderloin medallions

Vegetable oil

$^1/_2$ bunch parsley, washed and dried

1 leek, washed thoroughly and julienned

4 small square wonton skins

2 cups Black Bean Sauce (recipe follows)

1 cup Mushroom and Onion Compote (see page 271)

Mix the olive oil, salt, and pepper and toss the pork medallions in it. Grill over a hot fire to the desired doneness, being careful not to over cook.

Heat the vegetable oil in a deep-fryer to 350°F. Drop the parsley in the hot oil and deep-fry for 15 seconds. Remove from the oil and spread out on paper towels to drain. Keep warm for plate presentation. Cool the oil to 275°F. Fry the leeks until golden, about 2 minutes. Spread the leeks out on paper towels to drain.

Increase the oil temperature to 350°F. Place a wonton skin in a small potato nest, mold, and fry until golden. Repeat with remaining 3 skins. Mix the parsley and leeks.

To serve, pour Black Bean Sauce on a serving plate. Arrange pork medallions on the plate at 12, 4, and 8 o'clock. Spoon Mushroom and Onion Compote into a wonton cup. Place the cup in the center of the plate. Place a mound of the parsley and leek mixture on top of the cup. Serve immediately.

Patrick Yves Pierre-Jerome's Black Bean Sauce

MAKES 2 CUPS

1 tablespoon minced garlic

2 tablespoons extra-virgin
olive oil

One 11-ounce can black beans

One 11-ounce can creamed
corn

$^1/_4$ cup chopped, cooked
smoked bacon

1 tablespoon chopped fresh
thyme

$^1/_2$ tablespoon chopped fresh
sage

1 cup diced tomatoes

$^1/_4$ cup tomato puree

$^1/_2$ cup water

Salt and freshly ground
black pepper to taste

Sauté the garlic in the olive oil and add the remaining ingredients, stirring constantly over high heat to prevent scorching. Once the mixture is hot, stir and cover. Cook for 2 minutes. Season with salt and pepper. Keep warm until ready to serve.

Neck-bone Fricassee with Cuban Black Beans and Rice

Dozens of generations of African-American children have grown up cutting their teeth on neck bones. They epitomize "soul food."

4 pounds fresh pork neck bones, cut into pieces
$^1/_2$ teaspoon salt
$^1/_2$ teaspoon freshly ground pepper
$^1/_2$ teaspoon dried sage, crumbled
$^1/_2$ cup peanut oil
1 medium onion, diced
$^1/_2$ cup all-purpose flour
1 bay leaf
1 sprig fresh sage
2 egg yolks
$^2/_3$ cup heavy cream
2 tablespoons sherry vinegar
$^1/_4$ teaspoon ground allspice
Salt and freshly ground black pepper to taste
4 cups Cuban Black Beans and Rice (see page 96)

Preheat the oven to 325°F.

Season the neck bones with salt, pepper, and dried sage. In a large skillet, heat the oil over medium heat and sauté the neck bones and onion in batches on all sides until browned well. Remove the neck bones. Stir in the flour to make a roux and cook 3 to 4 minutes, then return the bones to the pan and add enough water to cover. Bring to a boil and stir. Reduce the heat and simmer until the sauce thickens. Add the bay leaf and fresh sage, cover, and braise in the oven until the neck bones are tender, 1 to $1^1/_2$ hours. Remove from the sauce, set aside, and keep warm.

Degrease the sauce. Reduce by one quarter over high heat until it reaches the desired consistency. Strain. In a small bowl, combine egg yolks and cream. Stir a small amount of hot sauce into egg yolks to temper it and add it to the sauce. Bring to just below a simmer, do not boil. Season with the vinegar, allspice, and salt and pepper to taste. Pour the sauce over the neck bones and serve hot with Cuban Black Beans and Rice.

Pan-fried Pork Chops Smothered in Creole Sauce

MAKES 8 SERVINGS

It is amazing how adding a spicy, Creole-inspired sauce can give pork chops a new attitude and a silky new texture.

$^1/_4$ cup peanut oil

$^1/_2$ cup all-purpose flour

$^1/_2$ teaspoon salt

$^1/_4$ teaspoon cayenne pepper

Eight 6-ounce center cut loin pork chops

3 cups Creole Sauce (see page 287)

Preheat the oven to 325°F.

Heat the oil in a skillet over medium-high heat. In a bowl combine the flour, salt, and pepper. Dust the pork chops in the flour, shaking off any excess. Fry chops in the hot oil until brown, about 3 to 4 minutes on each side. Remove the chops from the skillet, place in a baking pan, and pour Creole Sauce over them. Cover and cook in the oven until the chops are tender, about 45 to 50 minutes. Correct the seasoning, if needed. Serve hot with Steamed Buttered Rice (page 114).

Patrick Clark's Roasted Rack of Pork with Cider-Pepper Glaze

Pork has always been part of American culture, but it is experiencing a resurgence of interest, now that farmers are producing leaner hogs. This is a modern interpretation of a very old dish.

1 cup olive oil

1 tablespoon fresh rosemary

1 tablespoon fresh thyme

1 tablespoon fresh sage

1 tablespoon fresh savory

4 cloves garlic, chopped

3 pork rib racks with 8 ribs each

Salt to taste

Olive oil to sear meat

2 cups Cider-Pepper Glaze
   (recipe follows)

Combine the oil, herbs, and garlic and rub all over the pork racks. Refrigerate overnight.

Preheat the oven to 325°F.

Remove the pork from the marinade and wipe off and discard all the herbs and garlic. Season the racks with salt. Heat some olive oil in a large skillet and sear the ribs on all sides until brown, about 10 minutes. Place meat on a roasting rack and cook in the oven about 40 minutes. Increase heat to 350°F and brush with Cider-Pepper Glaze. Cook an additional 10 to 15 minutes, brushing and basting with the glaze. Remove to a platter and let rest before carving into chops.

Patrick Clark's Cider-Pepper Glaze

1 quart unsweetened dry
   apple cider

1 Rome apple, peeled, cored,
   and cut into chunks

1/4 cup cider vinegar

1/4 cup honey

2 teaspoons mustard seed

5 juniper berries, crushed

3 cloves garlic, minced

2 sprigs fresh thyme

1 tablespoon cracked peppercorns

Combine the cider, apple, vinegar, honey, mustard seed, juniper berries, garlic, and thyme in a saucepan and bring to a boil. Reduce the heat to simmer and cook for 20 minutes. Strain into a clean pot. Add the peppercorns and reduce over medium-high heat to a thick consistency. Serve at room temperature. Store covered in the refrigerator. This glaze will keep refrigerated for 3 to 4 days.

CLIFTON WILLIAMS'S ROAST RACK OF PORK WITH MADEIRA JUS LIE

MAKES 6 SERVINGS

Clifton wanted to create a dish that was upscale, but still affordable. This dish has all the character of a rack of lamb, but costs much less. To get a pork rack, have the butcher trim the fat cap from a center-cut pork loin roast. French the pork ribs by slicing between the ribs and removing all the meat up to 1 inch from the end.

2 cloves garlic, minced

1 teaspoon salt

$^1/_2$ teaspoon freshly ground black pepper

$^1/_2$ teaspoon cayenne pepper

2 teaspoons paprika

1 tablespoon water

2 pork rib racks with 8 ribs frenched

$^1/_2$ cup Madeira

2 tablespoons butter, softened

Salt and freshly ground black pepper to taste

Preheat the oven to 350°F.

In a small bowl, mix the garlic, salt, black and cayenne pepper, paprika, and water to make a paste. Rub evenly over the pork, then place racks fat side down in a roasting pan. Roast in the oven for 25 minutes. Turn the racks bone side down and finish cooking for an additional 20 minutes. Remove from the oven and set aside to rest for 15 minutes before slicing.

Strain the pan juices and degrease. Place the pan over medium-high heat and deglaze pan with the Madeira, cooking until reduced by half. Add the strained juices and simmer 2 to 3 minutes. Stir in the butter to finish the sauce. Season with salt and pepper to taste. Arrange 3 slices of pork on a plate with Garlicky Mashed Potatoes with Leeks (page 100) and Black-eyed Pea Salsa (page 267). Nap the pork with jus lie.

SAUTÉED BONELESS PIG'S FEET
WITH CHAMPAGNE VINAIGRETTE

Pig's feet are something that grows on you. When I was young, I turned up my nose at them, like so many young people do. As I got older I developed a taste for them, and the sharp taste of the vinegar that goes well with them. The good thing about this recipe is that you remove the bones to allow them to slice easily as you eat them. Serve as a main course with potato salad, greens, and hot corn bread.

4 pig's feet, front feet only, split in half

2 teaspoons salt

$1/2$ cup cider vinegar

1 small onion, quartered

1 bay leaf

3 ribs celery, coarsely chopped with leaves

BREADING

1 cup all-purpose flour

$1/2$ teaspoon salt

$1/2$ teaspoon freshly ground black pepper

4 eggs, beaten

2 cups yellow cornmeal

1 cup peanut oil

CHAMPAGNE VINAIGRETTE

2 cups Brown Sauce (see page 285)

3 tablespoons champagne vinegar

1 tablespoon Louisiana hot red pepper sauce

Wash the pig's feet and place in a large stockpot with cold water to cover. Bring to a boil, then reduce the heat and simmer for 1 hour, skimming as needed. Add the salt, vinegar, onion, bay leaf, and celery. Add more water as needed to ensure that the feet are covered. Return to a boil, reduce the heat to simmer, and continue to cook until the feet are tender, 1 to $1^1/2$ hours. Remove the pig's feet from the broth and set aside to cool.

Remove the bones from the feet. Form the meat into the shape of a log and place in a baking pan. Cover and refrigerate to set.

For the breading, in a bowl, combine the flour, salt, and pepper and dust the feet in the breading mixture. Beat eggs in a separate bowl. Dip the coated feet in the eggs and roll in cornmeal. Cover and return to the refrigerator to chill.

Meanwhile, prepare the champagne vinaigrette. Combine the Brown Sauce, champagne vinegar, and Louisiana hot red pepper sauce.

In a large skillet or sauté pan, heat the oil over medium-high heat and sauté the feet until golden brown and hot through, about 3 to 4 minutes per side. Serve hot on a pool of champagne vinaigrette.

SIMMERED CHITTERLINGS COUNTRY STYLE WITH HOG MAWS

MAKES 8 SERVINGS

My mother had a love-hate relationship with "chit'lins" or "wrinkle steak" as they are sometimes called. She loved to eat them, hated to smell them cooking. She also refused to eat chit'lins cooked by just anybody because she didn't think they took enough care when cleaning them.

The exception was our next door neighbor Miss Noreen Alsberry, a professional cook from Front Royal, Virginia. Miss Noreen volunteered in the kitchen at our church, Bethel AME, in Harrisburg. Whenever there was a church fund-raiser, Mom Pan would send me after two or three orders of just chit'lins—no hog maws (pig stomach).

As I grew older, I learned to cook the hog maws and the chit'lins from my sister Mary Francis.

4 pounds hog maws
1 large onion, quartered
4 cloves garlic
4 ribs celery, coarsely chopped
2 bay leaves
2 teaspoons red pepper flakes
1 teaspoon freshly ground
   black pepper
2 tablespoons salt
10 pounds chitterlings
$1^{1}/_{2}$ cups cider vinegar

Wash the hog maws, remove the fat and all membrane, and cut into 1-inch pieces. Place the hog maws in a small stockpot and cover with water. Add half the onion, 2 cloves garlic, 2 ribs celery, 1 bay leaf, 1 teaspoon red pepper flakes, $^{1}/_{2}$ teaspoon pepper, and 1 tablespoon salt. Bring to a boil, then reduce the heat to simmer and cook until the hog maws are tender, $1^{1}/_{2}$ to 2 hours.

Wash the chitterlings in cold water, separating them a piece at a time. Turn them inside out and clean them, scraping and removing any particles and most of the fat. Place the chitterlings in a large stockpot and cover with water. Add the remaining onion, garlic, celery, bay leaf, red pepper flakes, pepper, and salt. Bring to a boil, then reduce the heat to simmer and cook for 30 minutes. Add the vinegar and simmer until the chitterlings are tender, $2^{1}/_{2}$ to 3 hours. Drain the hog maws and add to the chitterlings and continue to simmer 10 minutes. Serve hot with your favorite hot sauce.

CHEF'S TIP

You can avoid some of the smell associated with cooking chitterlings by making sure to remove as much of the fat as possible.

Souse Meat

At the Elegant Taste of Heritage benefit dinner held in the summer of 1994 at the Grand Hyatt Hotel in Washington, D.C., I added this souse meat to some mixed greens, fresh tomatoes, and a champagne vinaigrette for an upscale salad.

1 large hog's head, split

6 pig's feet, split

4 pig's ears

1 cup cider vinegar

2 tablespoons chopped fresh sage

1 tablespoon red pepper flakes

1 tablespoon salt

FOR MIXING SOUSE

1 cup cider vinegar

1 red bell pepper, blanched and diced

1 green bell pepper, blanched and diced

1/2 tablespoon red pepper flakes

1 teaspoon dried sage, crumbled

1 teaspoon salt

1 teaspoon cayenne pepper

Have your butcher split the hog's head, remove the eyes and brain and scald and scrape it clean so it is ready to cook. Place the pig's feet, pig's ears, and hog's head in a large stockpot and cover with water. Bring to boil, add the vinegar, fresh sage, red pepper flakes, and salt. Reduce the heat to simmer and cook until the meat is tender and pulls easily away from the bone, 4 to 5 hours, adding more water as needed.

Drain and allow to cool. Remove the meat from the bones, mash, and place in a large mixing bowl with the vinegar, red and green bell peppers, red pepper flakes, dried sage, salt, and cayenne pepper. Mix well and transfer to medium-size loaf pans lined with plastic wrap. Cover and refrigerate overnight to set. Serve, sliced julienne, on a salad or with crackers.

SOUTHERN MIXED GRILL

MAKES 6 SERVINGS

I created this recipe for a Black Faculty and Staff fund-raiser at California State Polytechnic University in Pomona. Seven other African-American chefs joined me in preparing this dinner. It was a very special night of heritage.

MARINADE

$^1/_8$ teaspoon salt

$^1/_8$ teaspoon freshly ground black pepper

$^1/_8$ teaspoon cayenne pepper

1 teaspoon paprika

2 teaspoons chopped fresh sage

$^1/_2$ cup peanut oil

FOR THE GRILL

Six 3-ounce boneless, skinless chicken breast halves

Six 3-ounce boneless pork loin chops, sliced

$^1/_2$ teaspoon salt

$^1/_2$ teaspoon freshly ground black pepper

Six 4-ounce Chitterling Sausages (see page 203)

2 tablespoons peanut oil

1 large sprig sage

In a bowl combine the salt, black and cayenne pepper, paprika, chopped sage and oil. Add the chicken and allow to marinate 3 to 5 minutes. Season the pork with salt and pepper. Grill the chicken and pork over medium coals on each side until done, about 3 to 4 minutes. Brush the sausage with oil and grill. Turn to brown evenly, 2 to 3 minutes on all sides. To serve, arrange on heated plates with Savannah Red Rice (page 116) and Cornmeal Crepe Pouch Filled with Mixed Greens (page 91).

⋯⋯⋯⋯⋯

Chapter 9

Breads, Rolls, and Biscuits

I F YOU THOUGHT CORN BREAD WAS MERELY A HUMBLE SIDE DISH JUST FOR SOUTHERNERS, shame on you. Corn bread can be to today's menus what French bread is in France: A food meant to be eaten lathered with sweet cream butter, its purpose to sweep across the plate, sopping up crumbs and traces of sauces and gravies too delectable to be left behind.

It's true, corn bread is one of the decades-old backbone foods of Southern cooking. Just mention bread and dinner in an African-American or Southern household or restaurant and there will be a resounding refrain: "Corn bread!"

But its cakelike crumb also makes corn bread sturdy enough to stand up under rich sauces, yet delicate enough to be baked in muffin tins or shaped like ears of corn and served with soup. That's why you'll find it is intrinsic to so many chef's menus as well, spiked with everything from herbs to fresh vegetables and chiles.

The basic recipe for corn bread is versatile, lending itself well to an assortment of other baked goods. In the old days, Granny served up a spartan version of the mix in big, spongy cakes called hot water cornbread and served them alongside vegetables to give meals an added boost of nutrition. She crumbled leftover corn bread into the stuffing for Sunday's roast chicken. When the occasion called for something more special, she would simply whip up a few egg whites and fold them into the batter, to make a corn bread soufflé she called spoon bread.

Indeed, cornmeal has played an important role in the theater of African-American cookery—whether we spoon a little into our aromatic yeast dough to make rolls more exciting or use it to give tender fish fillets a crispy coating.

Because not even its most ardent fans (like me) eat corn bread everyday, I offer yeast breads and some of my favorite recipes for biscuits, too, which you can serve in the traditional manner, or cut them with tiny cookie cutters for a more decorative presentation.

These days, some folks complain there is no time for the day-long exercise of baking fresh breads from scratch. But spend one Saturday morning with your hands in a sticky bowl of fresh, aromatic dough and you'll see why I believe homemade buttermilk biscuits and yeast breads are worth every bit of the effort. It may not make you nostalgic enough to hang the wash out on a line, but it will definitely change the way you think about canned biscuits, prepared hot roll mix, and bread machines.

COUNTRY LOAF BREAD

MAKES 2 LOAVES

In the East, when the weather turns cold and gray, there are two ways to keep bread on the shelf in your kitchen: Buy all you can at the supermarket, or bake this wonderful, aromatic loaf.

One .06-ounce cake yeast or
  1 tablespoon active dry yeast
1 cup warm water (110 to 115°F)
1 cup milk, scalded and cooled
  to lukewarm
2 tablespoons shortening
2 tablespoons sugar
2 teaspoons salt
5 cups bread flour
$1/4$ cup ($1/2$ stick) butter, melted

Dissolve the yeast in the water in the bowl of an electric mixer. Add the milk, shortening, sugar, and salt. Allow the mixture to stand until it begins to foam. Add the flour and mix until smooth with the mixer set on medium speed. Turn the dough out onto a floured surface and knead until smooth and elastic, about 6 to 7 minutes. Roll the dough into a ball and place in a well-greased bowl, turning to coat on all sides with melted butter. Cover the bowl and let the dough rise in a warm place until doubled, about 2 hours.

Turn out onto well-floured surface, punch down, and shape into 2 loaves and place in 9 × 5-inch loaf pans. Allow to rise 30 to 45 minutes. Reshape the loaves, cover with a towel, and allow to rise again until doubled. Preheat the oven to 350°F and bake 45 to 50 minutes. Turn the bread out onto racks to cool. Brush with the melted butter.

CHEF'S TIP
Brush fresh-from-the-oven warm bread with melted butter to give the loaf a soft crust.

CLIFTON WILLIAMS'S CRACKED BLACK PEPPER BREAD

MAKES 1 LOAF

African-American cuisine is known for its fondness for spice and this bread, with its delicious aroma from crushed black peppercorns, upholds the tradition nicely. You can work it in to the bread crust, across the top, or mix it in the dough for less bite and excellent flavor.

1 package active dry yeast
$^1/_2$ cup (1 stick) butter
$^1/_2$ teaspoon salt
1 cup warm water (110 to 115°F)
$^1/_2$ tablespoon freshly cracked
   black pepper
3$^1/_4$ cups all-purpose flour
1 tablespoon melted butter

In a small bowl, dissolve the yeast, butter, and salt in the warm water. Add the pepper. Gradually stir in about 3 cups of the flour, then work in the remaining flour with your hands. Knead the dough until smooth and satiny, about 10 minutes. Place in an ungreased stainless-steel bowl, cover, and let rest 10 minutes. Shape the dough into a loaf and place in a lightly greased 9 × 5-inch loaf pan. Brush the top lightly with melted butter. Cover and let rise in a warm place until doubled in bulk, about 30 to 40 minutes. Preheat the oven to 400°F and bake until done, about 35 minutes.

KYM GIBSON'S GRUYÈRE MUSTARD LOAF

MAKES 2 LOAVES

The cheese in this bread makes the loaves brown fast, so tent it with greased waxed paper while it bakes to protect the delicate crust.

2 envelopes active dry yeast

1 teaspoon sugar

$^1/_3$ cup warm water (110 to 115°F)

$1^1/_2$ cups milk, at room temperature

1 egg yolk, beaten

5 cups bread flour

1 tablespoon salt

1 tablespoon dry mustard

1 tablespoon Pommery mustard

$^1/_4$ cup ($^1/_2$ stick) unsalted butter, melted

$1^1/_4$ cups Gruyère cheese

Combine the yeast, sugar, water, milk, and egg yolk in a small bowl. Stir to dissolve. Sprinkle $^1/_2$ cup of flour over mixture and let stand 15 minutes. Combine the remaining flour, salt, dry mustard, Pommery mustard, and butter in a large bowl. Add to the yeast mixture. Blend in the Gruyère cheese. Knead for 5 minutes on a lightly floured surface. Place in a greased bowl and lightly cover with greased waxed paper. Store in warm place until doubled in bulk.

Punch the dough down. Place on a floured surface, cut in half, and form loaves. Place in greased loaf pans and cover with greased waxed paper, sealing to close. Allow the dough to rise for 40 minutes. Preheat the oven to 400°F and bake the loaves with the greased waxed paper cover for 25 minutes. Reduce oven temperature to 350°F, remove the waxed paper, and bake until brown.

LEAH CHASE'S MONKEY BREAD

MAKES 6 TO 8 SERVINGS

*Leah likes her monkey bread rich with melted butter, but you can get away
with using just half of what is called for, if you wish.*

1 cup milk
1/2 cup (1 stick) butter
1/4 cup sugar
1 teaspoon salt
1 package active dry yeast
3 1/2 cups all-purpose flour
1/2 cup (1 stick) butter, melted

In a saucepan heat the milk, butter, sugar, and salt until the butter
melts. Remove from the heat and allow to cool to 110 to 115°F.
Add the yeast and let stand until dissolved. Stir and let rest for 4 to
5 minutes.

In a large bowl, combine the liquid ingredients with the flour, stirring
well. Cover and allow to rest in a warm area until doubled, about
1 1/2 hours. Punch the dough down and form into 2-inch balls. Flatten
them a little then dip each one in melted butter.

Layer the balls in a greased 10-inch tube or Bundt pan. Cover with a
dry kitchen towel and let rise in a warm place until doubled, 45 to
50 minutes. Preheat the oven to 75°F and bake for 30 to 40 minutes.
Cool in the pan for 5 minutes, then turn out onto a serving plate.

Pan-fried Hot Water Corn Bread

MAKES 6 SERVINGS

In my mother's day, this bread was called "hardtack." She made big, spongy cakes with crunchy edges, which was perfect for sopping up pot likker or her rich gravies.

If you want to make them for guests, just make them a little smaller.

1 1/2 cups white cornmeal
2 tablespoons all-purpose flour
1 tablespoon baking powder
3/4 teaspoon salt
1 1/2 teaspoons sugar
1 1/2 cups boiling water
1/3 cup vegetable oil

In a bowl, combine the cornmeal, flour, baking powder, salt, and sugar. Pour in the boiling water while stirring. Heat the oil in a skillet until hot, about 375°F. Drop 1/3 cup of the batter into 2 1/2-inch round cakes, about 1/2 inch thick. Cook until golden, about 3 to 4 minutes on each side. Drain the cakes on paper towels. Serve hot.

Plantation Hoecake

MAKES 6 SERVINGS

This is a legendary recipe that is surrounded by fable. It has been said the slaves used to bake this ridiculously simple recipe under the heat of the blazing Southern sun on the blades of the hoes they used in the cotton fields. A hot cast-iron skillet works just as well.

2 cups yellow cornmeal
1 cup all-purpose flour
2 teaspoons baking powder
1 teaspoon salt
1 tablespoon sugar
3/4 cup buttermilk
1/2 water
1/2 cup bacon drippings

In a bowl, combine the cornmeal, flour, baking powder, salt and sugar. Mix in the buttermilk, water (add a little more if needed), and 1 1/2 tablespoons of the bacon drippings. Form the batter into 3-inch cakes and flatten. In a large skillet, heat the remaining bacon drippings over medium heat and fry the hoecakes, turning once, until golden brown, about 3 to 4 minutes on each side. Serve hot.

Southern Buttermilk Biscuits

These traditional biscuits are so flaky and good, it's hard to decide just how many servings this recipe will make. Like the advertisement for an irresistible potato chip once said, "Nobody can eat just one."

4 cups all-purpose flour
2 tablespoons baking powder
1 teaspoon baking soda
1 teaspoon salt
1 1/2 teaspoons sugar
2/3 cup (1 1/3 sticks) butter, softened
1 1/4 cups buttermilk
1/4 cup water
1/4 cup butter, melted

Preheat the oven to 425°F.

In large bowl, combine the flour, baking powder, baking soda, salt, and sugar. Cut in the softened butter until the mixture resembles coarse meal. Combine the buttermilk and water and stir into the dry ingredients until thoroughly moistened. The dough will be crumbly. Turn out onto a lightly floured surface and knead lightly 3 or 4 times until the dough comes together. Roll the dough to a 3/4 inch thickness, then cut with a 2-inch biscuit cutter. Place the biscuits on a lightly greased baking sheet and prick with a fork to allow steam to escape. Brush the tops with melted butter. Bake until brown, 15 to 20 minutes.

CHEF'S TIP
For a more attractive presentation when serving these biscuits to guests, try cutting them with a 1-inch serrated biscuit cutter.

GRANNY'S SPOON BREAD

MAKES 6 SERVINGS

When Granny wanted something a little different than the old standby, corn bread, she would whip up a cornmeal soufflé. You can toss in a few stalks of chopped asparagus or broccoli florets, some really good ham or a sprinkle of shredded cheese and have a truly fine addition to any luncheon or brunch menu.

3 cups milk
1½ cups white cornmeal
¼ cup (½ stick) butter
1 teaspoon salt
2 teaspoons baking powder
4 eggs, separated

Preheat the oven to 325°F.

Combine 2 cups of the milk and cornmeal in a saucepan and stir until blended. Cook over low heat until thick, about 10 minutes. Remove from the heat and stir in the butter and salt. Dissolve the baking powder in the remaining 1 cup of milk. In a separate bowl, beat the egg yolks. Gradually stir about one quarter of the hot cornmeal mixture into the egg yolks, stirring well, then pour the yolk mixture back into the hot cornmeal mixture and mix well. Beat the egg whites in another bowl until stiff peaks form and fold into the cornmeal mixture. Pour the mixture into a buttered 3-quart casserole and bake for 1 hour. Serve hot with additional butter, if desired.

Darryl Evans's Down-home Hushpuppies

Herbs take these hushpuppies to a level beyond traditional.

1 cup yellow cornmeal
1/2 cup all-purpose flour
1/2 cup corn flour
1 tablespoon baking powder
3/4 teaspoon cayenne pepper
1/2 teaspoon salt
1/2 teaspoon freshly ground
   black pepper
1/4 teaspoon white pepper
1/2 teaspoon dried thyme leaves
1/4 teaspoon dried oregano
2 cloves garlic, minced
1/2 cup minced onion
1/4 cup minced green onions
2 eggs
1 cup milk
1/2 cup vegetable oil
Oil for frying

Mix all the dry ingredients in a large bowl. Stir in the garlic and onions, add the eggs, then the milk. Heat the oil and add to batter. Heat some oil in a deep-fryer to 350°F. Drop by heaping tablespoonfuls into the hot oil. Cook until golden brown.

SOUTHERN HUSHPUPPIES

By now, virtually everyone has heard the old tale that a cook created this recipe to quiet the hungry pups excited by the smell of fish cooking in the kitchen. It works just as well on kids and adults.

2 cups yellow cornmeal
1 teaspoon dried sage
1 teaspoon salt
$^1/_2$ teaspoon cayenne pepper
$^1/_2$ teaspoon freshly ground
  black pepper
1 small onion, minced
$^3/_4$ cup milk
1 egg, beaten
Vegetable oil

In a bowl, combine the cornmeal, spices and onion. Beat in the milk and egg. Gather single tablespoons of the dough into 1-inch balls. Heat the oil in a deep-fryer to 370°F and cook the hushpuppies until golden brown. Drain well.

EARLEST BELL'S BACON AND CHEDDAR CHEESE MUFFINS

MAKES 1 DOZEN

When corn bread is on the menu several times a week, you are always looking for new ways to present it. Need another idea?

$1^1/_2$ cups all-purpose flour
$^1/_2$ cup yellow cornmeal
2 tablespoons sugar
3 teaspoons baking powder
$^1/_4$ teaspoon salt
$^3/_4$ cup canned corn kernels
4 slices bacon, cooked and
  chopped
$^3/_4$ cup diced cheddar cheese
1 cup milk
$^1/_4$ cup vegetable oil
1 egg, beaten

Preheat the oven to 400°F.

In a medium bowl, combine the flour, cornmeal, sugar, baking powder, and salt. Mix well. Stir in the corn, bacon, and cheese.

In another bowl, combine the milk, oil, and egg. Mix well. Combine the liquid and dry mixtures, mixing thoroughly. Spray a 12-cup muffin pan with nonstick vegetable spray and pour in the batter. Bake for 20 to 25 minutes or until a toothpick comes out clean when inserted. Serve hot.

COUNTRY CORN BREAD

I never really understood why Granny melted butter in her cast-iron skillet and then poured the sizzling butter into her corn bread batter. All I knew was that it tasted like a little chunk of heaven. Today, I know it's the secret to a light, airy center and crispy edges. You'll want to eat it at every meal.

1 cup yellow cornmeal
1 cup all-purpose flour
2¹/₂ teaspoons baking powder
¹/₂ teaspoon baking soda
2 tablespoons sugar
1 teaspoon salt
2 eggs, beaten
1 cup buttermilk
¹/₄ cup (¹/₂ stick) butter

Preheat the oven to 425°F.

Combine the cornmeal, flour, baking powder, baking soda, sugar, and salt in a large bowl. In a small separate bowl, combine the eggs and milk. Combine the liquid and dry ingredients. Place the butter in a 9-inch cast-iron skillet and place in the oven until the butter is sizzling. Pour the hot butter into the batter and stir well. Pour the batter into the hot skillet and bake until a wood pick inserted in the center comes out clean, about 20 to 25 minutes. Cut into wedges and serve hot with creamy butter.

PATRICK CLARK'S BUTTERMILK CORN BREAD

MAKES 8 SERVINGS

By now everyone knows corn bread is a staple on African-American menus. Here it is imbued with chili powder and chives for a hint of Southwestern living.

1 cup yellow cornmeal
1 cup all-purpose flour
1 teaspoon baking soda
2 teaspoons baking powder
$^1/_2$ teaspoon chili powder
$^1/_4$ cup sugar
1 teaspoon salt
1 egg
1 cup buttermilk
$^1/_4$ cup ($^1/_2$ stick) butter, melted
2 tablespoons minced chives

Preheat the oven to 400°F.

In a medium bowl, mix together the cornmeal, flour, baking soda, baking powder, and chili powder. Stir in the sugar and salt. Beat the egg into the buttermilk and add to dry ingredients. Blend in the butter and chives. Pour into a greased 9-inch round pan or corn-cob shaped pans or muffin tins. Bake until the corn bread is golden and a wood pick inserted in the center comes out clean, about 20 to 25 minutes. Allow to cool for a few minutes before cutting into wedges. Serve with butter.

PRINCE AKINS'S GEORGIA CORN STICKS

MAKES 1 DOZEN

At Georgia, Prince is always looking for ways to infuse excitement into the menu. This bread stands in nicely when the guests and the cooks tire of biscuits, rolls, and loaf breads.

$1^1/_3$ cups yellow cornmeal
$^1/_3$ cup all-purpose flour
1 teaspoon baking powder
$^1/_2$ teaspoon baking soda
$^1/_2$ teaspoon salt
1 tablespoon sugar
1 cup buttermilk
2 eggs, beaten
3 tablespoons butter, melted

Preheat the oven to 425°F.

In a bowl, combine the cornmeal, flour, baking powder, baking soda, salt, and sugar. Add the buttermilk and eggs, stir, then pour in the melted butter and continue to stir. Heat two well-greased cast-iron corn-stick pans in the oven until hot, about 3 to 4 minutes. Remove the pans from the oven, pour the batter in the hot pans, filling only two-thirds full. Bake until golden, about 15 to 20 minutes. Remove from the pan and serve with butter.

Old-fashioned Cornmeal Yeast Rolls

MAKES 4 DOZEN

James Beard often enjoyed cornmeal bread sliced and toasted for breakfast. But these little rolls, with the surprise crunch are so good, you'll want to serve them at other meals, too.

1 cup warm water (110 to 115°F)
2 tablespoons honey
1 package active dry yeast
1¹/₂ cups lukewarm milk
1 cup cornmeal
¹/₄ cup sugar
³/₄ cup (1¹/₂ sticks) butter, softened
2 eggs, lightly beaten
2 teaspoons salt
6 cups all-purpose flour
Melted butter

In the bowl of an electric mixer, combine the water and honey, then dissolve the yeast in the mixture. Stir in the milk, cornmeal, sugar, butter, eggs, salt, and 2 cups of the flour. Beat with the mixer set on medium speed until smooth. Stir in enough additional flour to make a thick dough.

Turn the dough out onto a lightly floured surface and knead until smooth and elastic, about 4 to 5 minutes. Place the dough in a greased bowl, turning to coat on all sides. Cover and let rise in warm place until doubled, about 1¹/₂ hours. Punch the dough down, then shape into 1-inch balls. Grease four 12-cup muffin tins, then place 3 balls in each greased muffin cup. Cover with a towel and let rise until doubled, about 30 to 45 minutes. Preheat the oven to 400°F and bake until light brown, about 15 to 20 minutes. Brush with melted butter before serving.

Cheddar Cheese Biscuits

MAKES 1¹/₂ DOZEN

Whether you split these biscuits and drown them in a rich cream gravy, or cut them into small pieces, stuff them with ham, and serve on a luncheon buffet, one thing is certain: You'll love them.

2 cups all-purpose flour
1 tablespoon baking powder
¹/₄ teaspoon salt
6 tablespoons shredded sharp cheddar cheese
1 tablespoon butter, melted
1 cup milk

Preheat the oven to 425°F.

In a large bowl, combine the flour, baking powder, salt, and cheese. Lightly mix in the butter and enough milk to form a soft dough, about ²/₃ cup or slightly more. Turn the dough out onto a lightly floured surface and pat into a ¹/₂-inch-thick circle and cut with a 2-inch biscuit cutter. Brush the biscuits with the remaining milk and bake 12 to 15 minutes. Serve hot.

MISS BERT'S HOMEMADE FIST ROLLS

MAKES 3 DOZEN

The first time I smelled bread baking it was probably these rolls in the oven of my next-door neighbor Miss Bert Alsberry, mother of Miss Noreen, a professional cook. Like every good baker, Miss Bert awoke early in the morning to get these rolls ready for her friends and family in the Cumberland Street neighborhood of Harrisburg, Pennsylvania. You could consider yourself blessed if you came home and found some of Miss Bert's bounty on your table. Your family will think so too.

$^3/_4$ cup shortening
$^3/_4$ cup sugar
1 cup boiling water
2 packages active dry yeast
1 cup warm water (110 to 115°F)
2 eggs, lightly beaten
7 cups all-purpose flour
2 teaspoons salt
$1^1/_2$ teaspoons baking powder
$^3/_4$ teaspoon baking soda
Melted butter

In the bowl of an electric mixer, cream together the shortening and sugar until light and fluffy. Stir in the boiling water and set aside. In a small bowl, dissolve the yeast in the warm water. Set aside. Add the eggs to the shortening mixture, mixing well. Stir in the dissolved yeast.

Combine 5 cups of flour with the salt, baking powder, and baking soda. Beat the dry ingredients into the wet mixture. The dough will be sticky. Turn the dough out onto a heavily floured board and knead in about $^1/_2$ cup additional flour, or enough to make a stiff dough. Place the dough in a greased bowl, turning to coat on all sides. Cover and let rise until doubled, about $1^1/_2$ to 2 hours.

With greased hands, pinch the dough into 2-inch pieces and roll into balls. Place in two greased 9-inch round cake pans or a small baking pan. Cover the pans and let the dough rise until doubled, about $1^1/_2$ hours. Preheat the oven to 400°F and bake until golden, about 20 minutes. Brush with melted butter immediately.

CHEF'S TIP

To be sure your bread dough has completely risen, press two fingers into the dough after the first rising. Remove your fingers. If the dough springs back, it needs more time to finish rising.

Edna Lewis's
Baking Powder Biscuits

MAKES 1 DOZEN

Hardly anyone will admit they still use lard in these health-conscious days, but most everyone will agree lard lends a unique flavor to baked goods, especially these old-style biscuits.

2 cups all-purpose flour
4 teaspoons baking powder
1 teaspoon sugar
$^1/_2$ teaspoon cream of tartar
1 teaspoon salt
$^1/_2$ cup lard
$^3/_4$ cup milk
$^1/_4$ cup ice water

Preheat the oven to 450°F.

Combine the flour, baking powder, sugar, cream of tartar, and salt in a bowl. Cut in the lard until the mixture resembles coarse crumbs. Make a well in the center of the mixture. Beat in all the milk and water, as needed, to make a smooth dough. Using an electric mixer, knead 30 seconds. Roll or pat dough to a $^1/_2$ inch thickness. Cut with a floured $2^1/_2$-inch biscuit cutter, dipping the cutter in flour after every biscuit. Place the biscuits on an ungreased baking sheet and bake until golden, about 10 to 12 minutes. Serve hot with rich, creamy butter.

SWEET POTATO BRIOCHE

MAKES 1 DOZEN

Brioche is a wonderfully rich and sweet yeast bread that is even better when a bit of sweet potato is stirred into the mix.

2 packages active dry yeast

$^1/_4$ cup warm water (110 to 115°F)

1 cup mashed, baked sweet potatoes

$^1/_4$ cup sugar

$1^1/_2$ teaspoons ground cinnamon

$^1/_2$ teaspoon ground nutmeg

2 teaspoons salt

$2^1/_4$ cups cake flour

$2^1/_4$ cups bread flour

6 medium eggs

$1^1/_2$ cups (3 sticks) butter, softened

2 egg yolks

2 teaspoons water

In the bowl of an electric mixer, combine the yeast and warm water and stir to dissolve. Add the sweet potatoes, sugar, cinnamon, nutmeg, salt, and flours. Using a dough hook, begin to beat the mixture. Beat in the eggs and butter and mix until the dough begins to pull away from the sides of the bowl, about 7 to 8 minutes. Cover the bowl with a moist towel and refrigerate 2 to 3 hours. Punch the dough down and knead a few minutes.

Grease a 12-cup muffin tin. Smooth the dough into balls and place seam-side down in the muffin tin. Butter your finger and push it down into the center of each roll, making a $^1/_2$-inch indentation. Cover loosely with buttered parchment paper and set aside until doubled, about $1^1/_2$ to 2 hours. Combine the egg yolks and water and brush the rolls with the egg wash. Preheat the oven to 400°F and bake 35 to 40 minutes. Remove from the oven and turn out onto a wire rack, top side up, to cool. Serve warm with butter, if desired.

CHEF'S TIP
Be sure to use medium eggs in this recipe. Larger eggs will make the dough too moist and batterlike.

TIMOTHY DEAN'S COUNTRY BRIOCHE

MAKES 1 LOAF

$^1/_3$ cup warm water (110 to
    115°F)

1 package active dry yeast

3$^1/_3$ cups cake flour (retain
    1 cup for flouring surfaces)

2 cups bread flour

$^1/_3$ cup sugar

2$^1/_2$ teaspoons fine sea salt

6 large eggs, at room temperature

1$^1/_4$ cups (2$^1/_2$ sticks) unsalted
    butter, softened and cut into
    1-inch cubes

3 ounces slab bacon, sliced,
    cooked crisp, and coarsely
    crumbled

In a small bowl, combine the water and yeast and let stand 10 minutes, then stir with a spoon until the yeast is dissolved. Set aside.

In the large bowl of an electric mixer fitted with dough hooks, sift together the flours, sugar, and salt. Add the eggs and beat for 1 minute at low speed. Stop the machine, scrap the dough off the dough hook, and return the machine to low speed and beat 5 minutes more. Add the butter cubes one quarter at a time, beating for about 1 minute after each addition. Add the crisp bacon. Continue beating until the butter is completely blended into the dough, 10 to 15 minutes more. Place dough in a large floured mixing bowl and cover with plastic wrap. Set aside in a warm place until doubled, about 3 hours.

Turn the dough out onto a floured work surface and gently work the air out of it by folding it over several times while lightly pressing it down. Return the dough to the bowl, cover with plastic wrap and refrigerate overnight. Very generously butter a 9 × 5-inch loaf pan. Turn the dough out onto a floured work surface and with floured hands shape dough into a 15 × 10-inch rectangle about 2 inches thick. Cut the rectangle in half lengthwise with a pastry scraper or a large knife to form two 10-inch rectangles. Cut each rectangle crosswise into 8 equal-size pieces. (Each piece should be about 2$^1/_2$ inches long by 1$^1/_4$ inches wide and 2 inches thick.) Roll each piece of dough gently between your palms to form it into a smooth log, about as long as the width of the loaf pan. (If using a larger loaf pan, arrange 8 of the logs crosswise in the pan to make a single layer, then form a second layer with the remaining 8 logs placed crosswise. If using the smaller pans, arrange 8 logs crosswise in each pan, fitting them snugly together to make a single layer.)

Let the dough rise, uncovered, in a warm place until it is about $^1/_2$ inch above the top of the pan, about 3 hours. Preheat the oven to 350°F and bake until done and well browned on top, 35 to 40 minutes. Remove from the oven and immediately turn the brioche out onto a wire rack. Let the bread cool about 10 minutes and serve.

Chapter 10

Cakes, Pies, and Desserts

S OME SAY YOU CAN NEVER BE TOO RICH OR TOO THIN. I SAY YOU CAN NEVER HAVE ENOUGH dessert. Just think about all the buttery-rich sweets you've eaten in African-American homes and restaurants over the years and you'll agree: We love dessert.

Historically, family gatherings and the sweet things served at these times were a happy diversion from the harsh realities of life. Big Mama, and countless women like her, labored to transform leftover ingredients like rice and stale bread, fruit from the garden, and whatever else was at hand into the seductive cobblers and creative puddings that made life worth living.

On sticky summer evenings, home-churned ice cream became the treat of choice. That's when Granddad got into the act, supervising the children as they took turns at the old hand-cranked contraption.

But today, Granny's fried-fruit pies, rich chocolate fudge cake, 7-Up cake, and those sticky sweet potato and pecan pies that appeared when the family gathered on the fourth Sunday in July to celebrate the birth of new babies, congratulate graduates, or welcome new brides and grooms to the clan, reappear as the legacy of a generation of truly fine cooks.

At their side, a new breed of magnificent desserts has emerged from Aunt Dolly's humble creations. As you'll see from our recipe collection, juicy peaches and sweet potatoes are still at center stage, but they arrive at the table bathed in a rich crème brûlée or tucked in delicate dumpling pastry. Mom Pan's pound cake tastes just as dense and rich as ever, but for a more elegant presentation, we paint the serving plate with fruit puree and add a spray of crème anglaise.

And, don't worry that Barbara won't recognize her peach cobbler under my our spectacular brandy custard sauce. She'll be too busy chewing.

EARLEST BELL'S BREAD PUDDING

Earlest made bread pudding for the first time in 1975, while working at the Playboy Club in Chicago. Charles Mayes, an African-American chef of polished skill, helped him improve upon his mother's recipe. This is the result.

2 cups stale bread cubes
1 quart milk
3 eggs, beaten
3/4 cup sugar
1/8 teaspoon salt
1/4 teaspoon ground nutmeg
1 tablespoon vanilla
1/2 cup raisins
2 tablespoons butter

Preheat the oven to 350°F.

Soak the bread in the milk until soft, about 5 minutes. Blend or mix together the eggs, sugar, salt, nutmeg, vanilla, and raisins and mix thoroughly. Combine the bread with the egg mixture, add the butter, and mix thoroughly. Pour into a greased 13 × 9-inch baking pan and bake until golden brown, about 45 minutes. Allow to cool. Serve warm with your favorite vanilla or rum sauce.

CREPES WITH COUNTRY FRIED APPLES

The heady scent of apples, cinnamon, and butter baked in a pie is an American tradition. But for a fancy presentation the mixture is sautéed, then cradled in delicate crepes and served with a light custard sauce.

$3/4$ cup all-purpose flour

$1/2$ tablespoon granulated sugar

$1/8$ teaspoon salt

3 eggs

$7/8$ cup milk

$1/4$ cup clarified butter

3 cups Country Fried Apples
(see page 93)

1 tablespoon superfine sugar

$1/2$ tablespoon ground cinnamon

Crème Anglaise (see page 294)

Combine the flour, granulated sugar, and salt in a bowl. In a separate bowl, mix the eggs and milk together. Stir the liquid ingredients into the dry ingredients until well mixed. The batter will be thin.

Heat a 6-inch skillet or crepe pan over medium heat until hot. Remove from the heat, brush lightly with the clarified butter, then add 3 tablespoons of the batter to the pan, swirling to coat the bottom with a thin layer of batter. Return the pan to the heat and cook until the crepe is lightly browned, about 1 minute. Turn and cook 30 seconds on the other side. Remove the crepe to a plate and keep warm. Repeat with the remaining batter, placing waxed or parchment paper between each crepe to prevent sticking.

Preheat the oven to 375°F.

With the attractive side facing down, place 1 tablespoon Country Fried Apples on one end of each crepe. Roll up and place in a buttered baking dish. Combine the superfine sugar and cinnamon and sprinkle over the finished crepes. Bake to heat through.

Spoon Crème Anglaise on individual serving plates and top with 2 crepes.

CHEF'S TIP

Cover tightly and freeze any remaining crepes.

KYM GIBSON'S APPLE CAKE

MAKES 8 SERVINGS

If this updated version of Granny's old applesauce cake, luxuriously sweet with a perfume of brandy, doesn't make you a fan of contemporary African-American cuisine, nothing will.

4 cups peeled and thinly sliced
   Granny Smith apples
$1/4$ cup brandy
2 cups all-purpose flour
$3/4$ teaspoon salt
1 tablespoon ground cinnamon
1 teaspoon ground nutmeg
$1^1/_2$ teaspoons baking soda
3 eggs
1 cups vegetable oil
2 cups sugar
2 teaspoons vanilla
$3/4$ cups shelled walnuts or
   pecans, coarsely chopped

Soak the apples in the brandy for 10 minutes. Sift the flour, salt, cinnamon, nutmeg, and baking soda together and set aside.

Preheat the oven to 350°F.

In the bowl of an electric mixer, combine the eggs and oil and beat on medium speed. Blend in the sugar and vanilla until creamy. Gradually add the flour mixture and mix until completely blended. Fold in the apples and nuts. Pour into a greased and floured Bundt pan. Bake for 40 to 45 minutes. Cool 10 minutes in the pan, then unmold.

OLD-FASHIONED COCONUT CAKE

MAKES 12 TO 16 SERVINGS

This is one of those spectacular, showy desserts that grandmothers used to make for church socials and bake sales. Substitute a pineapple or coconut filling for a change of pace.

3 cups cake flour

2¹/₂ teaspoons baking powder

¹/₂ teaspoon salt

1 cup (2 sticks) butter

2 cups sugar

4 eggs

1 cup milk

1 teaspoon lemon extract

1 teaspoon vanilla

Lemon Filling (recipe follows)

Boiled Frosting (recipe follows)

¹/₂ cup flake coconut, toasted

Preheat the oven to 375°F.

Combine the flour, baking powder, and salt in a bowl. In a large bowl and using an electric mixer, cream together the butter and sugar on medium speed until light. Add the eggs, one at a time, beating well after each addition. Add the dry ingredients to the mixture, alternating with the milk and beginning and ending with the flour mixture. Stir in the lemon and vanilla extracts. Pour the batter into three greased and floured 9-inch round baking pans. Bake until a wood pick inserted in the center comes out clean, about 20 to 25 minutes. Remove from the oven and cool in the pans for 10 minutes. Turn out onto wire racks to cool completely. Spread Lemon Filling between the layers and frost liberally with Boiled Frosting. Sprinkle with toasted coconut.

LEMON FILLING

MAKES 2¹/₄ CUPS

¹/₃ cup all-purpose flour

1 cup sugar

¹/₄ teaspoon salt

³/₄ teaspoon water

3 tablespoons grated lemon zest

1 cup freshly squeezed lemon juice

4 egg yolks, beaten

In a medium saucepan, combine the flour, sugar, salt, and water and stir well. Stir in the lemon zest and juice and cook over medium heat, stirring constantly, until the mixture comes to a boil and thickens. With a wire whisk, gradually stir one quarter of the hot lemon mixture into the egg yolks, then whisk into the remaining mixture and return to a boil. Cook 1 to 2 minutes, stirring. Cool at least 2 hours.

BOILED FROSTING

1/2 teaspoon cream of tartar
1 1/2 cups sugar
1/8 teaspoon salt
1/2 cup hot water
4 egg whites, at room
    temperature
1/2 teaspoon lemon extract
1/2 teaspoon coconut extract

Combine the cream of tartar, sugar, and salt in a heavy saucepan. Stir in the water. Cook over medium heat, stirring constantly, until clear. Cook, without stirring, to the soft-ball stage (240°F) on a candy thermometer.

Meanwhile, beat the egg whites to soft peaks. With the mixer running, slowly add the hot syrup. Add the extracts and continue beating until stiff peaks form and the frosting is thick enough to spread.

TIMOTHY DEAN'S CHOCOLATE SOUFFLÉ

MAKES 4 SERVINGS

Timothy's hedonistic love of dark chocolate pound cake sometimes makes him feel a little guilty. He can hardly resist it. You will feel the same way about his airy soufflé.

1 1/2 cups milk
4 1/2 ounces unsweetened
    chocolate, chopped
2 tablespoons crème de cacao
1/4 cup granulated sugar
5 tablespoons butter
1/4 cup all-purpose flour
4 eggs, separated
2 egg whites
Powdered sugar

Preheat the oven to 400°F.

In a saucepan, combine the milk, chocolate, crème de cacao, and granulated sugar and stir over low heat until the chocolate melts. Melt the butter in a separate saucepan, stir in the flour, and cook over medium heat for 1 minute. Remove from the heat and gradually stir in the chocolate mixture. Place over high heat and stir until the mixture boils and thickens. Transfer to a large bowl and stir in the egg yolks. Beat the egg whites in another bowl until soft peaks form. Fold egg whites into chocolate mixture. Butter six 8-ounce soufflé or custard cups and sprinkle with additional granulated sugar. Pour the batter into the cups, filling about three-quarters full and sprinkle with granulated sugar. Place the soufflés on a baking sheet and bake until puffed and browned well, about 20 to 25 minutes. Dust with powdered sugar.

MOM PAN'S POUND CAKE

*In the old days, nearly everyone had their own variation of pound cake, whether
7-Up, ginger ale, or milk went into the recipe. Licking Mama's old wooden spoon from
a hand-beaten pound cake or eating a small (test) tube cake that my mother made specially
for me was the best part. Thanks, Mama.*

2 cups all-purpose flour
$^3/_4$ cup cake flour
$^1/_2$ teaspoon salt
1 cup (2 sticks) butter, softened
$2^1/_2$ cups sugar
4 eggs
1 teaspoon lemon extract
1 teaspoon vanilla
1 cup milk

Preheat the oven to 325°F.

Combine the flours and salt in a bowl and set aside. In a large bowl
with an electric mixer, cream the butter until light. Gradually beat in
the sugar, mixing until fluffy. Beat in the eggs, one at a time, beating
well after each addition. Beat in the extracts. Add the flour mixture to
the batter, alternating with the milk and beating just until mixed. Do
not overbeat. Pour the batter into a greased and floured 10-inch tube
pan. Bake until a wood pick inserted in the center comes out clean,
about 90 minutes. Cool in the pan for 10 to 15 minutes. Turn the
cake out onto a wire rack and cool completely.

CHEF'S TIP

This cake is delicious as is, or serve on a pool of pureed berries that
have been sweetened and spiked with a splash of Grand Marnier or
Amaretto liqueur.

BANANAS FOSTER

MAKES 8 SERVINGS

This tasty dessert was created in New Orleans and is now enjoyed all over the country.

$^1/_2$ cup (1 stick) butter

1 teaspoon ground cinnamon

1 cup packed dark brown sugar

$^1/_2$ cup banana liqueur

8 medium bananas, peeled, cut in half, and split lengthwise

$^1/_2$ cup dark rum

8 scoops vanilla ice cream

In a large skillet, melt the butter. Add the cinnamon and brown sugar and stir. Simmer over medium heat until the sugar dissolves, 3 to 4 minutes. Add the banana liqueur and blend well. Continue to simmer for 3 minutes more. Place the bananas in the hot sauce and simmer, basting constantly with the sauce until they are soft and lightly brown, about 6 to 8 minutes. Add the rum and allow to cook until heated. Ignite the sauce with a match and continue to baste the bananas with the sauce until the flames dies out.

Place a scoop of vanilla ice cream in the center of each dessert dish. Arrange 4 pieces of banana around each scoop of ice cream, then nap the sauce over the top.

BROWN SUGAR AND BLACK WALNUT POUND CAKE

This is a holiday favorite in the Randall home. It is perfect for those who want the flavor of nuts without all the chunks. For a festive dessert, top with a scoop of eggnog or creamy peach ice cream.

3 cups all-purpose flour
1 teaspoon baking powder
$^1/_2$ teaspoon salt
1 cup (2 sticks) butter, softened
2 cups packed dark brown sugar
1 cup granulated sugar
5 eggs
1 cup milk
1 teaspoon maple extract
$^1/_2$ teaspoon vanilla
1 cup finely ground black walnuts
$^1/_4$ cup maple syrup

Preheat the oven to 300°F. Combine the flour, baking powder, and salt in a bowl. Set aside.

In a large bowl and using an electric mixer, beat the butter until light. Beat in the sugars until well mixed, scraping down the sides of the bowl occasionally. Beat in the eggs, one at a time, beating well after each addition. Beat in the flour mixture, alternating with the milk. Fold in the extracts and nuts. Pour the batter into a greased and floured 10-inch Bundt pan and bake for 90 minutes. Cool in the pan for 5 minutes, loosen the cake from the sides of the pan, then turn out onto a rack to cool completely.

Heat maple syrup in a saucepan over high heat until reduced by half to make a glaze. Brush the cooled cake with the glaze.

BARBARA'S PEACH COBBLER

This traditional Southern dessert is a favorite at our house, as it is often requested by my oldest son, J. Christopher. Spoon it from the baking dish while still warm into attractive bowls and serve with vanilla ice cream.

2 cups plus 2 tablespoons granulated sugar
$1/2$ cup dark brown sugar, packed
$1/4$ cup all-purpose flour
$1/2$ teaspoon ground nutmeg
$1/8$ teaspoon ground cloves
$1^1/2$ teaspoons ground cinnamon
10 cups peeled, pitted, and sliced fresh peaches
$1/2$ teaspoon vanilla
2 teaspoons freshly squeezed lemon juice
$1/2$ cup (1 stick) butter
Pastry (recipe follows)
2 tablespoons butter, melted

Combine the 2 cups of granulated sugar, the brown sugar, flour, nutmeg, cloves, and cinnamon in a large Dutch oven. Add the peaches and set aside 15 minutes. Bring to a boil, then reduce the heat and cook over low heat, stirring occasionally to prevent sticking, until the peaches are almost tender and the mixture thickens, about 10 minutes. Add the vanilla, lemon juice, and butter. Stir gently and set aside.

Preheat the oven to 375°F.

Prepare the pastry as directed and spoon the peaches into it and top with the remaining crust. Trim the edge and flute. Combine the melted butter and the remaining 2 tablespoons of sugar. Brush the top of the cobbler with it, then prick to allow steam to escape. Bake until lightly browned, about 1 hour.

Pastry

4¹/₂ cups all-purpose four

1 teaspoon salt

1¹/₂ cups (3 sticks) butter

1 cup ice water, or more if needed

Combine the flour and salt in mixing bowl. Cut in the butter with a pastry blender until the mixture resembles coarse meal. Sprinkle the water evenly over the mixture 2 tablespoons at a time until moistened, adding more water if dough is too thick. Divide the dough in half. Roll half of the pastry ¹/₈ inch thick on a lightly floured surface. Fit it into a 9 × 13-inch baking dish. Roll the remaining pastry ¹/₈ inch thick for the top crust.

CHEF'S TIP

Place the cobbler on a baking sheet before baking to catch any juice that may drip from the pan. Substitute frozen sliced peaches if fresh are unavailable.

COUNTRY RICE PUDDING

MAKES 6 SERVINGS

*This old standby was a favorite of my customers at the Chester Inn,
in Chester, New Jersey. Serve in attractive stemware.*

4¹/₄ cups milk
1 cup short-grain rice
³/₄ cup sugar
¹/₈ teaspoon ground nutmeg
2 teaspoons grated lemon zest
¹/₄ teaspoon salt
1 egg, beaten
2 teaspoons bourbon
2 teaspoons vanilla
Cinnamon Sugar (recipe follows)

In heavy saucepan, combine the milk, rice, sugar, nutmeg, lemon zest, and salt. Bring to a boil, stirring occasionally. Reduce the heat to low and simmer, uncovered until tender and the mixture begins to thicken, about 20 to 25 minutes, skimming any foam as it accumulates on the surface. Stir in the egg and cook 2 minutes longer. Remove from the heat and stir in the bourbon and vanilla. Chill in individual serving dishes. Sprinkle with Cinnamon Sugar before serving.

CINNAMON SUGAR

¹/₄ cup sugar
1 tablespoon ground cinnamon

Combine the cinnamon and sugar and store tightly covered.

Edna Lewis's Fresh Blackberry Cobbler with Vanilla-flavored Whipped Cream

MAKES 6 TO 8 SERVINGS

This cobbler is another great Southern dessert. Edna prepared this heavenly blackberry cobbler for the dessert course at the first An Elegant Taste of Heritage fund-raising dinner, in Washington, D.C., at the Hay-Adams Hotel.

2 cups unbleached all-purpose
    flour
$1/2$ teaspoon salt
$1/2$ cup lard
$1/3$ cup cold water
1 cup sugar cubes, crushed
5 cups blackberries
4 thin slices butter
$3/4$ cup granulated sugar
2 teaspoons cornstarch
$1/4$ cup light cream
1 cups Vanilla-flavored
    Whipped Cream
    (recipe follows)

Sift the flour and salt into a large mixing bowl. Blend in the lard with a pastry blender or with your fingers. When it is well blended and fine-grained, sprinkle in the water all at once, and draw the dough together quickly, shaping it into a ball. Divide in half and let rest for a few minutes.

Preheat the oven to 425°F.

Roll out the dough and line an 8-inch baking pan. Sprinkle 2 or 3 tablespoons of the crushed sugar over the dough. Fill with the berries, adding the pieces of butter and sprinkling with the granulated sugar mixed with the cornstarch.

Wet the rim of the bottom crust and place the top pastry over it, pressing down to seal. Trim away the excess. With the handle of a dinner knife, make a decorative edge and then cut a few slits in the center to allow steam to escape. Brush the top with a thick brush of cream and sprinkle on the remaining crushed cube sugar. Place in the preheated oven, shut the door, and reduce the heat to 425°F. Bake for 45 minutes. Remove from the oven and set on a rack to cool slightly before serving. Serve with a dollop of Vanilla-flavored Whipped Cream on top.

CHEF'S TIP

You may cover the crust with waxed paper and refrigerate it until you are ready to assemble the cobbler. Roll and shape in the pan before refrigerating for easy handling.

Edna Lewis's Vanilla-flavored Whipped Cream

MAKES 1 CUP

1 cup heavy cream
3 tablespoons sugar
1 teaspoon vanilla extract

Pour the heavy cream into a clean, cold bowl and with a chilled whisk, whip the cream until nearly stiff. Add the sugar and vanilla and continue whipping until the cream is stiff.

CHEF'S TIP
When making whipped cream it is important that the bowl and the whisk be very cold. Place clean, dry utensils in the freezer or fill the bowl with ice water, place the whisk in the ice water, and let stand a few minutes before beating. Pour out the ice water and thoroughly dry the bowl and whisk before adding the cream.

Leah Chase's Poached Pears with Chocolate Hard Sauce

MAKES 8 SERVINGS

Chill the pears just long enough to cool them down slightly. If you make them in advance, keep the pears cold in the refrigerator, but bring them to room temperature before serving for the best flavor.

4 firm, ripe Bartlett pears
2 cups water
1^1/$_2$ cups sugar
2 whole cloves
^{1}/$_2$ cup (1 stick) butter
3 teaspoons chopped semisweet chocolate
1 teaspoon Godiva Chocolate Liqueur
8 maraschino cherries

Peel the pears, cut them in half, and core. Place the water in a saucepan. Add 1 cup of the sugar and the cloves and bring to a boil. Place the pears cut side down in the boiling syrup and cook until the pears are tender, about 5 minutes. Remove the pears and let cool. Place in the refrigerator to chill.

To make the hard sauce, beat the butter until fluffy and light. Gradually beat in the sugar. Add chocolate and liqueur and continue to whip until smooth. Place a spoonful of hard sauce in each pear half. Top each with a maraschino cherry. Serve cool.

Southern Gingerbread with Bourbon Cream

MAKES 18 SERVINGS

Fill the house with a ginger perfume on cold or rainy days with this quick dessert.

$^1/_2$ cup (1 stick) butter

$^3/_4$ cup granulated sugar

2 eggs

$2^1/_2$ cups all-purpose flour

$1^1/_2$ teaspoons baking soda

1 teaspoon ground cinnamon

$1^1/_2$ to 2 teaspoons ground
   ginger, or to taste

$^1/_2$ teaspoon ground cloves

$^1/_2$ teaspoon salt

1 cup molasses

1 cup hot water

BOURBON CREAM

2 cups heavy cream

$1^1/_2$ tablespoons powdered sugar

$1^1/_2$ tablespoons bourbon

Preheat the oven to 350°F.

Melt the butter in a saucepan over high heat. Cool to room temperature and add the granulated sugar and eggs. Mix well. In a bowl, combine the flour, soda, spices, and salt. In a separate bowl, mix the molasses and water. Add the dry ingredients to the butter-sugar mixture, alternating with the molasses mixture until mixed. Line a 9 × 13-inch baking pan with waxed paper and brush lightly with butter. Pour the batter into the pan and bake for 40 to 50 minutes. Allow to cool for 5 minutes, then cut into 2-inch squares to serve.

In a chilled bowl, whip the cream to rounded peaks. Add the powdered sugar and beat 30 seconds. Beat in the bourbon a little at a time, continuing to beat until stiff peaks form. Do not overbeat. Top the gingerbread squares with a spoonful of bourbon cream.

LEMON MERINGUE PIE

MAKES 8 SERVINGS

One slice of this cool, tangy lemon meringue pie and you'll wonder why it's been so long since you baked one.

1^1/$_2$ cups water

^{1}/$_3$ cup cornstarch

^{1}/$_4$ teaspoon salt

^{1}/$_2$ cup cold water

1^3/$_4$ cups sugar

3 eggs, separated

2 tablespoons butter

^{1}/$_2$ cup freshly squeezed lemon
juice

1 tablespoon grated lemon zest

1 baked Southern Pie Shell
(see page 254)

^{1}/$_4$ teaspoon cream of tartar

^{1}/$_4$ teaspoon lemon extract

Bring the 1^1/$_2$ cups water to a boil. Dissolve the cornstarch and salt in the cold water. Add to the boiling water, stirring with a wire whisk. Allow to cook until thickened, about 8 to 10 minutes. Add 1^1/$_4$ cups of the sugar and bring to a boil, then remove from the heat. In a small bowl, beat the egg yolks. Beat a little of the hot liquid into the yolks, then add the yolk mixture to the hot mixture. Add the butter. Return to the heat and cook over low heat, stirring constantly, until the filling boils. Cook 1 to 2 minutes, then remove from the heat. Add the lemon juice and zest and beat with a wire whisk. Set aside for 30 minutes. Pour into the pie shell and let cool.

Preheat the oven to 400°F.

Beat the cream of tartar with the egg whites until frothy, then beat until soft peaks form. Gradually beat in the remaining ^{1}/$_2$ cup sugar and the lemon extract, and continue to beat until stiff peaks form, about 2 minutes. Spread the meringue onto the cooled lemon filling, spreading to the edge of the crust to seal. Bake until firm and golden, about 6 to 8 minutes. Allow to cool on a rack at room temperature, then refrigerate at least 3 to 4 hours before serving.

CHEF'S TIP

Topping the cooled filling with meringue will prevent weeping.

PRINCE AKINS'S STRAWBERRY SHORTCAKE

Fresh, ruby-red strawberries are a sign of spring and this dessert has always been a popular way of heralding the new season.

1 quart fresh strawberries
2 tablespoons sugar
2 cups all-purpose flour
4 teaspoons baking powder
$1/2$ teaspoon salt
1 pinch ground nutmeg
1 teaspoon cream of tartar
$1/2$ cup (1 stick) butter
2 egg yolks
$1/2$ cup milk
1 cup whipping cream
1 tablespoon confectionary
　sugar

Preheat the oven to 450°F.

Cut the strawberries into $1/4$-inch slices and place in a stainless-steel bowl. Sprinkle 1 tablespoon of the sugar over the berries.

In another bowl, double sift the flour and mix in the baking powder, salt, nutmeg, remaining 1 tablespoon sugar, and cream of tartar. Cut the butter into the mixture using a food processor or by hand, either with two forks or a pastry blender. Slowly add the egg yolks and milk to make a coarse dough. Roll the dough out on a lightly floured surface to a $1/2$-inch thickness. Cut into rounds, about 3 inches in diameter.

Place shortcakes on a greased baking sheet and bake for 10 to 12 minutes. Cool for 5 to 10 minutes and cut in half horizontally.

In a cold bowl and using a cold whisk, whip the cream until soft peaks form. Add sugar and continue to whip. Place the bottom half of a shortcake on a dessert dish, layer with whipped cream, strawberries, a dollop of whipped cream, then the shortcake top. Garnish with more strawberries.

SOUTHERN SWEET POTATO PIE

MAKES 8 SERVINGS

Some Southern cooks didn't bother to mash the sweet potatoes for their holiday custard pie; they simply cut them up and spread them in the pie crust, topped with the other ingredients. Here's a version of that heirloom recipe.

$^1/_2$ cup (1 stick) butter

$^1/_2$ cup packed dark brown sugar

2 cups cooked and mashed sweet potatoes

$^1/_2$ teaspoon ground nutmeg

3 eggs, lightly beaten

$^1/_3$ cup corn syrup

$^1/_3$ cup milk

1 teaspoon salt

1 teaspoon vanilla

1 unbaked Southern Pie Shell (see page 254)

Preheat the oven to 325°F.

Combine the butter and sugar in a bowl. Stir in the sweet potatoes, nutmeg, and eggs and mix well. Stir in the corn syrup, milk, salt, and vanilla. Turn mixture into the pie shell and bake 10 minutes. Reduce the heat to 325°F and bake 40 to 50 minutes longer.

CHEF'S TIP

To preserve the naturally sweet goodness of sweet potatoes, bake them for 45 minutes to 1 hour, instead of boiling, for use in recipes.

AUNT DOLLY'S SWEET POTATO PIE

Aunt Dolly used a fork to get a silky smooth sweet potato puree for this pie.
A ricer or food processor works better.

1 pound sweet potatoes, baked
  and pureed
$^1/_2$ cup (1 stick) butter, softened
$^1/_2$ cup granulated sugar
$^1/_2$ cup packed dark brown
  sugar
$^1/_4$ teaspoon salt
$^1/_2$ teaspoon ground nutmeg
1 teaspoon ground cinnamon
2 eggs, beaten
1 cup half-and-half
1 teaspoon vanilla
1 unbaked Southern Pie Shell
  (recipe follows)

Preheat the oven to 350°F.

Combine the potatoes, butter, sugars, salt, nutmeg, and cinnamon in a bowl. Beat with an electric mixer set on medium speed until creamy. Beat in the eggs, then reduce the speed to low and beat in the half-and-half and vanilla. Pour the batter into the pie shell and bake until set, about 50 to 60 minutes. Cool to room temperature before serving. Refrigerate any leftovers.

CHEF'S TIP

Put the sweet potatoes through a ricer to remove any strings and to achieve a perfectly smooth consistency for this pie.

SOUTHERN PIE SHELL

A dash of sugar is the surprise ingredient in this flaky, tender crust.
To use with savory fillings, omit the sugar.

$1^1/_2$ cups all-purpose flour
1 teaspoon sugar
$^1/_2$ teaspoon salt
$^1/_3$ cup butter, chilled
$^1/_3$ cup shortening, chilled
3 tablespoons water, or more
  if needed

Combine the flour, sugar, and salt in a bowl. Cut in the butter and shortening with a pastry blender or fork until the mixture resembles coarse meal. Add the water, stirring lightly with a fork. Form the dough into a ball and roll out to a $^1/_8$-inch thickness on a lightly floured board. Fold the dough in half and place on a pie pan. Fold back to cover the pan and trim the excess, leaving a 1-inch edge. Fold the edge under and flute the rim. Bake according to recipe directions.

Patrick Yves Pierre-Jerome's Flourless Chocolate Cake with Raspberry Sauce

MAKES 10 SERVINGS

Virtually everyone recalls Grandmother's rich devil's food cake with chocolate fudge buttercream frosting. In this updated version, a raspberry coulis accentuates the dense chocolate torte.

1 pound semisweet chocolate, chopped
1 cup unsalted butter
8 eggs, separated
1$^1/_2$ cups sugar
2 tablespoons Frangelico liqueur

RASPBERRY SAUCE
1 pint fresh or frozen raspberries
1 tablespoon raspberry liqueur
$^1/_4$ cup sugar
$^1/_4$ cup chardonnay
Mint sprigs

Preheat the oven to 350°F.

Melt the chocolate and butter in the top of a double boiler. Cool to room temperature. Whip the egg yolks and sugar until thick and pale. Beat in the Frangelico. Whip the egg whites until stiff. Fold one third of the chocolate into the yolks. Fold in one third of the whites. Fold in the remaining chocolate and whites. Butter and flour a 10-inch springform pan. Pour in the batter and bake for 25 to 30 minutes. The cake edges will be set, but the center will still be soft. Cool in the pan and chill overnight.

For the sauce, place the raspberries in a blender or food processor and puree until smooth. Strain the puree through a fine strainer to remove the seeds. Heat the puree in a saucepan over low heat. Add the liqueur, sugar, and wine. Stir and remove from the heat. Cool and refrigerate until ready to serve.

When ready to serve, remove the cake from the pan, slice with a hot knife, and serve with raspberry sauce and a fresh mint sprig.

DEVIL'S FOOD LAYER CAKE

MAKES 10 TO 12 SERVINGS

For a change of pace, bake half the recipe for this moist and tender cake, cut it into thin slices, and serve on a puddle of pureed, sweetened berries or a fruit coulis.

2 cups all-purpose flour

2 cups sugar

³/₄ cup unsweetened cocoa powder

3 teaspoons baking powder

¹/₄ teaspoon salt

¹/₂ cup half-and-half

¹/₂ cup milk

¹/₂ cup (1 stick) butter, melted

¹/₄ cup vegetable oil

3 eggs

2 teaspoons vanilla

Chocolate Frosting (recipe follows)

Preheat the oven to 350°F.

In a mixing bowl, combine the flour, sugar, cocoa, baking powder, and salt. In a separate bowl, mix the half-and-half, milk, butter, oil, and eggs. Beat into the dry ingredients just until mixed, about 1 minute. Stir in the vanilla. Pour batter into two greased and lightly floured 9-inch cake pans. Bake until a wood pick inserted in the center comes out clean, about 30 to 35 minutes. Allow to cool 10 minutes, then remove from the pans and cool completely on wire racks. Place one cake layer on a large plate and spread with chocolate frosting and top with the second layer, top side up. Frost the sides and top of the cake.

CHOCOLATE FROSTING

MAKES ABOUT 4 CUPS

³/₄ cup (1¹/₂ sticks) butter, softened

3 cups powdered sugar

¹/₂ cup unsweetened cocoa powder

¹/₄ cup half-and-half

¹/₂ teaspoon vanilla

In a bowl, cream together the butter and 1 cup of the sugar. Add the cocoa, remaining sugar, half-and-half, and vanilla. Beat until smooth.

Sweet Potato Crème Brûlée

Chefs know the secret to a perfectly glazed custard is to caramelize the sugar with a blow torch or under a salamander. At home you can use the broiler, but watch carefully. It browns quickly.

7 egg yolks

6 tablespoons plus $1/2$ cup sugar

$1/2$ cup baked and mashed sweet potatoes

2 tablespoons toasted coconut

1 teaspoon ground cinnamon

$1/2$ teaspoon ground nutmeg

3 cups heavy cream, scalded

1 tablespoon vanilla

Combine the egg yolks and 6 tablespoons sugar in the top of a double boiler. Beat over simmering water until thickened—the mixture should form a ribbon when the whisk is removed. Remove from the heat occasionally so the custard doesn't cook too fast. Add the sweet potatoes, coconut, cinnamon, and nutmeg and mix well. Slowly whisk the hot cream into the egg-yolk mixture. Cook over hot water, stirring occasionally, until the custard is thickened, about 40 to 45 minutes. Stir in the vanilla. Spoon into 4-ounce custard or ramekins and refrigerate at least 1 hour before caramelizing the top.

Sprinkle each crème brûlée with 1 tablespoon sugar. Place under the broiler until the sugar browns, about 1 to 2 minutes. Refrigerate 15 minutes to allow the crust to set. Serve at room temperature.

BAKED APPLE DUMPLINGS

When apple pie just isn't elegant enough, apples cradled in a delicate dough will impress guests.

2 cups all-purpose flour
1 cup cake flour
2 teaspoons baking powder
$^3/_4$ teaspoon salt
$1^1/_4$ cups ($2^1/_2$ sticks) butter, softened
$^1/_2$ cup milk
$^1/_4$ cup half-and-half
6 cooking apples
$^1/_4$ cup packed dark brown sugar
1 teaspoon Cinnamon Sugar (see page 247)

CINNAMON SAUCE

2 cups sugar
2 cups water
$1^1/_2$ tablespoons butter
$^1/_2$ teaspoon ground cinnamon
$^1/_4$ teaspoon ground nutmeg
1 teaspoon grated lemon zest

$1^1/_2$ cups Crème Anglaise (page 294)

Preheat the oven to 375°F.

In a large bowl, combine the flours, baking powder, and salt. Cut in 1 cup of the butter with a pastry blender until the mixture resembles coarse meal. Combine the milk and half-and-half and slowly add the mixture to the bowl, stirring to form a tender dough. Roll the dough into a 21 × 14-inch rectangle $^1/_4$ inch thick on lightly floured board. Cut into 6 squares.

Peel and core the apples. Place one apple in the center of each dough square. Place 2 teaspoons brown sugar in the center of the apple and sprinkle with Cinnamon Sugar. Dot with the remaining $^1/_4$ cup butter, using about 2 teaspoons for each apple. Moisten the edges of the dough with a little cool water. Fold the edges toward the center of each apple and pinch the corners together to seal. Place the dumplings in a lightly buttered 13 × 9-inch baking pan. Bake for 30 to 35 minutes.

In a saucepan, combine the sugar, water, butter, spices, and lemon zest. Bring to a boil, then reduce the heat and simmer, stirring, until the sugar dissolves, about 5 to 6 minutes. Keep warm until serving time.

Cover the bottom of each serving plate with $^1/_4$ cup Crème Anglaise. Place the dumpling on top and pour cinnamon sauce over the dumplings. Serve immediately.

Darryl Evans's Lemon Pistachio Tuile Cookie Basket with Marinated Berries

MAKES 8 SERVINGS

This light and eye appealing dessert is an example of "Me being me," Darryl says.
You could try pecans for a more Southern flair. Figs, blackberries—
even muscadines, will give a rustic taste.

$^1/_3$ cup granulated sugar

1 teaspoon powdered sugar

1 tablespoon bread flour

$^1/_4$ cup cake flour

$^1/_3$ cup egg whites (about 5 egg whites)

7 tablespoons butter, melted

$^1/_4$ teaspoon vanilla

3 tablespoons fresh lemon juice

3 teaspoons lemon zest

$^1/_4$ cup pistachio nuts, chopped

MARINATED BERRIES

1 pint each fresh blackberries, strawberries, and raspberries, rinsed

$^1/_3$ cup orange juice

3 tablespoons orange zest

2 tablespoons Grand Marnier (optional)

1 tablespoon powdered sugar

TO FINISH THE DISH

1 cup heavy cream, whipped

8 sprigs mint

Preheat the oven to 350°F.

Sift together the sugars and flours and place in a mixing bowl. Add the egg whites, melted butter, vanilla, lemon juice, and zest. Spread the batter into 4-inch circles on a greased baking sheet (about 4 cookies to a sheet). Sprinkle with the chopped pistachios, then bake until lightly brown.

Remove from the oven and place each cookie over the bottom of a soup cup to make a basket. Be sure to face the nut side into the cup. Work fast or the cookies will set before you put them on the can.

Combine the berries with the orange juice and zest, Grand Marnier, and powdered sugar. At serving time place the berries in the basket and top with whipped cream and a sprig of fresh mint.

PEACHES BAKED IN PUFF PASTRY

MAKES 8 SERVINGS

This showstopping dessert was created for a dinner honoring actress and restaurateur Marla Gibbs at Cal-Poly, Pomona. It has continued to wow guests at Elegant Taste of Heritage dinners.

2 cups sugar
1 tablespoon ground cinnamon
$^1/_2$ teaspoon ground nutmeg
8 squares puff pastry, each cut into a 4-inch square
8 ripe peaches, peeled, pitted, and cut in half
2 cups sliced peaches
$^1/_4$ cup peach brandy
1 teaspoon freshly squeezed lemon juice
Brandy Custard Sauce (see page 293)
Candied Pecans (recipe follows)
Mint sprigs

Preheat the oven to 350°F.

Combine 1$^1/_2$ cups of the sugar and the cinnamon and nutmeg. Roll each puff pastry square into a $^1/_4$-inch-thick circle. Place two peach halves together to form a whole peach, then place one in the center of each pastry circle. Sprinkle the sugar mixture the over peaches. Form the dough into a ball to seal in the peaches and place on a baking sheet lined with greased parchment paper. Pierce the puff pastry with a fork, then bake until golden, about 20 to 25 minutes. Set aside.

Puree the sliced peaches, brandy, lemon juice, and the remaining $^1/_2$ cup sugar in a blender until smooth. Strain through a fine sieve and refrigerate, covered, until serving time.

To serve, coat the serving plates with Brandy Custard Sauce. Spoon some peach sauce into center of the custard sauce. Using a wood pick, draw parallel lines from the center of the peach sauce through the Brandy Custard Sauce to make an attractive spider web design. Place a baked peach in the center of each plate and arrange 4 pecans around each peach. Garnish with mint.

CANDIED PECANS

2 cups sugar
$^1/_2$ cup water
1 tablespoon Grand Marnier
$1^1/_2$ tablespoons butter
2 cups pecans

In a saucepan, bring the sugar, water, and Grand Marnier to a boil. Cook the mixture to soft-ball stage (240°F) on a candy thermometer. Remove the pan from the heat, add the butter, and beat with a wooden spoon until the mixture is just ready to set. Quickly add the pecans and continue to beat until the mixture crystallizes. Turn the candy onto a greased, cool surface to cool. When cool, use forks to separate the pecans.

CHEF'S TIP

If fresh peaches are not available use frozen. Choose canned peaches only as a last resort.

PEACH AND SUN-DRIED CHERRY DUMPLINGS

MAKES 8 SERVINGS

Dumplings poached in stewed fruit is a tradition from the old South. I put the fruit in the dumplings and serve them with a rich custard sauce.

2¹/₂ cups all-purpose flour

2 tablespoons butter, melted

2 tablespoons sugar

¹/₂ package active dry yeast

1 egg yolk

¹/₂ cup milk

¹/₈ teaspoon salt

1 tablespoon grated lemon zest

PEACH-CHERRY FILLING

¹/₂ cup water

¹/₂ cup sun-dried cherries

¹/₄ cup sugar

¹/₂ teaspoon ground cinnamon

2 fresh peaches, peeled, pitted,
    and cut into ¹/₂-inch cubes

1 tablespoon brandy

TO FINISH THE DISH

Brandy Custard Sauce
   (see page 293)

2 tablespoons powdered sugar

1 teaspoon ground nutmeg

In bowl of an electric mixer, combine the flour, butter, sugar, yeast, egg yolk, milk, salt, and lemon zest. Attach the dough hook and mix until smooth. Shape the dough into a ball and cover with a towel. Allow to rest 30 to 40 minutes in warm place (the dough will not rise). Place on a lightly floured board and cut into 16 pieces.

To make the filling, bring the water and cherries to a slow boil in a saucepan. Remove from the heat and set aside 15 minutes to reconstitute cherries. Drain, reserving the cherry juice. Bring the juice to a boil and add the sugar and cinnamon. Reduce the heat to simmer and cook until thickened. Add the peaches, cherries, and brandy and cook until the fruit is tender. Remove from the heat and set aside to cool.

Flatten each piece of dough into a 3-inch circle and spoon 1 tablespoon filling in the center of each. Fold the corners to seal dough and shape into balls. Allow the dumplings to rise, covered with a towel, until doubled. Cook in boiling salted water about 9 minutes. Turn and continue to cook 9 minutes longer, covered. Remove from the water with a slotted spoon and allow to drain.

Place each dumpling on a serving plate. Nap with Brandy Custard Sauce and sprinkle with the powdered sugar mixed with the nutmeg.

CLIFTON WILLIAMS'S SWEET BREAD PUDDING WITH CREAM

MAKES 8 SERVINGS

*Clifton takes a good thing and makes it even better, here using leftover
Danish from the freezer instead of stale bread.*

$^1/_2$ cup packed brown sugar

$^1/_2$ cup (1 stick) butter, at room
   temperature

2 tablespoons white corn syrup

3 eggs

1 cup granulated sugar

1$^3/_4$ teaspoons vanilla

2 teaspoons ground nutmeg

1 teaspoon ground cinnamon

Pinch salt

$^1/_4$ cup ($^1/_2$ stick) butter, melted

2 cups low-fat (2%) milk

$^1/_2$ cup raisins

5 cups cubed stale Danish rolls

1 cup heavy cream

1 tablespoon vanilla

2 cups Crème Anglaise (see page
   294) or other vanilla sauce

Preheat the oven to 300°F.

Mix together the brown sugar, butter, and corn syrup and sprinkle the mixture in the bottom of a 13 × 9-inch baking pan. In a large bowl, beat the eggs until well mixed and frothy, about 3 to 5 minutes. Add the granulated sugar, vanilla, nutmeg, cinnamon, salt, and melted butter. Beat well. Stir in the milk and raisins. Add the Danish to the mixture and soak for 20 minutes, patting the Danish down into the liquid occasionally. Remove the Danish and place it in the prepared pan. Bake until the pudding is well-rounded and puffy, about 50 to 65 minutes. Immediately invert on a serving tray but do not remove the pan. Let rest for 15 minutes. Remove the pan, allowing the sauce to spread over the top of the pudding.

With a wire whisk, whip the heavy cream, beating in the vanilla. To serve, place about $^1/_4$ cup of Crème Anglaise or vanilla ice cream in each dessert plate, then spoon the warm Danish pudding on top. Serve with the whipped cream.

Patrick Clark's White Chocolate Banana Cream Pie

MAKES TWO 9-INCH PIES

Patrick likes to use Callebaut or Valrhona white chocolate in his desserts.

PIE CRUST
$^1/_2$ cup plus 1 tablespoon
   shortening
$^1/_4$ cup ($^1/_2$ stick) unsalted butter,
   cut into 1-inch pieces
$^1/_2$ teaspoon salt
2 cups all-purpose flour
3 tablespoons ice water

FILLING
4 cups milk
1 vanilla bean, split
$1^1/_4$ cups sugar
Pinch salt
5 egg yolks
$^1/_2$ cup cornstarch
5 ounces white chocolate,
   coarsely chopped
6 medium ripe bananas

WHITE CHOCOLATE
WHIPPED CREAM
4 ounces white chocolate
3 cups heavy cream
2 cups banana liqueur
$^1/_4$ cup powdered sugar
1 chunk white chocolate, about
   2 ounces, for garnish

To make the crust, combine the shortening, butter, and salt until blended. Rub in the flour until the mixture is crumbly. Using a fork, stir in the water a little at a time until a dough begins to form. Knead just until the dough comes together. Wrap and refrigerate for 1 hour.

Preheat the oven to 350°F.

Divide the dough in half and roll out into circles. Line two 9-inch pie plates and crimp edges high. Prick with a fork or line with pie weights and bake until golden brown. Set aside to cool.

To make the filling, bring 3 cups of the milk to a boil with the vanilla bean, 1 cup of the sugar, and the salt. Cover and set aside to infuse for 15 to 20 minutes. Beat the egg yolks, the remaining $^1/_4$ cup of sugar, cornstarch, and remaining 1 cup of milk together until smooth. Add a small amount of the hot mixture to the yolk mixture. Return the milk mixture to a boil, then whisk in the tempered yolk mixture and bring to a boil, whisking constantly until thick. Remove from the heat and remove the vanilla bean. Let cool for 5 minutes, whisking occasionally to prevent a skin from forming. Whisk in the chopped chocolate.

Slice the bananas $^1/_4$ inch thick and divide among the two pie shells. Pour the white chocolate custard over the bananas and smooth the tops. Place lightly buttered waxed paper rounds over each pie, inside the rim of the crust, and let the pie cool in the refrigerator until cold.

To make the topping, melt the 4 ounces of white chocolate in the top of a double boiler over simmering water. Place it in a large bowl and set aside. Whip the cream, liqueur, and powdered sugar until firm but soft peaks form. Whisk one third of the whipped cream into the warm chocolate, then quickly fold the mixture into the remaining whipped cream. Divide evenly among the two pies. Shave white chocolate from remaining chunk over the pies.

Chapter 11

Wines and Extras

MAYBE YOU WERE RAISED ON A FARM, WHERE ONIONS, CELERY, FRESH HERBS, GARLIC, AND all sorts of peppers grew in the garden just outside your back door. They were invaluable in recipes. You remember corn that was so fresh you rushed inside to cook it in a hot kettle of boiling water to preserve that fresh-picked flavor. Or peas that snapped when they were popped from the pod.

If you have tasted tomatoes fresh from the vine, nibbled raw green beans still wearing the morning dew, and experienced slender carrots still blushing with a smudge of soil, then you know these are flavors you want to linger forever. You want to satisfy a nagging taste for the sweetness of Concord grapes or ruby red strawberries long after the season has passed.

In the old days, the answer was food preservation—canning, pickling, marinating, and sweetening perishable produce; meats were smoked, cured, and salted. Not only did it allow families to savor the best of the season's harvest, it helped them save money. And, though most often it was about survival during the harsh winter months, sometimes it was done just for fun.

Now that many of us have moved to the city doesn't mean we have to settle for woody tomatoes and peaches that taste like Styrofoam or uninformed produce managers who think escarole and endive look anything alike.

These days, most every major city has a farmer's market and shopping there can be like taking a nostalgic trip back to a simpler time. Unlike the average supermarket, you will find all sorts of different sausages and unusual cuts of meats, and some of the freshest fruits and vegetables imaginable. Don't be surprised if you come away with armloads of food, quite possibly far more than your family can eat before it goes bad. That's when you do what Uncle Dick's generation did.

Of course, many people say they don't have time to cook, much less put up fruits and vegetables. All that chopping and sterilizing just takes too long. With the suggestions on the following pages, nothing could be farther from the truth.

Over the years, dandelions have been used for beer and wine and tossed with a bacon vinaigrette for a tangy, French-style salad. Here their blossoms are tamed with the piquant flavor of citrus in Granny's Dandelion Wine.

Apple dishes are some of the easiest for preserving and Southern Apple Butter is a great place for beginning food preservers to start.

Once you get the hang of it, you may discover that hot buttermilk biscuits taste better with homemade jam; that a simple hamburger takes on a whole new charm when garnished with your very own cucumber pickles.

You may not put up enough to need a root cellar, but it does have a nostalgic ring.

CLIFTON WILLIAMS'S
BLACK-EYED PEA SALSA

MAKES 2 PINTS

*African-American cuisine has been influenced by an assortment of other cultures. This dish,
which is similar to Texas caviar, has a Southwest flair.*

$^1/_4$ cup finely diced tomato

$^1/_2$ cup finely diced onion

$^1/_2$ cup finely diced green pepper

1 cup finely diced celery

1 cup finely diced lean smoked
ham

2 tablespoons finely diced
serrano chiles

1 pound black-eyed peas,
cooked

2 tablespoons extra-virgin
olive oil

$^1/_4$ cup seasoned rice vinegar

$^1/_4$ teaspoon salt

$^1/_8$ teaspoon freshly ground
black pepper

$^1/_2$ tablespoon chopped fresh
parsley

In a large bowl, combine the tomato, onion, green pepper, celery, smoked ham, chiles, and black-eyed peas. Stir well. Combine the remaining ingredients and pour this dressing over the salsa and mix well. Refrigerate until needed.

COUNTRY CHOWCHOW

This is one of those wonderful recipes that was created as a way to preserve the season's best. The best thing about chowchow is it doesn't require processing in a hot water bath. Serve a spoonful with collard greens—it is like the butter on a biscuit or the frosting on a cake.

6 cups chopped green cabbage
(about 1 large head)
2 cups diced green tomatoes
(about 4 medium)
2 cups diced green pepper
1 cup diced red pepper
2 cups diced onions
1 teaspoon minced garlic
3 tablespoons salt
$2^3/_4$ cups distilled vinegar
2 cups sugar
2 teaspoons celery seed
2 teaspoons dry mustard
1 teaspoon mustard seed
1 teaspoon turmeric
$^1/_2$ teaspoon ground ginger
$^1/_4$ cup grated fresh horseradish

In a large bowl, combine the cabbage, tomatoes, green and red peppers, onions, and minced garlic, and sprinkle with the salt. Cover and refrigerate for at least 4 hours. Drain off any liquid that accumulates.

In a saucepan, combine the vinegar, sugar, celery seed, dry mustard, mustard seed, turmeric, ginger, and horseradish. Simmer for 10 to 12 minutes, add the vegetables, stir, then turn up the heat and bring the mixture to a boil. Reduce the heat and continue to simmer for 12 to 14 minutes. Pour the chowchow into sterilized pint jars with tight-fitting lids and refrigerate until needed.

CRANBERRY RELISH

MAKES 2 CUPS

Cranberries and oranges have a natural affinity, and adding white wine makes a good thing even better. Served alongside roast turkey, this relish will dazzle your holiday guests.

2 cups fresh cranberries
$1/_4$ cup chardonnay
$1/_2$ cup sugar
1 cup fresh orange juice
2 teaspoons orange zest

Bring the cranberries, wine, and sugar to a boil in a saucepan. Stir in the orange juice and orange zest, reduce the heat to simmer, and cook for 15 minutes. Remove the mixture from the heat and cool. Refrigerate until ready to serve.

CURED SALTED MACKEREL

MAKES 12 FILLETS

In some homes, pickling is the preferred method for preserving mackerel, but my family likes curing with salt.

Twelve 6- to 8-ounce Spanish mackerel fillets
2 cups coarse sea salt

Fillet the mackerel or have it done at the fish market, then place a layer of salt in the bottom of a stone crock. Arrange 2 or 3 fillets on top of the salt, then repeat the layering once. End with a layer of salt. Cover the crock and refrigerate for 2 weeks or more. As the fish cures, it will create its own brine.

PATRICK CLARK'S
FIG AND APPLE CHUTNEY

MAKES 4 CUPS

This is a takeoff on applesauce that may drive purists nuts. Patrick gets inspiration from all ethnicities, which is why his dishes are so popular. "We have to push the boundaries," he says.

6 dried mission figs, thinly
   sliced
2 tablespoons sugar
1 cup ruby port
$^1/_2$ cup red wine vinegar
2 teaspoons mustard seed
$^1/_2$ teaspoon ground cinnamon
$^1/_2$ teaspoon ground allspice
2 whole cloves
$^1/_4$ teaspoon cayenne pepper
$^1/_4$ teaspoon salt
1 medium red onion, finely
   chopped
$2^1/_2$ pounds Granny Smith
   apples, peeled, cored, and cut
   into $^1/_2$-inch pieces
1 teaspoon finely grated
   orange zest
1 teaspoon finely grated
   lemon zest
1 teaspoon freshly squeezed
   lemon juice

In a nonreactive medium saucepan, combine the figs, sugar, port, vinegar, mustard seed, cinnamon, allspice, cloves, cayenne pepper, and salt. Bring to a boil over high heat, then reduce the heat to medium and simmer, stirring occasionally, until the figs are tender, 10 to 15 minutes. Add the onion and cook until tender, about 10 minutes longer. Stir in the apples and simmer over moderate heat, stirring often, until the chutney is thick and chunky, about 30 minutes. Stir in the orange zest and lemon zest and juice and cook 2 minutes longer. Transfer to a bowl and let cool.

CHEF'S TIP
This chutney can be refrigerated for up to 3 days. Let return to room temperature before serving.

Mom Pan's Applesauce

MAKES 6 TO 8 SERVINGS

Fresh apples from the Broad Street Market could mean many things, from fried apples for breakfast to apple dumplings, but you could be sure there was going to be some of Mom Pan's homemade applesauce in the refrigerator.

8 Granny Smith Apples
$^{1}/_{2}$ teaspoon salt
1 cup sugar
$^{1}/_{8}$ teaspoon freshly ground
    nutmeg
$^{3}/_{4}$ cup water

Wash, peel, and core the apples, cut them into quarters, and place them in a large saucepan. Sprinkle the apples with the salt, sugar, and nutmeg. Cover the pan and cook the apples over medium heat for 8 to 10 minutes. Remove the cover, add the water, and cook over low heat until the apples are soft. Strain the applesauce and add more sugar, if needed.

Patrick Yves Pierre-Jerome's Mushroom and Onion Compote

MAKES 1 CUP

1 cup diced mushrooms
1 cup diced onions
$^{1}/_{4}$ cup dry sherry
$^{1}/_{8}$ teaspoon salt
$^{1}/_{8}$ teaspoon freshly ground
    black pepper

Sauté the mushrooms over high heat until brown. Remove the mushrooms from the pan and add the onions and sauté until brown. Combine the mushrooms and onions and add the sherry and simmer until the liquid has evaporated. Season with salt and pepper and keep warm until ready to serve.

ROASTED RED PEPPERS

MAKES 1 1/2 CUPS

Roasting has become a popular treatment for vegetables on modern menus.
Hold the peppers over a bowl as you peel away the charred skin to be sure you
capture every drop of the delicious roasted juices.

4 red peppers

Roast the red peppers over a hot flame, using metal tongs, or under the broiler until they are charred all over. Place the peppers in a brown paper bag, seal it, and set aside until cool enough to handle, about 15 minutes. Remove the charred skin, and cut each pepper in half to remove its seeds. Refrigerate the peppers, covered, until ready to use.

EDNA LEWIS'S SINGLE-ACTING BAKING POWDER

MAKES 1/2 CUP

1/4 cup cream of tartar
2 tablespoons baking soda
3 tablespoons cornstarch

Combine all the ingredients, mixing well. Store the baking powder in a glass jar with a tight-fitting lid. It will keep for a month or more.

SMOKED CATFISH

MAKES 5 POUNDS

The flavor of smoked salmon and catfish come together marvelously in this dish. Usually hot smoking is done at temperatures ranging from 150 to 250°F so that the slowly roasted fish or meat absorbs a hearty, smoky flavor. The high temperature also ensures that the fish or meat remains tender and juicy. But be warned, smoking is not an exact science. You'll have to practice until you get the hang of it. Improvise.

5 pounds catfish fillets, trimmed
2¹/₂ quarts Smoked Fish Brine
(recipe follows)

Place the catfish fillets in the brine, making sure that they are completely covered, and allow to soak for 5 hours. Remove the fish from the brine, place it on a rack, and allow to air-dry for 1 hour, using a fan set on low at a 4-foot distance. This will create a dry surface, which will help the fillets absorb the smoke better. When they are completely dry, place the fillets on a rack and smoke for 45 minutes according to the instructions accompanying the smoker.

CHEF'S TIP
There are small versions of commercial smokers, usually consisting of a metal box with a gas or electric heating element on the bottom. Be sure to assemble the unit correctly, with the wood chips placed in a pan over the heat and the fish or meat on a rack over the savory smoke.

SMOKED FISH BRINE

MAKES 2¹/₂ QUARTS

1 cup salt
2 cups packed brown sugar
1 tablespoon garlic juice
1 tablespoon onion juice
¹/₃ medium potato, peeled
2 quarts warm water

Combine the salt, brown sugar, garlic juice, and onion juice in a large bowl or plastic container to make a brine. Place the potato in the brine and gradually add water until the potato just sinks.

SOUTHERN APPLE BUTTER

MAKES 3 PINTS

Homemade apple butter tastes so delicious on fresh-baked breads and it is so easy to make,
you will wonder why you didn't try it sooner.

3 pints apple cider
15 medium Granny Smith
    apples, washed, cored, and
    peeled (about 5 pounds)
1 cup packed dark brown sugar
$^1/_2$ teaspoon ground cloves
$^1/_2$ teaspoon ground allspice
1 teaspoon ground cinnamon
$^1/_4$ teaspoon salt

In a large saucepan, bring the cider to a boil. Reduce the heat and simmer until the cider reduces by half, about 20 to 30 minutes. Add the apples, stirring continuously, and cook until the apples are tender, about 15 to 20 minutes. Place the apples and liquid through a sieve or puree them in a food processor. Return the mixture to the saucepan and add the brown sugar, cloves, allspice, cinnamon, and salt. Return to a simmer and cook, stirring often, until the mixture is thick and smooth, about 25 to 30 minutes.

Pour the apple butter into 3 hot sterilized jars, leaving about $^1/_2$-inch of space at the top. Loosely seal the jars and place on a rack in a canning pot, partly submerged in boiling water. Completely seal the jars and add more boiling water to cover the jars by at least 1 inch. Return the water to a boil and allow the jars to remain in the boiling water for 5 to 6 minutes. Remove and store in a cool, dry place. Refrigerate after opening.

UNCLE DICK'S EGGNOG

MAKES 6 SERVINGS

There are people who believe that the way to show hospitality is by offering guests something to eat
or drink when they visit your home. I can't ever remember visiting Uncle Dick's house during the
Christmas holidays without being offered some of his famous homemade eggnog.

6 eggs, separated
1 cup sugar
$^3/_4$ cup bourbon
$^1/_4$ teaspoon vanilla
$^1/_2$ teaspoon freshly ground
    nutmeg
2 cups heavy cream, whipped
1 cup half-and-half

In a large mixing bowl, place the egg yolks and gradually beat in $^1/_2$ cup of the sugar with a wire whisk until light and lemon-colored. Stir in the bourbon, vanilla, and nutmeg.

In a separate bowl, beat the egg whites until stiff. Beat in the remaining $^1/_2$ cup of sugar. Fold the egg whites into the egg-yolk mixture. Fold in the whipped cream and stir in the half-and-half. Beat well. Chill overnight and serve cold.

UNCLE DICK'S PEACH WINE

MAKES 3 QUARTS

Wine-making was a tradition at Uncle Dick's house. He made wine from just about every fruit that was grown in his yard, including grapes, plums, apricots, pears, and my favorite, peaches. He took pleasure in watching his guests' enjoyment of whichever wine was offered. He would always take a sip with you, but I never saw him drink any store-bought liquor. He even owned and operated two hotels with bars and never drank in them.

10 pounds ripe peaches, washed
4 quarts water
4 pounds sugar
1 package active dry yeast
1/4 cup lukewarm water

Wash the peaches and cut them in half. Place them in a large stainless-steel pot. Cover with the water and bring to a boil, then reduce the heat to simmer and cook 30 to 40 minutes. Remove from the heat to cool. Strain the cooled fruit through cheesecloth and measure 4 quarts of liquid into a stone crock. Add the sugar. Dissolve the yeast in the lukewarm water and stir into the crock. Cover the crock with a clean, double layer of cheesecloth and tie it tight.

Store the crock in a cool, dark place undisturbed for 4 weeks. Remove the cheesecloth from the crock, strain the wine into sterilized bottles, cork the bottles, and allow the wine to age in a cool, dark, place for at least 6 months. The wine improves with age. Serve chilled.

GRANNY'S DANDELION WINE

Although I never saw her drink any herself, Granny used to make this wine for family and friends to share at picnics and family gatherings. I spent many days hand-picking dandelion blossoms at the country home my father purchased outside of Harrisburg, Pennsylvania. We called it the country club because it gave black people a private picnic area.

3 quarts dandelion blossoms, stems removed

4 quarts boiling water

1 lemon, cut into pieces

2 Valencia oranges, cut into pieces

3 pounds sugar

1½ teaspoons active dry yeast, or 1 yeast cake dissolved in 2 tablespoons warm water

Wash the dandelion blossoms thoroughly and place them in a large soup pot. Pour in the boiling water being sure it covers the dandelions and bring to a boil again. After the water boils, remove the pot from the heat, let cool, and pour the contents into a large crock. Set aside undisturbed for 3 days and nights. Strain the liquid through a cheesecloth into a large soup pot. Bring the liquid to a boil and add the lemon, oranges, and sugar. Stir, then remove from the heat. Cool the liquid, then return it to the large crock and add the yeast. Store the liquid, covered, in a cool place for 10 to 14 days. Strain the wine, bottle it, and store it in cool place.

Chapter 12

The Basics: Stocks, Sauces, and Gravies

ALTHOUGH EVERY GOOD CHEF ALWAYS HAS A FRAGRANT POT OF VEAL STOCK CLOSE AT hand for finishing his finest creations, most African-American cooks don't realize how much they too rely upon richly flavored stock.

Sometimes we start with leftovers: a ham bone, a turkey or chicken carcass, or a few fish bones. Other times, crisply cooked bacon, ham hocks, salt pork, or streak-of-lean and streak-of-fat goes into the stockpot, along with a few mild vegetables and water.

If we want soup, we simply add a few chopped vegetables and puree the mix. Thickened with cream, butter, milk, and a few pieces of shellfish, you call the brew a bisque. Reduce and stir in a roux or butter and aromatic vegetables and you've produced a fine sauce.

A full-bodied stock is, arguably, the most indispensable part of fine cooking no matter who—chef or home cook—is stirring the pot. Still, most of us have gotten comfortable with shortcut cooking—dumping commercially prepared broth from a can to quick-cook recipes. Even though it takes more time and some advance preparation, you'll find it useful to have stocks you've made yourself in the freezer. Simply pour cooled stock into ice cube trays and freeze. Or, you may refrigerate it for about a week. Fresh stocks taste much better than anything you could pour out of a can or mix from a bottle of bouillon.

The components are essentially the same whether you are making lamb, veal, beef, fish, or chicken stock. The difference is fish and chicken bones are not browned before they are tossed into the stockpot. You'll have to skim the pot more often with veal and fish bones as they contain a good deal of gelatin.

The stock recipes in this book benefit from mildly aromatic vegetables like onions, celery, and carrots and a bouquet garni, but less often garlic or other vegetables with a strong flavor, which intensify and may overwhelm the other flavors as the stock cooks and reduces.

Unlike some cooks, we believe stocks are improved with a little salt. It helps extract the flavor from the ingredients in the pot and acts as a preservative when the stock is stored. But use caution. When the stock condenses, the saltiness is fortified. To be safe, you may simply add it at the end of the cooking time.

Another point to remember: Bring the stock to a slow boil to get a good beginning temperature, then reduce the heat to a gentle simmer. If you boil the stock too rapidly, it will be cloudy and may taste unpleasant.

The same principles translate to the other sauces and gravies in African-American cuisine. Barbecue sauce, tomato sauce, even pizza sauce taste better when you make them yourself. Our recipes are very forgiving and allow lots of room for your own inspiration.

Stocks

CHICKEN STOCK

MAKES 2 QUARTS

4 pounds chicken bones, cut
  into 3-inch pieces if desired
  and rinsed
3 quarts water
1 medium carrot, coarsely
  chopped
1 medium onion, coarsely
  chopped
2 ribs celery, coarsely chopped
2 teaspoons salt (optional)
3 sprigs fresh parsley
2 sprigs fresh thyme
1 bay leaf
3 whole peppercorns

In a large stockpot, combine the bones and water. Bring them slowly to a boil, then reduce the heat and simmer for 2 hours, skimming the stock as needed. Add the carrot, onion, celery, salt, parsley, thyme, bay leaf, and peppercorns and continue to simmer 2 hours more. Strain. Allow to cool completely and skim off any fat. Cover and refrigerate. The stock will keep 2 to 3 days refrigerated, or it can be frozen.

CHEF'S TIP
Store chicken backs, necks, and the bones from poached chicken in the freezer tightly sealed in freezer bags for making stock.

FISH STOCK

MAKES 1 QUART

3 pounds fish bones, broken
  into pieces
1 1/2 quarts water
1/2 cup diced onion
1/2 cup diced celery
1/2 cup diced carrot
1/8 cup mushroom trimmings or
  sliced mushrooms (optional)
2 sprigs parsley
1 bay leaf
1 teaspoon salt (optional)
1/2 teaspoon ground white pepper

In a large stockpot, combine the fish bones, water, onion, celery, carrot, mushrooms, parsley, bay leaf, salt, and pepper. Bring slowly to a boil, then reduce the heat and simmer, skimming the stock as needed, for 40 to 45 minutes. Strain and allow to cool. Skim off any fat. Cover and refrigerate. The stock will keep 1 to 2 days refrigerated, or it can be frozen.

LAMB STOCK

MAKES 3 CUPS

Bones from 1 leg of lamb
$^1/_4$ cup diced celery
$^1/_4$ cup diced carrot
$^1/_4$ cup diced onion
$1^1/_2$ quarts water
1 bay leaf
1 sprig rosemary
3 whole black peppercorns
3 sprigs fresh mint

Preheat the oven to 375°F.

Place the lamb bones in a baking pan and brown them in the oven for 30 to 40 minutes. Place the browned bones in a stockpot and add the celery, carrot, onion, water, bay leaf, and rosemary. Bring the stock to a boil, then reduce the heat and add the peppercorns and mint. Simmer for 2 hours. Strain. Cover and refrigerate. The stock will keep 2 days refrigerated, or it can be frozen.

SHRIMP (SHELLFISH) STOCK

MAKES 1 QUART

$^1/_4$ cup peanut oil
$1^1/_2$ pounds shrimp shells, from
   5 pounds of peeled shrimp
1 rib celery, coarsely chopped
1 small carrot, coarsely chopped
1 small onion, coarsely chopped
2 cloves garlic, coarsely chopped
2 quarts water
$^1/_4$ cup dry white wine
2 tablespoons tomato paste
1 sprig parsley
1 sprig fresh thyme
2 black peppercorns
1 bay leaf

Heat the oil in a stockpot over medium heat. Add the shrimp shells and sauté for 3 to 4 minutes, stirring until the shells look dry. Add the celery, carrot, onion, and garlic, and continue to sauté for 2 to 3 minutes. Add the water, wine, tomato paste, parsley, thyme, peppercorns, and bay leaf. Bring the stock to a boil, then reduce the heat and simmer for 1 hour. Strain the stock through a fine mesh strainer. Return to the heat and boil until reduced to 1 quart. The stock will keep 2 to 3 days refrigerated, or it can be frozen.

SMOKED HAM STOCK

MAKES 1 QUART

2 pounds smoked ham hocks, split

1 1/2 quarts water

1 rib celery, coarsely chopped

1 medium carrot, coarsely chopped

1 medium onion, coarsely chopped

1 sprig fresh thyme

3 peppercorns

1 tablespoon seasoned salt

In a large stockpot, combine the hocks, water, celery, carrot, onion, thyme, peppercorns, and seasoned salt. Cover and simmer for 1 1/2 to 2 hours. Strain the stock, remove the skin from the ham hocks and discard it. Dice the meat and reserve it to add to vegetables or soup. Cool and refrigerate. The stock will keep 3 to 4 days refrigerated, or it can be frozen.

VEAL (BROWN) STOCK

MAKES 1 QUART

3 pounds veal bones

1/2 cup coarsely chopped onion

1/2 cup coarsely chopped carrot

1/2 cup coarsely chopped celery

1/4 cup coarsely chopped leeks

2 quarts water

1 cup canned whole peeled tomatoes, chopped

1 bay leaf

1 sprig parsley

4 black peppercorns

2 teaspoons salt

Preheat the oven to 400°F.

Place the veal bones in a roasting pan and roast for 30 minutes. Turn the bones and roast 30 minutes more. Add the onion, carrot, celery, and leeks, and cook until the vegetables brown. Remove the roasting pan from the oven and place the bones in a large stockpot. Drain the vegetables and add them to the pot. Add cold water to cover, then add the tomatoes, bay leaf, parsley, peppercorns, and salt. Bring the stock to a boil, then reduce the heat and simmer for 7 to 8 hours. Strain the stock through a fine sieve. Allow to cool and refrigerate. The stock will keep 2 to 3 days refrigerated, or it can be frozen.

CHEF'S TIP
Knuckle bones contain the most cartilage and gelatin and are best for making stock. Neck bones and shank bones can also be used.

OYSTER BROTH

MAKES 2 PINTS

½ cup (1 stick) butter

1 pint Eastern oysters, shucked and drained, liquor reserved

2 cups half-and-half

1 cup heavy cream

¼ teaspoon ground white pepper

⅛ teaspoon cayenne pepper

¼ teaspoon salt

Melt ¼ cup of the butter in a skillet. Add the oysters and sauté on both sides until edges begin to curl. Remove the oysters from the pan. Add 1 cup reserved oyster liquor, half-and-half, and cream. Bring to a boil, then reduce heat and simmer until reduced by half. Season with salt and white and cayenne peppers. Stir in the remaining ¼ cup butter and oysters. Keep hot.

TASSO TOMATO BROTH

MAKES 1 QUART

1½ pounds fresh Italian plum tomatoes

¼ cup (½ stick) butter

½ cup finely diced onion

1 teaspoon minced garlic

¼ cup finely diced celery

¼ cup finely diced green pepper

2 teaspoons sugar

1 tablespoon tomato paste

2 tablespoons thyme

½ teaspoon cayenne pepper

2 cups water

1 tablespoon salt

½ tablespoon freshly ground black pepper

2 cups heavy cream

¼ pound tasso ham, julienned

In a pot of boiling water, blanch the tomatoes for 30 to 40 seconds. Remove and shock them in an ice water bath to stop the cooking. Peel the tomatoes and remove and discard the seeds. Dice the tomato flesh and set it aside.

Melt the butter in a saucepan. Add onion, garlic, celery, and green pepper and sauté over medium-high heat for 2 to 3 minutes. Stir in the tomatoes and cook for 3 to 4 minutes. Stir in the sugar, tomato paste, thyme, cayenne, water, salt, and black pepper. Bring the mixture to a boil, then reduce the heat and simmer until the broth thickens, about 20 to 30 minutes.

In a small saucepan, bring the heavy cream to a boil, then reduce the heat and simmer until the cream reduces by half; set aside.

Place the tomato mixture in a food processor fitted with a metal blade. Puree until the mixture is smooth, then strain through a fine sieve into the saucepan. Bring the broth to a boil and add the ham and reduced cream. Simmer for 2 minutes, then remove from the heat.

TOMATO BROTH

MAKES 1 QUART

1/4 cup (1/2 stick) butter

1/2 cup diced yellow onion

3 cloves finely chopped garlic

1/4 cup diced celery

1 cup dry white wine

3 cups Shrimp (Shellfish) Stock
(see page 280)

1 cup Pomi strained tomatoes
or any heavy tomato sauce

1/4 cup tomato paste

1/8 teaspoon salt

1/8 teaspoon freshly ground
black pepper

1/8 teaspoon cayenne pepper

1 tablespoon sugar

1 tablespoon finely chopped
fresh thyme

2 tablespoons softened butter

Heat the butter in a saucepan over medium heat. Sauté the onion, garlic, and celery 2 to 3 minutes. Add the white wine and shellfish stock and bring the mixture to a boil, then reduce the heat to a simmer. Add the strained tomatoes, tomato paste, salt, black pepper, cayenne, sugar, and thyme. Simmer the broth for 30 minutes.

Remove the broth to a blender and blend until smooth. Strain it back into the pot through a fine sieve and correct the seasoning, if needed. Whisk in the butter, a little at a time. This will keep 2 to 3 days refrigerated.

Sauces

BACKYARD BARBECUE SAUCE

MAKES 1 GALLON

While operating Rent-A-Chef Catering Service in Sacramento and northern California,
I catered my share of picnics and barbecues. The largest, for a group from Arkansas called
the Searchers, was for about 700 guests. They loved this sauce.

$^1/_4$ cup peanut oil
1 tablespoon minced garlic
$^1/_2$ cup finely chopped onion
6 cups tomato sauce
2 cups ketchup
1 quart water
$^1/_2$ cup prepared mustard
$^1/_4$ cup fresh lemon juice
$^1/_2$ cup cider vinegar
$^1/_4$ cup Worcestershire sauce
1 cup firmly packed brown sugar
1 teaspoon cayenne pepper
$^1/_2$ tablespoon red pepper flakes
2 teaspoons salt
1 teaspoon freshly ground
 black pepper
$^1/_4$ cup cornstarch
$^1/_4$ cup water

Heat the oil in a stockpot over medium-high heat. Add the garlic and onion and sauté until the onion is transparent. Do not let the garlic or onion brown. Stir in the tomato sauce, ketchup, and water and bring to a boil. Whisk in the mustard, lemon juice, vinegar, Worcestershire sauce, and brown sugar. Whisk until the sauce is blended well.

Reduce the heat to a simmer and cook for 5 to 10 minutes, then add the cayenne, red pepper flakes, salt, and black pepper. Simmer for 1 hour.

In a small bowl, mix the cornstarch and water, and add the mixture to the pot. Continue to simmer for 30 minutes.

Strain the sauce and correct the seasoning. Store in containers in the refrigerator for up to 3 months.

Brown Sauce

2 tablespoons butter

1/8 cup diced carrot

1/8 cup diced celery

1/4 cup diced onion

1/4 cup diced mushrooms

2 tablespoons all-purpose flour

2 cups Veal (Brown) Stock
   (see page 281)

1/3 cup champagne

1 teaspoon tomato paste

Salt to taste

Freshly ground pepper to taste

In a saucepan, melt the butter. Sauté the carrot, celery, onion, and mushrooms over high heat until brown. Stir in the flour and cook until the mixture turns brown, about 3 to 4 minutes. Stir in the veal stock, champagne, and tomato paste, stirring until the sauce has thickened and is smooth. Reduce the heat and simmer for 15 to 20 minutes. Season with salt and pepper. Strain the sauce and refrigerate it.

Plantation Sauce

MAKES 1 QUART

An African-American legacy handed down from generation to generation from the big house kitchen to the ribs houses of today.

1/4 cup (1/2 stick) butter

2 tablespoons dark chili powder

1 tablespoon paprika

1/2 cup finely diced onion

2 cloves garlic, minced

2 cups ketchup

2 teaspoons brown mustard

1 cup cider vinegar

1/2 cup Worcestershire sauce

2 tablespoons blackstrap molasses

1 tablespoon sugar

1/2 tablespoon red pepper flakes

1 teaspoon salt

1/2 teaspoon freshly ground
   black pepper

Melt the butter in a saucepan. Add the chili powder and sauté for 1 to 2 minutes over medium-high heat. Add the paprika, onion, and garlic, and sauté them until the onion is translucent. Add the ketchup, brown mustard, vinegar, Worcestershire sauce, molasses, sugar, red pepper flakes, salt, and black pepper. Bring the sauce to a boil, whisk it until it is well blended, then reduce the heat and simmer for 30 minutes. Remove the sauce from the heat, strain, and set aside to allow flavors to marry for 1 to 2 hours. Reheat the sauce before serving.

CARIBBEAN SAUCE

MAKES 1 QUART

This sauce was a big hit at a dinner I prepared for the Black Faculty and Staff Association honoring Dr. Hugh La Bounty, former president of Cal-Poly, Pomona, upon his retirement. The theme for the event was "A Caribbean Evening." The menu's first course was callaloo soup; the salad, spring greens with mango vinaigrette; main course, grilled Caribbean chicken with this wonderful sauce served with Hoppin' John (page 89), sautéed zucchini and yellow squash; and for dessert, tropical fruit strudel with rum custard sauce.

2 tablespoons peanut oil
1 small onion, finely diced
4 cloves garlic, minced
1 tablespoon chili powder
2 cups tomato sauce
$1/4$ cup soy sauce
$1/4$ cup cider vinegar
$1^1/2$ cups water
2 sprigs fresh thyme
1 whole Scotch bonnet pepper
1 ripe mango, peeled, seeded, and pureed
$1/4$ cup sugar
1 teaspoon salt
1 teaspoon freshly ground black pepper
2 tablespoons ground allspice
1 teaspoon ground nutmeg
1 teaspoon ground cinnamon
1 teaspoon ground thyme
1 teaspoon cayenne pepper
1 tablespoon cornstarch
$1/8$ cup water

In a saucepan, heat the oil over medium heat. Add the onion, garlic, and chili powder and sauté for 3 to 4 minutes. Stir in the tomato sauce, soy sauce, vinegar, water, thyme, and Scotch bonnet pepper. Bring the mixture to a boil, then reduce the heat to simmer.

Add the mango, sugar, salt, black pepper, allspice, nutmeg, cinnamon, thyme, and cayenne. Stir, then continue to simmer for 50 minutes to 1 hour, stirring occasionally. Taste and correct the seasoning.

In a small bowl, mix the cornstarch with the water. Stir the mixture into the sauce and cook until thickened, about 4 to 5 minutes. Stir and strain the sauce and refrigerate it, covered.

CREOLE SAUCE

1/4 cup (1/2 stick) butter

1 medium onion, coarsely chopped

3 cloves garlic, minced

1 medium green pepper, coarsely chopped

1/4 cup all-purpose flour

2 cups canned Italian plum tomatoes, left undrained and mashed

2 cups water

1 tablespoon chopped fresh thyme

1 bay leaf

1 teaspoon salt

1/2 teaspoon sugar

1/2 teaspoon freshly ground black pepper

1/2 teaspoon cayenne pepper

1 tablespoon chopped fresh parsley

In a saucepan, heat the butter over medium-high heat. Add the onion and garlic and sauté them until crisp-tender. Add the green pepper and sauté for 2 to 3 minutes. Stir in the flour to make a roux and cook the mixture for 1 to 2 minutes.

Add the tomatoes and their liquid, water, thyme, bay leaf, salt, sugar, black pepper, and cayenne. Stirring constantly, allow the sauce to cook over high heat for 4 to 5 minutes, then reduce the heat, add the parsley, and simmer for 20 minutes, stirring occasionally. Correct the seasoning.

CREOLE SOUR CREAM

2 cups sour cream

2 tablespoons finely chopped horseradish

1 teaspoon cayenne pepper

1 teaspoon paprika

1 teaspoon salt

1 tablespoon fresh lemon juice

1/2 tablespoon Worcestershire sauce

Combine all the ingredients and pour them into a squeeze bottle. Cover the bottle and refrigerate until serving time. This will keep for 3 to 4 days in the refrigerator.

Oyster Sauce

MAKES 2 PINTS

1/2 cup (1 stick) butter

1 pint Eastern Oysters, shucked and drained, liquor reserved

2 cups half-and-half

1 cup heavy cream

1/4 teaspoon salt

1/4 teaspoon ground white pepper

1/8 teaspoon cayenne pepper

Melt 1/4 cup of the butter in a skillet. Add the oysters and sauté over medium-high heat on both sides until the edges begin to curl. Remove the oysters from the pan. Add 1 cup of the reserved oyster liquor, the half-and-half, and cream. Bring the liquid to a boil, then reduce the heat and simmer until reduced by half. Season with salt, white pepper, and cayenne. Stir in the remaining 1/4 cup butter and the oysters. Keep hot until use.

Pizza Sauce

MAKES 2 CUPS

1 pound fresh Italian plum tomatoes

1/4 cup extra-virgin olive oil

3 cloves garlic, minced

2 tablespoons chopped fresh basil

1 tablespoon chopped fresh oregano

2 tablespoons red wine vinegar

1/2 teaspoon salt

1/4 teaspoon freshly ground black pepper

Blanch the tomatoes in boiling water for 1 minute, then remove the tomatoes to an ice water bath to stop the cooking. Peel them, remove and discard the seeds, and crush the tomatoes. Set aside.

In a saucepan, heat the olive oil over medium-high heat. Add the garlic, tomatoes, basil, and oregano and simmer for 2 to 3 minutes. Add the vinegar, salt, and pepper, and cook for 5 minutes. Puree the sauce and allow to cool until ready to use.

REMOULADE SAUCE

1 egg yolk

1 tablespoon paprika

2 tablespoons Creole mustard or
    any tasty whole grain mustard

1 tablespoon red wine vinegar

1 cup extra-virgin olive oil

½ cup celery, finely chopped

½ cup finely chopped green
    onions, green part only

2 teaspoons minced garlic

¼ cup chopped fresh parsley

1 tablespoon freshly grated
    horseradish

1 tablespoon fresh lemon juice

⅛ teaspoon cayenne pepper

½ teaspoon salt

¼ teaspoon freshly ground
    black pepper

2 dashes Tabasco sauce

In a mixing bowl, beat the egg yolk and paprika with a wire whisk. Whisk in the mustard and vinegar. Slowly add the oil in a thin stream, whisking briskly until the sauce thickens. Add the celery, green onions, garlic, parsley, horseradish, lemon juice, cayenne, salt, pepper, and Tabasco sauce. Stir the sauce until it is well combined and refrigerate it until use.

Roasted Red Pepper Sauce

2 tablespoons butter
2 tablespoons minced shallots
1 1/2 cups chardonnay
1 1/2 cups pureed Roasted Red
  Peppers (see page 272)
1 1/2 cups heavy cream
Salt to taste
Freshly ground black pepper
  to taste

Melt the butter in a skillet over medium-high heat. Sauté the shallots for 2 minutes. Add the wine and bring the mixture to a boil. Add the roasted red pepper puree and boil the mixture until it is reduced by half. Add the cream, reduce the heat, and simmer until the sauce thickens. Season with salt and pepper. Strain the sauce before use.

Tartar Sauce

1 1/2 cups mayonnaise
1 tablespoon minced onion
1 small dill pickle, finely
  chopped
1/2 teaspoon minced fresh chives
1/2 tablespoon prepared mustard
1 teaspoon Worcestershire sauce
3 dashes Tabasco sauce
1 teaspoon fresh lemon juice
1 teaspoon salt
1/8 teaspoon white pepper

Combine all the ingredients and mix well. Refrigerate until needed.

Gravies

EDNA LEWIS'S BROWN GRAVY

MAKES 3 CUPS

To be sure the gravy will be ready to serve when the chicken comes out of the pan, begin preparing the stock for this gravy as soon as you start preparing the chicken.

2 chicken backs and wing tips
1 rib celery, including leaves, chopped
1 onion, thickly sliced
3 cups water
$1/4$ cup reserved fat from the cooking chicken
$1/4$ cup all-purpose flour
Salt and freshly ground black pepper to taste

Combine the chicken backs and wing tips, celery, onion, and water in a saucepan. Cook over medium heat for 1 hour. Strain and set aside to cool. Degrease the stock.

When the chicken is half done, spoon $1/4$ cup fat from the pan into a 9-inch skillet. Stir in the flour and make a roux. Cook and continue to stir until the flour turns a dark chestnut brown. Remove from heat and add $2^1/2$ cups of chicken stock. Stir well and return to the heat. Bring to a simmer and cook over medium heat for 15 minutes. Season to taste with salt and pepper. If the gravy is too thick, add more stock or water. Spoon off any excess fat that rises to the top of gravy.

Giblet Gravy

MAKES 3 SERVINGS

1 chicken neck
1 chicken liver
1 chicken heart
1 chicken gizzard
1 teaspoon salt
$^1/_8$ teaspoon freshly ground
   black pepper
1 quart water
$^1/_4$ cup ($^1/_2$ stick) butter
$^1/_4$ cup all-purpose flour

Place the chicken giblets (neck, liver, heart, and gizzard) in a saucepan and sprinkle them with salt and pepper. Add the water and bring to a boil. Reduce the heat and simmer the mixture for $1^1/_2$ hours. Remove the giblets from the stock, cool them, then discard the neck. Finely dice the liver, heart, and gizzard. Reserve the stock (you should have about 3 cups).

Melt the butter in a skillet over medium-high heat. Add the giblets and sauté them for 2 to 3 minutes. Stir in the flour to make a roux and cook the mixture until brown, about 4 to 5 minutes. Stir in the reserved chicken stock. Bring to a boil, then reduce the heat and simmer until the gravy thickens, about 15 to 20 minutes. Correct the seasoning with salt and pepper, to taste.

Red-eye Gravy

MAKES 4 SERVINGS

4 slices Smithfield Virginia ham
   or other dry cured country ham
$^1/_4$ cup black coffee
$^1/_2$ cup water

Make a little cut in the fat around the edges of ham to prevent curling. Cook the ham slices in a heated skillet over medium-high heat until brown on both sides. Remove to a serving platter and pour off any excess fat. Deglaze the skillet with the coffee, stirring to loosen all the browned bits and pieces of "red" ham meat. Add the water, bring it to a boil, then reduce the heat and cook for 2 to 3 minutes.

Dessert Sauces

BRANDY CUSTARD SAUCE

MAKES ABOUT 1¹/₂ CUPS

This version of the sauce crème anglaise is spiked with a bit of brandy to torque up the flavor.

4 egg yolks
3 tablespoons sugar
¹/₈ teaspoon salt
1 teaspoon cornstarch
1³/₄ cups scalded milk
1 tablespoon brandy

In a mixing bowl, beat the egg yolks and sugar until the mixture is thickened and pale. Stir in the salt and cornstarch. Gradually stir in the milk.

Pour the mixture into a heavy saucepan and cook over low heat, stirring constantly, until the mixture thickens and lightly coats the back of a metal spoon, about 10 to 15 minutes. Remove the pan from the heat and cool it in an ice water bath.

Stir the brandy into the sauce and refrigerate, covered, until serving time.

CRÈME ANGLAISE

Crème anglaise is actually a thin vanilla custard often used as a sauce for rich tarts, but this version gets a boost of flavor from calvados. To serve it with your favorite dessert recipes, simply omit the apple brandy.

2 cups milk
6 egg yolks
$^1/_2$ cup sugar
1 teaspoon vanilla
1 tablespoon calvados

In a small saucepan, scald the milk and set it aside.

In a stainless-steel bowl, beat the egg yolks and sugar together until the mixture is thick and lemon-colored. In a double boiler, heat the egg and sugar mixture over simmering water, stirring constantly with a wooden spoon. Gradually add the milk and continue to cook and stir until the sauce thickens and coats the back of a metal spoon, about 15 to 20 minutes. Remove from the heat and cool the pan over ice water, stirring occasionally as the sauce cools.

Stir in the vanilla and calvados. Refrigerate the sauce, covered.

CHEF'S TIP
To make sure the sauce has the correct consistency, dip a metal spoon in the sauce toward the end of the cooking time. Remove the spoon from the sauce and wipe the back of it with your finger. If a clean streak appears, the sauce is done.

Menu Suggestions from Chef Randall

Spring

CONTEMPORARY DINNER FOR SPRING

Suggested wine: Fumé blanc

Sautéed Sea Scallops with Black Bean Cakes and Citrus Vinaigrette

Roasted Tomato and Okra Soup

Green Leaf Lettuce, Sliced Beets, Smithfield Ham, Bermuda Onion, and Georgia Peanuts with Peanut Oil Dressing

Suggested Wine: Merlot

Southern Fried Quail with Wild Mushroom Sauce

Smothered Cabbage

Down-home Potato Salad

Spoon Bread

Sweet Potato Crème Brûlée

FISH FRY DINNER FOR SPRING

Suggested wine: Chardonnay

J. R.'s Oyster Stew

Pan-fried Porgies with Savannah Red Rice

Smothered Cabbage

Country Rice Pudding

Plantation Hoecake

NEW ORLEANS DINNER FOR SPRING

Suggested wine: Cabernet sauvignon

Sweet Potato Smoked Louisiana Sausage Bisque

Red Leaf Lettuce, Butter-Leaf Lettuce, Grilled Spring Onions, Tomatoes, and Souse Meat with Champagne Vinaigrette

Suggested wine: Chardonnay

New Orleans Shrimp Creole with Steamed Buttered Rice

Country Succotash

Peach and Sun-dried Cherry Dumplings with Brandy Custard Sauce

Cheddar Cheese Biscuits

CARIBBEAN DINNER FOR SPRING

Suggested wine: Chardonnay

Caribbean Fish Tea

Limestone Lettuce, Mâche, Warm Fried Okra, Diced Tomato, and Roasted Corn with Fresh Basil Vinaigrette

Suggested wine: Cabernet sauvignon

Grilled Chicken Caribbean

Fried Plantains

Cuban Black Beans and Rice

Sautéed Zucchini, Tomatoes, and Mushrooms
Country Rice Pudding
Old-fashioned Cornmeal Yeast Rolls

Summer

COUNTRY BUFFET BREAKFAST MENU
FOR SUMMER

Suggested wine: Fumé blanc or champagne
Eggs cooked to order
Scrambled Eggs and Pork Brains
Virginia Ham with Red-eye Gravy
Country Fried Apples
Creamy Grits
Cheddar Cheese Biscuits
Southern Apple Butter
Pecan Waffles with Maple Syrup
Pan-fried Salmon Cakes
Country Sausage and Slab Bacon
Country Sausage with Milk Gravy
  Over Cheese Biscuits
Potato Pancakes

SUNDAY SUPPER FOR SUMMER

Suggested wine: White zinfandel
Dandelion Greens, Bibb Lettuce, New Potatoes,
  and Green Beans with Country Smoked
  Bacon Dressing
Suggested wine: Chardonnay
Uncle Dick's Deep-fried Chicken with Corn Fritters
Rustic Baked Macaroni and Cheese
Southern Collard Greens
Aunt Dolly's Sweet Potato Pie

FISH FRY DINNER FOR SUMMER

Suggested wine: Chardonnay
Leaf Spinach, Savannah Pickled Shrimp, and
  Marinated Peppers with Citrus Vinaigrette
Southern Fried Catfish Fillets with Hushpuppies
  and Tartar Sauce
Oven-roasted Potatoes

Creamy Coleslaw
Southern Sweet Potato Pie

PICNIC FOR SUMMER

Suggested wine: White zinfandel or chardonnay
Down-home Potato Salad
Creamy Coleslaw
Grilled Spareribs and Grilled Chicken with
  Backyard Barbecue Sauce
Barbecued Baked Beans
Mom Pan's Green Beans
Barbara's Peach Cobbler
Mom Pan's Pound Cake
Country Corn Bread

CARIBBEAN DINNER FOR SUMMER

Suggested wine: White zinfandel or chardonnay
Jamaican Pepper Pot (Callaloo)
Limestone Lettuce, Mâche, Warm Fried Okra,
  Diced Tomato, and Roasted Corn with Fresh
  Basil Vinaigrette
Sautéed Calypso Shrimp with Caribbean Sauce
Hoppin' John (Black-eyed Peas and Rice)
Fried Plantains
Sautéed Mustard Greens and Mushrooms
Sweet Potato Crème Brûlée
Country Loaf Bread

CUISINE OF BALTIMORE FOR SUMMER

Suggested wine: Fumé blanc
Baked Oysters Wrapped in Country Bacon
Maryland Cream of Crab Soup
Mixed Baby Lettuces, Fried Chicken, and Tiny
  Corn Fritters with Buttermilk Dressing
Suggested wine: Chardonnay
Deep-fried Lake Trout
Maryland Crab Cakes
Oven-roasted Potatoes
Creamy Coleslaw
Barbara's Peach Cobbler
Country Loaf Bread

CONTEMPORARY DINNER FOR SUMMER

Suggested wine: Cabernet sauvignon
Beef Tenderloin Soup
Limestone Lettuce, Mâche, Warm Fried Okra,
   Diced Tomato, and Roasted Corn with Fresh
   Basil Vinaigrette
Suggested wine: Chardonnay
Grilled Salmon Fillets with Cilantro Vinaigrette
Oven-roasted Potatoes
Smothered Cabbage
Baked Apple Dumplings with Cinnamon Sauce
Miss Bert's Homemade Fist Rolls

Fall

CONTEMPORARY SOUTHERN DINNER FOR FALL

Suggested wine: Chardonnay
Mixed Baby Lettuces, Fried Chicken, and Tiny
   Corn Fritters with Buttermilk Dressing
Suggested wine: Fumé blanc or champagne
Simmered Chitterlings Country Style with
   Hog Maws
Southern Collard Greens
Rustic Baked Macaroni and Cheese
Down-home Potato Salad
Barbara's Peach Cobbler
Pan-fried Hot Water Corn Bread

PENNSYLVANIA DUTCH FEAST FOR FALL

Suggested wine: Chardonnay
Dandelion Greens, Bibb Lettuce, New Potatoes,
   and Green Beans with Country Smoked
   Bacon Dressing
Pennsylvania Dutch Chicken Corn Soup
Baked Spareribs and Sauerkraut
Whipped Potatoes
Country Fried Apples
Southern Gingerbread with Bourbon Cream
Country Loaf Bread

CONTEMPORARY SOUTHERN DINNER FOR FALL

Suggested wine: Fumé blanc
Chit'lin Pizza on a Cornmeal Crust
Soft Greens and Marinated Black-eyed Peas
   with Roasted Red Pepper Vinaigrette
Suggested wine: Cabernet sauvignon
Sautéed Calf's Liver with Slab Bacon and
   Country Fried Apples
Pan-fried Green Tomatoes
Creamed Potatoes
Brown Sugar and Black Walnut Pound Cake
   with Vanilla Ice Cream
Country Loaf Bread

Winter

CREOLE FEAST FOR WINTER

Suggested wine: Chardonnay
Shrimp Custard with Roasted Red Peppers and
   Remoulade Sauce
Fresh Corn and Oyster Soup
Suggested wine: Merlot
Pan-fried Pork Chops Smothered
   in Creole Sauce
Steamed Buttered Rice
Mom Pan's Green Beans
Crepes with Country Fried Apples
Monkey Bread

CONTEMPORARY SOUTHERN DINNER FOR WINTER

Suggested wine: Sauvignon blanc
Baked Oysters Wrapped in Country Bacon
Wilted Spinach, Mustard Greens, Grilled Red
   Onions, Sliced Artichokes, Smithfield Ham
   and Red-eye Gravy
Suggested wine: Merlot
Oven-braised Pot Roast with Potato Pancakes
Stewed Okra and Tomatoes

Devil's Food Layer Cake with Chocolate Frosting
Sweet Potato Brioche Rolls

CONTEMPORARY SOUTHERN DINNER FOR WINTER

Suggested wine: Fumé blanc
Catfish Stew with Cornmeal Dumplings
Suggested wine: Merlot
Braised Short Ribs of Beef in Natural Gravy
 with Fresh Horseradish
Savannah Red Rice
Smothered Cabbage
Suggested wine: Moscato d'oro
Southern Gingerbread with Bourbon Cream
Southern Buttermilk Biscuits

RANDALL'S HOLIDAY DINNER FOR WINTER

Suggested wine: White zinfandel
Green Leaf Lettuce, Sliced Beets, Smithfield
 Ham, Bermuda Onion, and Georgia Peanuts
 with Peanut Oil Dressing
Suggested wine: Chardonnay
Oven-roasted Garlic-Rosemary Chicken
 with Corn Bread Dressing and Giblet Gravy
Mom Pan's Baked Ham
Mom Pan's Green Beans
Mom Pan's Candied Sweet Potatoes
Miss Bert's Homemade Fist Rolls
Lemon Meringue Pie
Mom Pan's Pound Cake

SUNDAY DINNER FOR WINTER

Suggested wine: Sauvignon blanc
Baby Romaine and Spicy Fried Oysters with
 Caesar Dressing

Suggested wine: Chardonnay
Roasted Capon Stuffed with Sweet Potato
 Dressing
Giblet Gravy
Creamed Potatoes
Country Succotash
Baking Powder Biscuits
Old-fashioned Coconut Cake with Lemon
 Filling

MARDI GRAS FEAST FOR WINTER

Suggested wine: Sauvignon blanc
Catfish Fingers with Remoulade Sauce
Suggested wine: Merlot
Creole Seafood Gumbo
Baby Romaine and Spicy Fried Oysters
 with Caesar Dressing
Chaurice Sausage with Louisiana Red Beans
 and Rice
Mom Pan's Candied Sweet Potatoes
Bananas Foster
Country Corn Bread

CONTEMPORARY DINNER FOR WINTER

Suggested wine: Chardonnay
Cream of Boiled Peanut Soup
Leaf Spinach, Savannah Pickled Shrimp, and
 Marinated Peppers with Citrus Vinaigrette
Suggested wine: Pinot noir
Braised Lamb Shanks with Ragout of White
 Beans, Sweet Corn, and Baby Carrots
Rice Pilaf
Peach and Sun-dried Cherry Dumplings with
 Brandy Custard Sauce
Old-fashioned Cornmeal Yeast Rolls

Featured Chefs: Their Menus, Recipes, and Stories

When chef John Sedlar opened Saint Estephe in Manhattan Beach, California, there was a raging controversy as to how to define his artfully presented dishes.

"Is he doing nouvelle French food with some ingredients from his New Mexican childhood, or is he crafting an elegant level of Southwest cuisine utilizing French techniques?" experts asked.

Contemporary African-American chefs share this conundrum. The cuisine we create echoes authentic African-American heritage cooking, with its Old-World ingredients, while embracing classical technique. This doesn't mean there is a schizophrenic battle going on in our heads. We have a mission, however paradoxical, to make the established "soul food" more respectable.

It's a daunting task. The words "soul food" mean different things to different people. It is usually connected to slavery and poverty which some people just don't want to think about anymore. Or it is confused with Southern cooking, which our ancestors helped create, but as great African-American cooks moved away from the South to other parts of the country, their culinary expertise transcended that regional restriction. They took their cooking traditions along with them and used them with new ingredients, or they learned new ways to cook traditional foods.

African-American cuisine has also been considered hearty country cooking, enriched with fresh ingredients like lamb, oysters, and veal, and healthy preparation techniques because that symbolize what a lot of us ate growing up. But to limit the discussion of African-American cuisine to soul food is to paint an incomplete portrait. All of those facets need to be preserved.

We need to remember the slavery-inspired soul food because of its spirit of innovation. It is a testament to the cooks who made a lot out of a little, who knew how to cook and cook well, so they could bring all the flavors out of food, whatever the source.

And of course, we need to return to the farm-inspired way of country cooking, especially today when supermarkets have made fresh herbs, fruits, vegetables, and seafood so readily available.

That is why it is so important to introduce you to this elite group of African-American chefs.

Their cooking can be complex, reflecting inspired skill. Or it may be more simple fare that takes advantage of the freshest possible ingredients and artfully prepares and attractively presents them on individual plates.

Whichever, their menus are a refreshing example of the splendor of all African-American cuisine is meant to be.

As you will see, their backgrounds represent a wide spectrum. Some have received a culinary education;

others are self-taught. Each one has an unparalleled love of cooking, learned as a rite of passage in their families. And it shows.

In African-American families, recipes were not handed down on paper, originally because our ancestors couldn't read or write. They transferred recipes verbally, through folktales and hands-on experience in the kitchen. Youngsters observed their mothers, grandmothers, and aunts, and adopted their culinary styles. Both girls and boys alike were recruited to fetch water, chop vegetables, wash greens, and stir the pot.

"Mother took great care with the food she fed her large family and our assorted guests," says cooking great Edna Lewis. "I suppose I just naturally followed her example."

African Americans did the cooking in some very fine places beginning with a few simple recipes they received from the mistress of the house, which they memorized and improvised. Over the years, however, they received little, if any, written credit for the cuisine they were responsible for creating.

There are, of course, a few exceptions to that rule. One was an unnamed slave whose recipes were compiled by her Kentucky mistress in a collection of "colored cook's" recipes, which included puff pastry, mousse, cream puffs, roasted tenderloin, veal, lots of oysters, bisques, and French sauces. James Hemings, a slave cook for Thomas Jefferson, was another. Hemings was taken to France by Jefferson so he could master the art of fine cooking. He apprenticed under caterer Monsieur Combeaux and continued with a pastry chef until he eventually earned the title *chef de cuisine* in Jefferson's kitchen.

As free men, our grandfathers worked their way up the ranks in restaurant kitchens and as Pullman porters. They were assigned a task, and they performed it—whether as saucier, line cook, *mise en place* for the station, performing prep work, broiling the steaks, sautéeing, baking, or creating plate presentation. Few were as fortunate as Hemings.

Some of the very best, including Chef Robert W. Lee, of the Harrisburger Hotel, Harrisburg, Pennsylvania, were part of a great migration of Southern chefs in the 1930s and 1940s. Through this pipeline of servitude between Pennsylvania and Atlanta, low-wage Southern chefs were shipped North to restaurants that needed their culinary expertise.

For the first time, cooks began to be promoted to the rank of executive chef. At least five of the country's finest chefs (Leroy Hill, John Hooks, Jimmy Broton, George Hawkins, and Douglas Lee, Chef Robert Lee's nephew), all started out at the Harrisburger, Lee recalls. Then they went on to work elsewhere. They brought their families along, some of whom were trained and became executive chefs in other cities as well.

They left Atlanta not with broad responsibilities, but as laborers who had been cutting meat, peeling, chopping, mopping, washing dishes, and running errands for a chef. They honed their skills under the tutelage of great chefs, and eventually were able to move to the manager level, becoming responsible for the overall operation, even though they were still considered domestic workers, along with maids and housekeepers. In 1977 the U.S. Department of Labor changed the classification, at the urging of Hungarian chef and author Louis Szathmary of the Bakery Restaurant in Chicago.

Some of the elite chefs you will read about on the following pages traversed a similar heritage trail, entering the food service industry through the back door. Others also received their first exposure to cooking from the family and quickly realized that they wanted a successful culinary career. They pursued specialized culinary training and business education. Some, like Patrick Clark, have even studied abroad.

Whatever the route, each deserves special attention for the gift they have bestowed on America through the glittering culinary legacy they are sharing with us.

We raise our glasses and offer them this toast: To African-American cuisine: It is more than soul food; it's about cooking with the soul.

Clifton Williams

Executive Chef
The Safari Club
Los Vegas, Nevada

LIKE SO MANY OF HIS CONTEMPORARIES, CLIFTON GOT AN EARLY START IN THE KITCHEN, TRAINING WITH his father, the chef and owner of the Monterey restaurant in Newark, New Jersey. His father continued to be an influence as Clifton first completed an apprenticeship, then following in his father's footsteps, became owner and manager of a Newark coffee shop for several years.

But during the late 1960s, while I was cooking in northern New Jersey at Llwellyn Farms Restaurant, I met Windy and we grew together as cooks and as friends. It was natural that he should come to work for me when I returned to Pennsylvania to become the executive chef at Gallen Hall Country Club, near Reading, Pennsylvania.

Time passed and I moved on. I recommended that Windy replace me at Gallen Hall. Sadly, we lost contact for about eleven years. During that time, his career goals came into clear focus. He enrolled at the Culinary Institute of America and worked full time, graduating with honors in 1975. Clifton's first post was at the famed Playboy Towers Hotel in Chicago. Next, he journeyed to Kentucky, taking on the position of executive chef at Casa Grisanti Restaurant in Louisville.

We were reunited in 1983 while attending the American Culinary Federation's National Convention in Salt Lake City, Utah, and we made a pact

that night during dinner atop the Mountain at Snow Bird Ski Lodge never to lose contact again. We never have.

For seventeen years, Clifton was the executive chef at the Executive Inn Rivermont in Owensboro, Kentucky. Later, he opened Clifton's New Gateway Bar and Grill Restaurant in Muddy, Illinois.

Clifton has many affiliations and has received numerous awards including the Honorable Order of the Golden Toque, the American Academy of Chefs and Oxford's Who's Who—The Elite Registry of Extraordinary Professionals. He is the president and a charter member of Les Amis d'Escoffier Society of Kentucky and a member of the Honorable Order of Kentucky Colonels.

Clifton's career has been greatly influenced by his family history. Many of the dishes he prepares were inspired by the food created by his great-great-grandmother, who was a slave. The difference, he says, is "We are more skilled than we were before, more organized and more adept at cooking for large masses and large numbers than we were before. And we learned to integrate or mix other ethnic foods into our own style of cooking."

For instance, Clifton still prepares black-eyed peas, "But I don't have to boil them with a ham hock and I can make it part of a cold salad. We've been doing this a long time.

"I would hope like all the other nationalities, we would be allowed to take responsibility for the great variety of foods and spices we have that have influenced American cooking."

Clifton has been very supportive and has worked with me on many ventures. He has participated in the Taste of Heritage dinners and is a founding trustee of the A Taste of Heritage Foundation.

•

A MENU BY CHEF CLIFTON WILLIAMS

Sautéed Shrimp with Linguine (page 12)

Orange Slices and Watercress Drizzled with Spicy Oil (page 71)

Roast Rack of Pork with Madeira Jus Lie (page 212)

Garlicky Mashed Potatoes with Leeks (page 100)

Black-eyed Pea Salsa (page 267)

Sweet Bread Pudding with Cream (page 263)

Cracked Black Pepper Bread (page 220)

•

Darryl Evans
Executive Chef
The Four Seasons Hotel
Atlanta, Georgia

COUNTRY AND HOME-STYLE DISHES ARE AS MUCH A PART OF DARRYL'S CULINARY PERSONALITY AS THOSE that start with classical technique. But don't think his vision is unclear.

Although he does cook with some foods that African Americans haven't traditionally eaten, he likes to think his menus reflect a mix of "the best of the best": ingredients that are indigenous to African Americans wedded to those from other cultures.

That is one reason why he has been recognized as one of the nation's top young chefs. He won three gold medals and one silver medal in 1988, and a gold medal in 1992, in the culinary Olympics held in Frankfurt, Germany. He was named Culinarian of the Year for 1991 and 1992 by the Greater Atlanta Chefs. In 1993, Darryl participated in the World Cooks' Tour for Hunger in Johannesburg, South Africa, sponsored by the American Culinary Federation. And he was awarded first prize in 1994 in the national competition, A Taste of Excellence.

His interest in the culinary arts began when he was twenty-two, during an apprenticeship with Certified Master Chef Thomas Catherall at the Cherokee Town and Country Club in Atlanta. During his eight-year tenure, Darryl was promoted to sous chef, and later opened the Azalea Restaurant in Atlanta.

I first got to know Darryl during these years and have followed his career ever since. We talked periodically by telephone and got reacquainted each year at American Culinary Federation conventions. By 1992, Darryl had achieved the title of executive chef, joining the Athens Country Club in Athens, Georgia. As executive chef at the Vinings Club in Atlanta, Georgia, in 1993, Darryl added heart-healthy and delicious "spa cuisine" to his repertoire. He began redefining the art of fine dining in 1994 when he decided to further his career at Anthony's in Atlanta.

Since his appointment in 1995 to executive chef at the Occidental Grand Hotel in Atlanta, he has striven to uplift Southern cuisine to a stylish new level. He has been an avid supporter of the Taste of Heritage Foundation, preparing a course for two of its fund-raising dinners. He is a founding trustee of the Foundation.

"I give a little bit of my personality," Darryl says. "But I don't have to cover it up or add things to disguise it and make it something that it is not.

"I get upset when people say soul food is just black-eyed peas and collard greens. That part was comfort food to African Americans and to white Americans in the South; they ate a lot of the same foods we ate."

◆

A MENU BY CHEF DARRYL EVANS

Corn and Roasted Pepper Chowder (page 42)

Pan-fried Almond- and Pecan-crusted Breast of Chicken
with Honey Glaze (page 163)

Smoked, Grilled Salmon Fillets on Couscous with Balsamic Vinaigrette
and Caramelized Vidalia Onions (page 141)

Lemon Pistachio Tuile Cookie Basket with Marinated Berries (page 259)

Down-home Hushpuppies (page 226)

◆

Earlest Bell

Executive Chef
J. W. Marriott Hotel
Washington, D.C.

WHEN NANCY ROSS RYAN DISCOVERED EARLEST WHILE WRITING A STORY ON AFRICAN-AMERICAN CHEFS for *Restaurant Institutions* magazine, she was very impressed. He was a talented young man, who at the time was apprenticing at Chicago's Drake Hotel. He sounded like someone I should meet. He was, after all, an ambitious African-American chef establishing himself in the industry.

A native of Bogalusa, Louisiana, Earlest completed his apprenticeship under Leo Waldermeir at the Drake Hotel and was immediately assigned to the task of preparing dinners in the hotel's fine dining restaurant, the Cape Cod Room. He remained in the Chicago area for a time, with management positions at the Knickerbocker Hotel and the Chicago Hilton and Towers.

"I started out watching my mother and grandmother cook in Louisiana a long time ago," Earlest says. "I remember the smells and the noise that the pans made and the herbs and spices and sneaking some of the food when they went out of the kitchen. I started from there."

Eventually, Earlest was lured to Florida, to participate in a management training program offered by Walt Disney World. He became the executive banquet chef for the Marriott hotel at the Orlando World Center and held the post for five years. In 1995, he was named executive chef of the J. W. Marriott Hotel in Washington, D.C. He has studied abroad and has been recognized as An Outstanding Young Man in America.

"I put everything together, but never forgot the basics of cooking from my background," Earlest says. "I got classical training in school and combined my training with my African-American heritage, making food taste good and look good. Our heritage is all about food."

Earlest believes that cooking is a universal language and the fundamentals are all the same no matter what your ethnicity.

"Even with fusion cuisine you have the basic fundamentals: You have to know how to poach and how to fry."

Earlest is a founding trustee of the Taste of Heritage Foundation.

•

•

Earlest Bell
Executive Chef
J. W. Marriott Hotel
Washington, D.C.

WHEN NANCY ROSS RYAN DISCOVERED EARLEST WHILE WRITING A STORY ON AFRICAN-AMERICAN CHEFS for *Restaurant Institutions* magazine, she was very impressed. He was a talented young man, who at the time was apprenticing at Chicago's Drake Hotel. He sounded like someone I should meet. He was, after all, an ambitious African-American chef establishing himself in the industry.

A native of Bogalusa, Louisiana, Earlest completed his apprenticeship under Leo Waldermeir at the Drake Hotel and was immediately assigned to the task of preparing dinners in the hotel's fine dining restaurant, the Cape Cod Room. He remained in the Chicago area for a time, with management positions at the Knickerbocker Hotel and the Chicago Hilton and Towers.

"I started out watching my mother and grandmother cook in Louisiana a long time ago," Earlest says. "I remember the smells and the noise that the pans made and the herbs and spices and sneaking some of the food when they went out of the kitchen. I started from there."

Eventually, Earlest was lured to Florida, to participate in a management training program offered by Walt Disney World. He became the executive banquet chef for the Marriott hotel at the Orlando World Center and held the post for five years. In 1995, he was named executive chef of the J. W. Marriott Hotel in Washington, D.C. He has studied abroad and has been recognized as An Outstanding Young Man in America.

"I put everything together, but never forgot the basics of cooking from my background," Earlest says. "I got classical training in school and combined my training with my African-American heritage, making food taste good and look good. Our heritage is all about food."

Earlest believes that cooking is a universal language and the fundamentals are all the same no matter what your ethnicity.

"Even with fusion cuisine you have the basic fundamentals: You have to know how to poach and how to fry."

Earlest is a founding trustee of the Taste of Heritage Foundation.

•

Chicken and Dumpling Soup (page 38)

Twice-Cooked Fish Cakes (page 154)

Old-fashioned Beef and Oxtail Stew (page 33)

Bread Pudding (page 237)

Bacon and Cheddar Cheese Muffins (page 227)

•

Edna Lewis
Retired Chef and Cookbook Author
Atlanta, Georgia

AFTER YEARS OF ADMIRING EDNA AS A CHEF AND AUTHOR FROM AFAR, I DECIDED TO CALL HER AT GAGE and Tollner and introduce myself. We instantly became friends, communicating by telephone whenever we could. Over the years, she has been encouraging and supportive and she did not hesitate when I asked her to come from her home in Atlanta to participate in the first An Elegant Taste of Heritage fund-raising dinner. She is founding trustee of the Foundation.

It is fitting that Edna was born in Freetown, Virginia, a city originally settled by freed slaves. She soaked up the community's rich culinary history like a sponge and by the late 1940s had already become the chef at John Nicholson's Cafe Nicholson, on Manhattan's East Side. She has since taught cooking classes, worked as a caterer, and has been a visiting restaurant chef at such great places as Fearington House in Pittsboro, North Carolina, and Middletown Place in Charleston.

When she retired from Gage and Tollner, a landmark restaurant in Brooklyn, New York, with a 119-year-old interior, she had been chef for four years.

Cook's Magazine ranked her among its Who's Who in American Cooking in 1986. She has appeared as a guest chef at Robert Mondavi Vineyards and on the Great Chefs of France public television series. She was one of twelve of Beringer Vineyard's Great Women Chefs and she has been among the hosts at the James Beard Tribute to City Meals on Wheels for the past eight years.

Add to that impressive background, guest appearances in Bloomingdales' Great New York Restaurant Series, Macy's DeGustibus Lecture Series, Philadelphia's annual The Book and the Cook event, and the Smithsonian Institution's series on Creativity and American Cooking, and it's easy to see why Edna is so highly regarded in the culinary world.

She has penned three cookbooks: *The Edna Lewis Cookbook, The Taste of Country Cooking,* and *In Pursuit of Flavor.* She is the founder of the Society for the Revival and Preservation of Southern Food, whose mission is to revitalize and expand the endangered art of Southern cooking, and to increase public awareness and understanding of Southern culinary heritage through lectures, seminars, classroom instruction, publications, exhibits, and special events.

On the concept of African-American cuisine and soul food, Edna is emphatic: "I never really talk about soul food. When the slaves went home, they took food from the master's garden and they also had their own gardens."

It wasn't until years later, she explains, that soul food came into vogue as a way to define African-American cuisine. Soul food definitely is not what the slaves cooked in Africa.

"Soul food was something African Americans had at home, what they called food when they were skimping or living in ghettos. Then they took it upon themselves to be defined by that. Period."

•

A MENU BY CHEF EDNA LEWIS

She-crab Soup Charleston-Style with Benne Seed Biscuits (page 50)

Watercress, Romaine, and Green Leaf Lettuce with
Cider Vinegar Dressing (page 70)

Virginia Fried Chicken with Brown Gravy (page 168)

Whipped Potatoes (page 100)

Long-cooked Green Beans with Smoked Pork Shoulder (page 103)

Baked Tomatoes (page 86)

Fresh Blackberry Cobbler with Vanilla-flavored
Whipped Cream (page 248)

Baking Powder Biscuits (page 232)

•

John Harrison

Executive Chef
Old Original Bookbinders Restaurant
Philadelphia, Pennsylvania

I ALWAYS FELT GRATEFUL, IN THE DAYS WHEN VISITING MY MOTHER MEANT HOPPING ON A PLANE FROM California to Pennsylvania, to be routed through Philadelphia. It meant I could stop by and have dinner at the Old Original Bookbinders restaurant and see my good friend John.

John has been with the steak and seafood eatery for more than forty years. Beginning as a cook's helper, he caught on very quickly and it wasn't long before he was promoted to cook. He worked his way up the ranks and eventually took command of the kitchen, becoming executive chef.

When we met fourteen years ago, John was the executive chef at Bookbinders and I wanted to meet him and experience his cuisine. I made a reservation, made his acquaintance, and enjoyed the meal immensely.

Since then, John has been nationally recognized for his culinary expertise by *Philadelphia* magazine, *Ebony, Essence,* and *Upscale,* as well as other publications. He also has appeared in print and radio advertisements for Lawry's Seasoned Salt. In 1989, he was chosen to prepare a variety of dishes for the inauguration celebration for President George Bush, at the White House in Washington, D.C.

Not long after that John was diagnosed with diabetes and he took action. He changed his culinary style, borrowing from the cooking he had been doing at Bookbinders for the past forty-four years to help him redesign the food of his heritage. John customized a healthier eating plan for himself that still included all of his favorite foods, but John switched gears.

"Most of the food I fix at home is something like what I prepare in the restaurant. Sometimes, I make a fish salad—fresh salad greens with tuna—or add roasted or grilled chicken to get away from everything having to be fried."

But John is the first to admit it wasn't always this way. "In the old days, if I was invited to a party and they were having collard greens, pig's feet, and chopped barbecue, I would be the first guy to dive right in. But now I have to be very critical of what I eat.

"I'm trying to translate what I learned at the restaurant onto what I grew up eating."

◆

Clams Casino (page 22)

Grilled Breast of Chicken with Grilled Fruit (page 159)

Grilled Sirloin Steak à la Johnny (page 189)

Broccoli au Gratin (page 87)

Roasted Red Bliss Potatoes (page 104)

◆

Kym Gibson
Executive Chef
Chicago Omni Hotel
Chicago, Illinois

SOMETIMES PRAISE ARRIVES IN THE MOST SURPRISING WAYS. IT IS ALWAYS NICE TO RECEIVE TELEPHONE CALLS from people who are interested in supporting your projects. But when they volunteer to become active in promoting a cause it is really good news. One day in the fall of 1993, I received just such a call.

It was from a very encouraging and supportive young chef who worked at Blair House, the guest residence of the President of the United States. Her ambition: To get young students of the culinary arts placed in apprenticeship positions at Blair House. Since that call, she and I have become close friends, working tirelessly on that goal and more. She remains a valuable supporter of the Foundation and is one of its founding trustees.

You could say Kym is one of a new breed of African-American chefs who have emerged over the past few years. Raised on Long Island in New York, she relocated to Washington, D.C. to study at Howard University and upon graduation immediately pursued an education at Washington Culinary School. She held a number of culinary internships and worked at several of the capital's most prestigious hotels and restaurants. She went on to receive specialized training at the Culinary Institute of America.

Kym takes her craft seriously. In 1990, she accepted an invitation to become the sous chef at Blair House, preparing menus for heads of state from all over the world. Here, Kym says she learned the importance of staying true to culinary style.

"Whether the menu called for classical French, German sausage, or a Panamanian dish, that's what I did. The nationalities changed on a weekly basis."

So when Kym became the associate director and executive chef for the Children's Defense Fund at Haley Farm in Clinton, Tennessee, the 125-acre estate of the late Alex Haley, she knew she had a job to do.

It was the first job where she cooked for more African Americans than any other minority, but her style didn't change just because she was at the Alex Haley estate. "I didn't decide, 'Now I'm going to cook collard greens and chitterlings.'"

Kym's menu includes smoked meats such as tenderloin and marinated lamb chops on the grill; tomato pudding casserole, which resembles the old tomato pudding your grandmother used to make; collard green soup with ginger; cornbread salad; and chocolate pâté (fudge baked in a water bath) served with raspberry coulis. Reflecting her own multicultural heritage, she does a lot of Caribbean food.

"When I do African-American cooking I don't do chitterling soufflés. There's a difference between presentation and altering food to the point where you don't know what it is, where it becomes something that African Americans won't eat and neither will anyone else. I give them the same standard of excellence I would have given a head of state."

In early 1997, Kym accepted the position of Executive Chef at the Omni Hotel in Chicago.

◆

A MENU BY CHEF KYM GIBSON

Red Snapper Chowder (page 52)

Salmon Croquettes (page 149)

Curried Chicken (page 157)

Red Mint Rice (page 115)

Sautéed Green Tomatoes and Olives (page 101)

Dhal (page 97)

Apple Cake (page 239)

Gruyère Mustard Loaf (page 221)

◆

Leah Chase

Chef and Restaurateur
Dooky Chase Restaurant
New Orleans, Louisiana

Whenever I had the pleasure of visiting New Orleans, I always gave myself a gift, what I consider to be a unique dining experience in the hospitality industry: A wonderful feast at Dooky Chase Restaurant.

The experience is more than just eating a good meal. What is perhaps more significant is the special feeling you get when Leah pulls up a chair and sits down to welcome you. It is the epitome of true Southern hospitality. Despite a busy schedule of her own, Leah has been an invaluable friend who has always been happy to share her Creole magic with guests at Taste of Heritage dinners. She is a founding trustee of the Foundation.

She comes by her culinary style and grace naturally, even though growing up in a little town across the lake called Madisonville in Louisiana she would do "anything to keep out of the kitchen."

She found herself in the food service industry, in spite of herself, waiting tables in the French Quarter of the city when she was eighteen. It was the first time Leah had ever seen the inside of a restaurant, since at the time there weren't any establishments serving African Americans where she grew up.

To her surprise, she loved it and decided to own and run her own place. Today, Leah's creative cuisine and legendary Creole gumbo have made Dooky Chase a national treasure.

"I didn't intend to do any cooking at first," Leah remembers, but "I had so many ideas in my head about food and what to serve, and I've been in the kitchen ever since.

"I serve what I've been eating all my life, like the gumbos; we have had that from my grandmother on down. You can still do basically everything that has been done before without altering the taste. The foods that have to be fried you will still fry but you don't eat it everyday." Leah adds, "But we never did."

Leah has been recognized for her culinary talents in numerous publications including *McCall's, Ebony, Essence, Elle, Southern Living,* and *Cuisine.* She is featured in Brain Lanker's book, *I Dream A World, Portraits of Black Women Who Changed America,* and in Master Chef Nathaniel Burton's 1978 cookbook *Creole Feast.* Some of her favorite recipes have been collected in the *Dooky Chase Cookbook.*

She also is the recipient of humanitarian and leadership honors including the 1984 Candace Award (Coalition of 100 Black Women), the 1985 Freedom Foundation Award, the 1986 Women in the Fore Front Award, the 1987 Young Leadership Council Role Model Award, the 1988 Beautiful Activist Award, the 1989 Anti-Defamation League Torch of Liberty Award, the 1990 Human Understanding Award, the 1991 A. P. Tureaud Award of the NAACP, and the 1992 Weiss Award of the National Conference of Christians and Jews.

◆

A MENU BY CHEF LEAH CHASE

Corn and Crab Soup (page 39)

Creole Tomatoes and Green Bean Salad (page 63)

Pot Roast with Garden Vegetables (page 184)

Poached Pears with Chocolate Hard Sauce (page 249)

Monkey Bread (page 222)

◆

Patrick Clark

Executive Chef and Restaurateur
Patrick's
New York, New York

WHILE PATRICK AND I HAVE CORRESPONDED AND TALKED ON THE TELEPHONE FOR YEARS, IT WASN'T until he and his family moved to California that we became close friends. We share holiday dinners at each other's homes and his last child, Cameron, is my godson.

Patrick has been very supportive and has worked closely with me on many projects and dinners for the Taste of Heritage Foundation. He hosted the first dinner in Washington, D.C., while he was at the Hay Adams Hotel and he is a founding trustee of the Foundation.

It is amusing to imagine, just for a moment, what it was like for Patrick when he learned that he was being considered for the prestigious post of White House chef. Not bad for a kid from Brooklyn, whose father, a talented New York chef, knew the demands of the job and wanted no part of the occupation for his son.

Still, Patrick set his culinary career on course, training at New York City Technical College, where he earned his associate of arts degree in 1978. He continued his culinary education at Bournemouth Technical College in Great Britain, earning an apprenticeship at Braganza Restaurant in London.

But it was under the direction of French chef Michel Guerard, the father of *cuisine minceur*, at Les Pres et Les Source d'Eugine in Les Bains, France, that Patrick polished his skill.

Upon returning to the United States, the young chef accepted a journeyman's position at Regine's in New York City, followed by stints at New York's Le Coup de Fusil, La Bôite, and the Pear Tree.

Patrick may be best known for his instrumental role in building the reputation of two Manhattan establishments, The Odeon and Cafe Luxembourg, but he developed his own style of Frenchified American cuisine when he opened his own restaurant, Metro.

Disenchanted with the rigors of ownership, Patrick joined Bice Ristorante in New York, then was promoted and took over the reins at Bice in Beverly Hills.

Patrick returned to the East Coast to serve as executive chef at the prestigious Hay-Adams Hotel, on Lafayette Park, where heads of state and poet laureates dined on his upscale menu. And after just two short years, Patrick was lured back to New York City to revitalize New York's famed Tavern on the Green.

He has earned several awards, including the coveted Best Chef, Mid-Atlantic Region from the prestigious James Beard Foundation; the 1988 Chef in America National Medallion; the 1988 and 1989 Grand Master Chef Award; and the 1990 New York State Restaurant Associate Culinary Award for Achievement.

"Although coming up in my career, I didn't embrace the foods that were indigenous to my heritage, I never forgot them," Patrick says. "But now it seems like it's okay to do them also. I have done collard green ravioli with sea scallops, sweet potato flan with goat cheese and veal.

"That's where the art comes in. As culinary artists we're trained to take common everyday products and turn them into something that will be beautiful on the plate. You can take mundane, common things like pig's knuckles and feet and greens and put them under different guises."

◆

A MENU BY CHEF PATRICK CLARK

Bay Scallop Chowder (page 34)

Roasted Rack of Pork with Cider-Pepper Glaze (page 211)

Sweet Potato and Wild Mushroom Hash (page 111)

Braised Greens and Rutabaga (page 88)

Fig and Apple Chutney (page 270)

White Chocolate Banana Cream Pie (page 264)

Buttermilk Corn Bread (page 229)

◆

Patrick Yves Pierre-Jerome
Executive Chef
Cavalier Cafe
Clifton, New Jersey

I AM ALWAYS ANXIOUS TO MEET UP AND COMING AFRICAN-AMERICAN CHEFS, SO WHEN SCOTT Allmendinger, the food editor for *Restaurant Business* magazine, told me about Pierre at the American Culinary Federation convention in Honolulu, I was ecstatic. This dynamic young chef was operating St. Yves restaurant in Montclair, New Jersey, and was being very well received by the New Jersey dining community.

I had to meet him. I telephoned him when I returned to the mainland and we discovered a common thread. He was very receptive to my vision of uniting African-American chefs. Like myself, Pierre acquired his passion for cooking from his mother and grandmother. Aromatic memories of the dishes of his childhood haunted him, directing him to study at the Culinary Institute of America. After graduation in 1985, he went to cook with Francis Drillion at the U.N. Plaza Hotel in Manhattan, then it was off to France to study the art cooking alongside André Daguin. He worked in assorted capacities in restaurants in the New York City and New Jersey area before opening St. Yves in 1989.

"My grandmother had the ability to make dirty old sneakers taste great," Pierre says. "I just marveled at her love of cooking for the family, she cooked with genuine love. I was interested in allowing foods to taste like themselves without too much heavy manipulation, just allowing the true flavors to come through, but helping them to come through with style."

It was that style that made Pierre the subject of an article on American chefs in a 1990 issue of *Restaurant Business* magazine. He has received the following accolades: featured in the top five best restaurants in northern New Jersey by *New Jersey Monthly* magazine, rated four stars by the New Jersey *Star Ledger*, and rated three stars by *New Jersey Monthly* magazine.

Pierre is a founding trustee of the Foundation.

•

A MENU BY CHEF PATRICK YVES PIERRE-JEROME

Chilled Duo of Melon Soup (page 40)

Salmon Salad with Hot Onion Dressing (page 67)

Medallions of Pork Tenderloin with Black Bean Sauce (page 207)

Flourless Chocolate Cake with Raspberry Sauce (page 255)

•

Prince Akins
Chef de Cuisine
Georgia
Los Angeles, California

THE OLD FOLKS HAVE A SAYING: "THE LORD PUT US TOGETHER." LOOKING BACK, I SUPPOSE I HAVE ALWAYS thought my relationship with Prince was heaven-sent. When we met in the spring of 1993, I was consulting with Brad Johnson and Norm Nixon on their new Melrose Avenue restaurant, Georgia, and Prince was looking for a change. He explained that he was from Georgia and enjoyed Southern cooking. It seemed natural that he should head the kitchen at Georgia.

Prince had been cooking in restaurants all over Los Angeles and San Gabriel Valley since he arrived in California at the age of ten. At the tender young age of twelve, he began helping out in the kitchen of Chef's Restaurant in Arcadia, and continued to accept all sorts of kitchen duties there over the next eleven years.

To perfect his craft, Prince accepted a sous chef's post at the famed Parkway Grille in Pasadena, where he honed his skills for four years before being promoted to chef at Reflection's Restaurant. He was the executive chef at the Derby Restaurant near Santa Anita Race Track before coming on board at Georgia.

Though Prince did not pursue a culinary education, he has no regrets. "I was fortunate to work with some very knowledgeable people; it's good to have both," he says.

When he started at Georgia, he had not cooked strictly Southern-style beyond what he was doing for himself at home, but adds, "I knew what it was supposed to taste like. I think that what happens is you have to be able to have the mix, you use both ends of your background." But he emphasizes, "You don't ever forget your roots."

◆

A MENU BY CHEF PRINCE AKINS

Black-eyed Pea Soup (page 35)

Carpetbagger Steak (page 191)

Green Beans and New Potatoes (page 102)

Fried Corn (page 99)

Strawberry Shortcake (page 252)

Georgia Corn Sticks (page 229)

◆

Timothy Dean

Executive Chef
Odesia's Restaurant
Laguna, California

F ROM A CONSULTANT'S SPOT WITH ATLANTA'S FAMED GUNTHER SEEGER, TO OPENING A NEW RESTAURANT with two of this country's finest chefs, Roberto Donna and Jean Louis Palladin, to serving as Patrick Clark's sous chef, you could say Timothy is one very ambitious young man. It should come as no surprise that he started his culinary career at the tender age of fourteen, cleaning dishes and doing prep work in a small pizzeria in Clinton, Maryland.

Timothy learned to love cooking from his mother and grandmother in North Carolina. Growing up, his family enjoyed a different ethnic cuisine every night—Mexican, Italian, French, and a traditional Southern night of pork.

"I jumped in, grabbed a knife, and started cooking. It smelled so good it caught my attention," he says.

By sixteen, Timothy was ready to take on the world of restaurant hospitality, accepting a cook's job at the Best Western Hotel in Temple Hills, Maryland, and pursuing an informal apprenticeship under Jean Louis at the Watergate Hotel, all the while attending classes at Mackin Catholic High School. Over the next two years Timothy trained in all stations in the Watergate kitchen and was promoted to sous chef. He held that post for the next four years.

Timothy attended Howard University where he received a degree in business. He moved to Atlanta to work with Gunther and was excited to experience a chef of such esteem. Their collaboration was a big hit in the spring of 1992. Timothy returned to Washington, D.C., after a year to explore bistro cuisine at Roberto Donna and Jean Louis Palladin's wildly successful Pesce.

Patrick Clark, executive chef at the Hay-Adams Hotel in Washington, D.C., offered Timothy a sous chef's position in 1993. He was doing some prep work for Patrick's participation in the Taste of Heritage dinner at the Grand Hyatt Hotel in Washington, D.C., when I invited him to join us the following year and he has been very supportive.

After just one year with Patrick, Timothy returned to work for Jean Louis as chef de cuisine at Palladin Restaurant, a French bistro–style restaurant in the Watergate Hotel. He became chef de cuisine at the Bistro, the main restaurant at the ANA Hotel in Washington, D.C., in the spring of 1996.

A MENU BY CHEF TIMOTHY DEAN

Jumbo Lump Crab Cakes with Ratatouille (page 10)

Caesar Salad with Curried Scallops (page 61)

Poached Lobster with Black-eyed Peas and Sweet Yellow Corn (page 148)

Chocolate Soufflé (page 241)

Country Brioche (page 234)

About the Authors

JOE RANDALL IS A THIRTY-YEAR VETERAN OF THE HOSPITALITY AND FOOD SERVICE INDUSTRY. THE DEPTH and range of his experience and his dedication to professional excellence have earned him the respect of professional chefs as well as restaurant managers and owners. He is noted for his capacity to teach, guide, and advise others in the practical aspects of food quality and profitable food-service operations.

Chef Randall has worked his way up though the ranks from Air Force flight line kitchens to executive chef posts with hotels, country clubs, and several restaurants, including the award-winning Cloister Restaurant and the Showboat Restaurant in Buffalo, New York; and Baltimore's Fishmarket. His uncle, the Pittsburgh restaurateur and caterer Richard Ross, gave him a start and a early feel for a culinary career. He then completed apprenticeships under notable chefs Robert W. Lee at the Harrisburger Hotel and Frank Castelli at the Penn Harris Hotel in Harrisburg, Pennsylvania. He has owned and managed a catering firm and provided consultant services to many restaurant operators. He is most proud of the time spent working with Norm Nixon and Brad Johnson at Georgia in Los Angeles. Developing recipes and menus to establish a restaurant with a theme built around an authentic African-American cuisine was a joy. His broad experience, coupled with

his talent and enthusiasm for helping others learn the craft and systems of restaurant excellence, resulted in his serving on the faculty of four schools.

Chef Randall's professional affiliations include the American Culinary Federation and the American Academy of Chefs. He founded A Taste of Heritage Foundation, a nonprofit organization that addresses career-related issues impacting African-Americans in the hospitality industry. Founded in 1993, the organization encourages African-Americans to be active in their approach to the development of their careers and urges them to take control and responsibility for the single most important aspect of their life's work: their education and training. The Foundation undertakes to achieve three major objectives. They are: 1) To create an educational instrument for social change, to promote understanding and public interest. Chef Randall hopes to expand peoples' perception of the contributions of African-Americans to the hospitality industry by presenting African-American chefs and restaurateurs as positive role models. 2) To enrich through food the culture of the American community at large. He does this by bringing traditional Southern cooking to a new level of appreciation by using experience and creativity in everything from contemporary styling to progressive regional cuisine. 3) To raise capital for the Taste of Heritage Scholarship fund to support those African-American students choosing to attend culinary schools.

Joe Randall has received many awards, including Distinguished Service from the National Institute for the Food Service Industry; gold, silver, and bronze medals for culinary competition; the Outstanding Service Award, City of Los Angeles; and the Meritorious Award for Performance and Professionalism conferred by the president of California State Polytechnic University, Pomona. In January 1992, he received the Black Men's Forum Distinguished Award for Outstanding Contributions and Service to the Community. In February 1995, Chef Randall was awarded a Lifetime Leadership Award for his efforts to advance the culinary contribution of African-American chefs by the Culinary Institute of America's Black Culinary Alumni.

Chef Randall has been heard on many radio talk shows: KABC's "Super Foodies," "The Hollywood Chef" with Vern Lanegrasse, on a South Carolina Public Radio interview show, and with Kathy Hughes WOR Talk Radio One Baltimore-Washington area. Chef Randall's recipes and the activities of the foundation have been featured in many magazine and newspapers articles: *Restaurant Institution* in 1985, 1994, and 1995, *Chef's Magazine* in 1993, *Fancy Foods Magazine* in 1993, *Restaurant Business* in 1993, *Nation's Restaurant News* in 1993, 1994, 1995, and 1997, *Food Arts* in 1994 and 1995, *American Visions* in 1992 and 1993, *Upscale* magazine in 1993, 1994, and 1996, *Black Traveler* magazine in 1996, *Chester Daily Local News* in 1997 and *About . . . Time* magazine in 1997.

Chef Randall stands behind his heritage. African-American Cuisine as he defines it is simple and delicious. It is a medley of flavors in concert unfolding like the blues; it is good for you when you are happy and will make you happy when you're sad. Joe teaches and lectures widely, giving culinary demonstrations for organizations all over the country and performs cooking demonstrations on many television stations from coast to coast.

TONI TIPTON-MARTIN IS THE FIRST AFRICAN-American food editor of a major metropolitan daily newspaper, *The Cleveland Plain Dealer.* Formerly, she was a member of the prestigious, award-winning food staff of *The Los Angeles Times,* and she held the post of food editor at a black weekly in Los Angeles, *The Wave Newspaper.* She is also a contributor to a cookbook series about the world's cuisines, *The United States of America: A Culinary Discovery.* A graduate of the University of Southern California School of Journalism, Martin has received several writing awards. She lives with her husband and three children in Shaker Heights, Ohio.

Index